THE RETURN OF THE AMASI BIRD

THE RETURN OF THE AMASI BIRD

BLACK SOUTH AFRICAN POETRY 1891 — 1981

EDITED BY TIM COUZENS
AND
ESSOP PATEL

Ravan Press   Johannesburg

Published by Ravan Press (Pty) Ltd.
P. O. Box 31134 Braamfontein 2017, South Africa
First Impression 1982
Copyright: The individual poets or their heirs
Copyright in this collection: Tim Couzens and
Essop Patel

Cover Artwork: Mzwakhe Nhlabatsi
Design: The Graphic Equalizer
ISBN 0 86975 195 6

Printed by Blackshaws (Pty) Ltd., Cape Town.

ACKNOWLEDGEMENTS

The Editors express their grateful thanks to all the contributors as well as the publishers of *Ilanga Lase Natal, Ipepa Lo Hlanga, Koranta Ea Becoana, Izwe Le Kiti, Abantu-Batho, Umtetli Wa Bantu, The Worker's Herald, Bantu World, Cape Standard, Democrat, Inkululeko, Drum, The Voice of Africa, Purple Renoster, Black Orpheus* (Nigeria), *The Classic, The New African* (South Africa & London), *New Coin, Contrast, BLAC Bulletin, Ophir, New Nation, UNISA English Studies Journal, IZWI, The New Classic, Donga, Presence Africaine* (France), *Staffrider, Wietie, Marang, Lovedale Mission Press, Heinemann Educational Books Ltd, Victor Gollanz, Ad Donker Publishers, Avon House, Ohio University Centre for International Studies and Troubadour Press,* for allowing them to publish these poems in this anthology: *The Return of the Amasi Bird* — Black South African Poetry 1891 — 1981. Every effort has been made to trace copyright holders and publishers, but where this has proved impossible, the editors and publishers would certainly be interested to hear from any persons who would be in a position to convey any information.

Contents

Introduction   1

**PART ONE: YOUR CATTLE ARE GONE
1892 — 1949**

I.W.W. Citashe   Your Cattle Are Gone   15

Chapter One: Africa: My Native Land

I.W. Wauchope   To Us A Son Is Born   16
A.K. Soga   Ntsikana's Vision   17
                       Death and Life   18
                       Santa Cruz: The Holy Cross   18
Robert Grendon   Tshaka's Death   19
'Vespertilio'   'Ilanga'   26
Robert Grendon   A Glimpse of Umkomaas   27
                       To You Abantu   30
P. KaI. Seme   The Regeneration of Africa   35
Anon   Amagunyana's Soliloquy   35
AEK   The Spirit Song of
                          Mehlokazulu   38
John Dube   Welcome To Our Supreme
                          Chief   39
EMG   Ohlange   40
Mrs A.C. Dube   Africa: My Native Land   41

CONTENTS

Robert Grendon   A Tribute To Miss Harriet
                   Colenso   41

Chapter Two: My Country

Sol T. Plaatje	Song	45
	Mzilikazi's Song	45
	Song Of The Baca	46
Anon	Emakhaya	46
A.K. Soga	Daughter of Africa	47
M. Mphahlele	In Commemoration Of The Pass System Martyrs	47
Sol T. Plaatje	In Praise Of Langa	49
	Sweet Mhudi and I	49
'Alpha Beta'	Bars	50
PQR	A Game of Chess	51
NGM	An African Star — R.T. Caluza	52
PQR	Post Mortem	53
	Three Folk Poems	53
	The Death Of A Zulu	55
A.F. Matibela	Ohlange Is Our Shield	55
'Rollie Reggie'	My Country	57
HDT	To Satan	58
'Zulu'	Teachers' Meeting	59
'Zulu'	Our Dying Speech	61
'Zulu'	The Three Aborigines	62
R.R.R. Dhlomo	The Wailings of Rolfes R.R. Dhlomo	64
JM	The Firm Hand: An Unfinished Story	66
E.C. Jali	Despair	68
LR	'Civilised' Labour Policy	70

CONTENTS

E.C. Jali	The Poet's Defiance	71
S.M. Lekhela	A Bantu Lament	72
Violet Plaatje	'What Is In A Name?': In Memory of Sol T. Plaatje	73
A.B. Swarts	Be Of Good Cheer	75
'Makinidan'	Basuto Mother's Prayer	76
Anon	A Zulu Thought	77
Shep Maloy	Farewell My Lady	78
LHP	Remember	79
Stanley Silwana	Compensation	80
MG	Black And White	80
Stanley Silwana	Ode to Dr W.B. Rubusana, PhD	81
	I Sing Of Africa	82
LDR	The Struggle	83
Peter Abrahams	The Call Of The Sea	84
	The Negro Youth	85
Walter Nhlapo	The Revolution Song	85
	Up! My Race, Up!	86
LDR	The Defeat	87
Theodore Khunou	Our Future	88
W.J. Thabede	Winter And Our Little Poor	88
Walter Nhlapo	Black And White Before God	90
	They Are Gone — Gone Forever More	90

Chapter Three: Rhymes Of Solitude

E. Fanele	Spring	92
S.C. Faber	The Scolly	92
S.P. Maluleka	My Mother's Dream	93

CONTENTS

Peter Abrahams	Freedom	94
Walter Nhlapo	Late Queen Lomawu	95
Obed Mooki	Dedication To The New Offices Of The *Bantu World*	96
Walter Nhlapo	A Prayer For Africa	98
Shep Maloy	Dawn On Africa	99
Peter Abrahams	Heritage	100
Walter Nhlapo	The *Mendi*	101
Peter Abrahams	Little Grease-Men	102
P.J. Maree	Upon The Dealings Of Man	103
JRS	Onward, Ever Onward!	104
Walter Nhlapo	Mrs Charlotte M. Maxeke, BSc	106
Obed Mooki	Mother Maxeke, BSc	107
Walter Nhlapo	Amanzimtoti Institute, Farewell!	107
	First Romantic Night	108
J.W.L. Letsebe	Africa Is Calling	109
Peter Abrahams	Freedom's Child	110
	Self	113
	To White Workers	114
	Spring In A Coloured Woman	115
Anon	On Some White 'Friends'	116
Walter Nhlapo	War Dancer	117
Rahab Petje	Africa's Song Of Freedom	118
Herbert Dhlomo	Sweet Mango Tree	119
Anon	Salang Ka Khotsa	126
Mavis Kwankwa	'May Be'	127
Zini Mfeka	Hark! My Lonely Heart	128
Herbert Dhlomo	Drum Of Africa	129

CONTENTS

B.W. Vilakazi   In The Gold Mines   131
Gaur Radebe   An African To His
    Country   136
Herbert Dhlomo   Not For Me   138
    The Harlot   139
Obed Mooki   The African National
    Congress   141
J.J.R. Jolobe   To The Fallen   142
Anon   Shantytown   145
Herbert Dhlomo   'That Their Praise
    Might Be Reported'   146
    Because I'm Black   150
Walter Nhlapo   Africa   151
Herbert Dhlomo   Drought   152

PART TWO: WHERE THE RAINBOW ENDS: 1950 – 1960

Richard Rive   Where The Rainbow
    Ends   155

Chapter One: From The Heights Of The Maluties

EM   The God Of Formal
    Ways   156
Walter Nhlapo   Come, Freedom, Come!   157
    How Long, O God!   157
    Tomorrow   158
KVM   The Burly Sop   159
Herbert Dhlomo   Lindiwe Laughs   159
    O Mystic Love   161
Desmond Dhlomo   How Soon They Pass   161

CONTENTS

Desmond Dhlomo	Rise Up	162
Lewis Nkosi	To Herbert Dhlomo	163
Joshua Messan	The Beggar And The Lady	164
Can Themba	O Ghana	164
G.M. Kolisang	A Game Of Guessing	165
Can Themba	Ballad To The Coffee Cart	166

Chapter Two: Exile In Nigeria

Ezekiel Mphahlele	Exile In Nigeria	167

PART THREE: FROM SHARPEVILLE TO SOWETO: 1961 – JUNE 1976

Enver Docratt	The Slender Child Is Dying In The Bush	175

Chapter One: Things I Don't Like

Bessie Head	Things I Don't Like	176
Casey Motsisi	The Efficacy Of Prayer	179
Can Themba	Dear God	180
Modikwe Dikobe	A Worker's Lament	181
Arthur Nortje	Nothing Unusual	182
	Thumbing A Lift	183
Finn Pheto	It Is Night	184
Arthur Nortje	Discovery	187
Adam Small	And The Flesh Was Made Word	188
Keorapetse Kgositsile	Innuendo	189

CONTENTS

Dollar Brand (Abdullah Ibrahim)	Africa, Music And Show Business	190
Adam Small	Body	196
Basil Samhlahlo	Naked They Come	196
Stanley Motjuwadi	Taken For A Ride	198
	White Lies	199
Joyce Nomafa Sikakane	An Agony	200
Oswald Mbuyiseni Mtshali	Reapers In A Mieliefield	202
	The Washerwoman's Prayer	203
	I Will Tell It To My Witchdoctor	204
Mafika Mbuli	Out	205
P.M. Mabyane	A Dying Man	207
Adam Small	But O ...	208
Unus Meer	Gazal II	210
Farooqi Mather	My Country	211
Saffee Sidique	To This Day	212

Chapter Two: Beyond This Moment

Njabulo Ndebele	I Hid My Love In A Sewage	213
Z.B. Molefe	Jerusha's Dance	215
Clifford Nhau	The Widow	215
Mongane Serote	Alexandra	216
Njabulo Ndebele	More Impressive On The Mind	217
Mongane Serote	Lost Or Found World	218
Tenda Robert Rachitanga	The Shadow Behind Me	219

CONTENTS

Stanley Mogoba	Cement	220
Ilva MacKay	It's Not There!	221
Mafika Pascal Gwala	Just To Say . . .	221
Oswald Mbuyiseni Mtshali	Handcuffs	222
Mothobi Mutloatse	Six	223
	Wa'reng?	224
	On Marriage	225
	Mamellang	225
James Twala	A Sad Case	226
Nkathazo kaMnyayiza	The Durban Indian Market Fire	227
Kissoon Kunjbehari	Housewives	228
	Vulgar Neighbours	229
	Children Playing	229
Sipho Sepamla	Feeling Small	230
Shabbir Banoobhai	God, Please	231
Paul Vilakazi	Portrait Of An Intshumentshu	232
Sipho Sepamla	The Start Of A Removal	232
	Nibbling	233
Oswald Mbuyiseni Mtshali	Carletonville	235
	The Cross-Bearer	238
Mongane Serote	My Brothers In The Street	239
	Listen To Me	240
	For Don M — Banned	241
Oswald Mbuyiseni Mtshali	The Miner	242
Nkathazo kaMnyayiza	Do They Deserve It?	242

CONTENTS

Alexander Mthombeni	A Mum Calls Her Children	244
	The End Of The Dragon	244
	The Highway Road	245
Mike Dues	My Fishing Village Is	245
Christine Douts	My Township	245
Mbulelo Mzamane	South Of The Border	246
Z.B. Molefe	To Paint A Black Woman	247
Essop Patel	Baby Thembisa	248
Motshile Nthodi	Ghost	249
Lefifi Tladi	Notes From An Afrikan Calabash	249
Shabbir Banoobhai	The Border	250
Sipho Sepamla	Darkness	250
Christopher van Wyk	Agrarian Reform	251
John Samuel	Now We Shall Stand	252
Claude Noble	Significant Change	252
Nape 'a Motana	My Organs	253
Obed Kunene	Apartheid Falling	254
Lebona Mosia	Sister Sing The Blues	256
Leonard Koza	The Street Lamp	257
Fhazel Johennesse	Extra	258
Colin Smuts	Doornfontein	259
Fhazel Johennesse	The Bullfight	261
Sol Rachilo	The Anonymous Houseboy	261
Zinjiva Winston Nkondo	Always My People	263
	Africa	264
Sipho Sepamla	Beyond This Moment	265
Nkathazo kaMnyayiza	A Day In Our Life	266

CONTENTS

Sipho Sepamla   I Remember Sharpeville   269

Chapter Three: 'In Exile'

Peter Abrahams   Lonely Road   272
Bloke Modisane   Lonely   273
Peter Clarke   In Air   274
Arthur Nortje   In Exile   275
Keorapetse   For Melba   275
  Kgositsile
Mazisi Kunene   To Be Proud   276
                    The Echoes   277
                    Farewell   278
                    As Long As I Live   278
John Bruin   Light, Green-yellow   279
                      Luminescence, Tender
                    I Might Be A Better Lover
                      I Believe   279
Mongameli   Dead Freedom Fighter   280
  Mabona
Arthur Nortje   Poem: South Africa   281
                    My Country Is Not   282
Keorapetse   My People No Longer
  Kgositsile   Sing   283
Arthur Nortje   Promise   284
I. Choonara   Letter To Mamma   285
Cosmo Pieterse   Song (For Being)   286
                    Two Scenes: Boland and
                      Cape Town   287
                    District Six (Cape Town)   287
                    Song (We Sing)   288

CONTENTS

PART FOUR: PORTRAIT OF ONE'S LIFE: JUNE 16, 1976 — 1981

Matsemela Manaka   'Let Us Create And Talk
                     About Life'   289

Chapter One: Rustle In The Tall Dry Grass

A.G. Nguza   The Village River   290
                    Black Out   291
Nape 'a Motana   Another Black Boy   291
Essop Patel   Limehill   292
Ujebe Glenn   A Cry From The Cells   293
  Masokoane
Fanyana Mazibuko   The Voiceless Ones   295
Christopher   A Riot Policeman   296
  van Wyk
Modikwe Dikobe   These Black Hands   297
                    Counter 14   298
                    Time   299
                    Asseblief Baas   299
                    Dispossessed   300
Sipho Sepamla   Manchild   306
Nkathazo   Forgotten People   307
  kaMnyayiza
Mandla Ndlazi   Face   308
Oupa Thando   Like A Wheel   308
  Mthimkulu
Shabbir Banoobhai   For Fatima Meer: So
                      Much Love   309
Ingoapele   Black Trial   310
  Madingoane

CONTENTS

Bonisile Joshua Motaung	So Well Tomorrow	312
Christopher van Wyk	A Song Of Hope	313
Muhammad Omar Ruddin	When I Die	314
T. Makhetha	The New Anthem	315
Fhazel Johennesse	Before June The 16th	316
Mafika Pascal Gwala	There Is . . .	317
Leonard Koza	Let Me Be An Apple	318
James Matthews	Prison Sequence	319
Keith Adams	Morality Acts	323
Nthambelenl Phalanndwa	Voices From The Throat Of A Dead Man	324
Farouk Stemmet	Custodian Of Our Spirit	328
Jaki waSeroke	Whooping The Facets Of Knowledge	329
	How Was I Born?	330
Tshilidzi Shonisani Ramovha	The Ignoramus	331
Shafa'ath Ahmed Khan	Exhorting Minority	332
Chidi waPhaleng	The Silent Listener	334
Sipho Sepamla	The Exile	335
Christopher van Wyk	Candle	336
Noorie Cassim	We Know Love	336
Thamsanqa Zondo	Death Without Compromise	337
Matsemela Manaka	Don't Delay	338
Eugene Skeef	Afrika	339
Shadrack Phaleng	As A Child	340

CONTENTS

Molahlehi waMmutle	My Sanctuary	341
Mafika P. Mbuli	Demented	342
Achmat Dangor	An Exile's Letter Home	345
Farouk Asvat	The Journey Of A Slave	346
Bonisile Joshua Motaung	The Garden Boy	347
Mafika Pascal Gwala	The ABC Jig	348
Ingoapele Madingoane	Behold My Son	350
Essop Patel	How Long!	353
Nthambeleni Phalanndwa	Dogs Continue To Bark	353
Ben J. Langa	For My Brothers (Mandla and Bheki) In Exile	354
Christopher van Wyk	Injustice	356
Dikobe Martins	Time To Come Home	357
Mafika Pascal Gwala	Afrika At A Piece	358
Lindiwe Mvemve	The Rustle In That Tall Dry Grass	362
David Moja-Mphuso	Ghetto Boy	363
James Matthews	Trip To Botswana	365
Kriben Pillay	Eyes	366
Achmat Dangor	Piety	367
Farouk Asvat	The Solitaire	368

Chapter Two: Songs In The Wind

Vusi Mchunu	To The Fallen	369
Barolong Seboni	Punch-U-ation	370

CONTENTS

Makhulu waLedwaba	Freedom	371
Lefifi Tladi	Songs In The Wind	371
Mongane Serote	Time Has Run Out	372
Mandlenkosi Langa	They No Longer Speak To Us In Song	379
Pitika Ntuli	The Face	385
Njabulo Ndebele	The Revolution Of The Aged	386
Keorapetse Kgositsile	Mayibuye iAfrica	388
	The Child Of The Crisis	389
Mazisi Kunene	The Political Prisoner	390
	First Day After The War	391
Lindiwe Mabuza	Embracing Exile	392
Klaus Maphepha	Sacrifice	393
Rebecca Matlou	This Path	394
John Matshikiza	At The Dawn I Saw Africa	394
Victor Mota-panyane	Remember Me	396
Dennis Brutus	I Am The Exile	397

Chapter Three: Azanian Love Song

Jaki waSeroke	Our Points Of View	398
Achmat Dangor	The Silence Of The Rocks	399
Essop Patel	In The Shadow Of Signal Hill	400
Muhammad Omar Ruddin	Azanian Love Song	401

CONTENTS

Chapter Four: The Return Of The Amasi Bird

Daniel P Kunene   Do Not Ask Me   403

Index   405

Introduction

The struggles of black writers in South Africa have been long and hard. Almost all of the early poems printed here have never been published in book form. The black newspapers for a long time represented the sole outlet for the writers, who seldom got any feedback and no doubt soon became discouraged. The early poems in the section we call 'Your Cattle Are Gone: 1892 – 1948' are not presented with any exaggerated claim as to their literary merit. We do, however, press a claim for their value as an historical record which can give insight into the changing patterns of black *reaction* through one medium (poetry), and as a body of evidence that black poetry is not a recent phenomenon, neither are all its contemporary themes necessarily new. In considering the early work, though, the word *reaction* seems as appropriate as the word *resistance* is when we come to the poetry of the present. The poems are presented as far as possible in chronological order as they were published and, for one sensitive to the history of the period 1890 – 1950, they do represent a skeleton 'reactive history' of those blacks who were literate during this period — a comparatively small class, the educated elite.

The poems here presented are all poems originally written in English (except where otherwise stated). The choice of this language-form by the writers necessarily imposed certain constraints, or implied that the writer accepted, consciously or unconsciously, certain patterns of perception. This section cannot therefore claim to represent *all forms* of poetic reaction during this period. Poems printed in African languages and oral forms (such as work-songs, resistance songs etc.) are not included. To be fair, however, to each of these poems they should not be read as though timeless. The reader must try to project himself into history, and to read the works with an awareness of the limits of available idiom.

The earliest poem in English we have unearthed (perhaps earlier examples will be found in future) is one which fuses the birth of the author's child with the resurrection of Christ. The poem was signed with the initials 'I W W'. This use of initials or a pseudonym was a frequent device in the newspapers of the time, and it is not always possible to determine the true name of the author. In this case, however, we know that the author must have been Isaac W Wauchope. He also wrote as I W W Citashe — in Xhosa.

The early writers, it will be noticed, had a strong belief in Christianity and its benefits and they coupled this with a clear optimism about future progress. Though conscious of racial prejudice there was less sense of the assertive polarities that mark the work of later writers. This should not lead us to accuse them of political naivete. Indeed A K Soga, the second poet represented, was an editor of the newspaper *Izwi Labantu* and a founder of one of the earliest modern political organisations, a Cape regional forerunner of the South African Native National Congress. His poems about the cross that Diaz planted and about the earliest Christian convert, Ntsikana, recognise that the old ways of life have been irrevocably displaced and that new forms of social organisation are either inevitable or necessary.

In Natal, at the turn of the century, John Dube (later to be the first president of the S A N N C) came back from the United States where he had been a student. From the famous black American, Booker T Washington, Dube got the idea of starting an industrial training school which, situated some miles north of Durban, became known as Ohlange Institute. The school became the symbol of black ability to originate and maintain a viable project in the new 'civilisation'. In the 1912 poem by E M G (name unknown) the lights that shine from the school (situated on top of a hill) are not only directly representative of the new world (electricity) but are also a beacon to the valley promising enlightenment, the light of education and the Light of God. The removal of Ohlange from independent hands when it was taken over by Bantu Education in the fifties was a crushing blow for many.

Dube also started the newspaper *Ilanga Lase Natal* (The Sun of Natal) in 1903. 'Vespertilio', who writes its eulogy, was Robert Grendon (born in the territory which is now Namibia, son of a Herero woman and an Irish trader) who had a classical education. He taught at Edendale Training Institution and was for a while headmaster of Ohlange. He was also nicknamed 'Nongamu'. His poems are not untypical of the time — in his belief that Africa was a sleeping giant ready to be awakened. But he also believes that it *can* be awakened, that education and 'civilisation' are well within the capacity of blacks — an idea hotly denied by many whites certainly at that time, perhaps even now. His poem 'Umkomaas' is an unselfconscious nature poem which assumes that the land, the scenery is for all to enjoy and his 'To you, Abantu' is an exhortation to work, a eulogy to the dignity of labour and self-help.

At the beginning of the century the imaginative horizons of South African blacks, already stimulated by the travels of many, had begun to widen. Two poems from South Africans in America, one by the founder of the S A N N C (Seme) begin to see Africa as a whole political entity — a mighty alliance — and start to pursue the personification of Mother Africa (compare this with Serote's recent personification of Alexandra as a mother in *No Baby Must Weep*. For Msikinya the child, the new world, America, can teach the mother, the old world, Africa.)

The exact dates of the poems should be carefully noted for these might help us to understand the full meaning of the poems. The two poems of 1906 are a good example of this. They are by unknown writers and could have been written by anyone, white or black, but they appeared in *Ilanga Lase Natal*. They appeared in the year in which the last great open resistance on the battlefield took place — the rising of Bambatha. Extremely powerful poems, both assert present or future independence.

Bambatha's uprising began in February, 1906, so the poems should be seen as having very immediate and specific relevance. Indeed, Mehlokazulu was the most important leader to join the Bambatha uprising besides Sigananda, and he died with Bambatha on the 9th or 10th June, 1906. *The Spirit Song* was therefore of immediate consequence. The very publication of

these poems in the newspaper was significant for on
4 May Dube had written an article entitled *Vukani
Bantu* in which he had called on the Zulu people to
raise money to send a delegation to England to protest
against the compulsory labour system, pass laws and
high rents. He was brought before the Natal Governor
and forced to make a public renunciation and
apology. The title of his article as translated by the
government officials, was 'Arise, O People', and was
seen as a call for rebellion. This interpretation was
mistaken and we should remember also the opening
of Grendon's poem on Shaka, but Dube must have
had some sympathy for Bambatha while seeing the
inevitability of his failure. (For a fuller understanding
of the whole period Shula Marks's *Reluctant Rebellion*
is a crucial work.)

Another poem where the specific time is important
is that by Mrs A C Dube. It was published on the day
that Dinizulu was buried — the Zulu king who had
been, as an exile, outcast from his own land. It was
also the year of the Natives Land Act which had such
devastating consequences, turning thousands off the
land (events vividly recorded in Plaatje's *Native Life
in South Africa.*)

Many early poems (such as those on Caluza, Plaatje
and Rubusana) were eulogies to specific people. The
purpose and effect, conscious or unconscious, was to
create modern heroes to set beside the old — like
Shaka, Khama and Moshoeshoe. However, the values
looked for in these heroes should be carefully noted:
not all of them would win the respect of blacks today.
Other poems are satirical like that of H D T, or
love poems like those of Shep Maloy. One of these,
perhaps one of the best poems of the early select-
ion, is *Maybe*, written by one of the few woman

writers represented.

While the period before 1914 chronicled the last episode of open resistance on the battlefield and the rise of the new national organisation, the S A N N C (later renamed the African National Congress), the period during and after the First World War reflects the closing political net. Plaatje, 'P Q R', and 'Zulu' saw the effects of the destruction of African culture and made attempts to stop its total disappearance. 'The Death of a Zulu', a kind of sonnet, is a particularly fine effort. Many poems reflect a major concern of the A N C — the desire to destroy tribalism for the sake of national unity, though continuity is also stressed as in the poem where the blazer badge of Ohlange is the 'education shield'.

The poems become more claustrophobic from the advent of General Hertzog as Prime Minister in 1924, with his proposals to abolish the vote for blacks and his attempts to settle the land question. The agony of the towns, of slums, of squatters begins to creep in as a major theme. And new languages of resistance begin to appear from the late thirties onwards. The invasion in 1936 of the oldest independent African country (Ethiopia had been independent since the 3rd Century A D) by Italy brought both anger and despair and many blacks fought in the Second World War because they thought they were fighting for freedom, freedom in the world and freedom in their own country. The poetry of the forties represents a mixture of some hope, some defiance and some disillusion. The decade heralded the emergence of a major poet — Herbert Dhlomo — who wrote, in 1941, an extremely important long poem called *Valley of a Thousand Hills*. His poems must be read with some care because they are the bridge into the later generation of writers which included Ezekiel Mphahlele ('E M') and Lewis Nkosi and other writers of the *Drum* era. Dhlomo is a major transitional poet as well as being the first modern black playwright.

From a belief — in the early thirties — in the inevitability of progress he started along the path of disillusion after the Hertzog Acts of 1936 and, though always tempered, his anger increased during the forties, when he became an important early figure in the newly-formed Congress Youth League. He was also active in the behind-scenes manipulation of victory for Luthuli in the A N C presidential choice.

After World War II the pace of world-wide decolonisation increased. India gained independence in 1947, Ghana in 1957. In South Africa thousands of blacks had fought in North Africa and elsewhere and Jolobe's poem 'To the Fallen' once again reflected the hope and belief of blacks in the gratitude of the people they helped win the war. An illusion. And the 1948 election seemed to entrench an inevitably bleak future. But by the early fifties a firm resolve had spread through the black population, the Defiance Campaign of 1952 cemented it and the A N C had found a permanent place as a mass movement in the hearts of the people. With a widening literate market and with a feeling that a new day was soon to dawn, *Drum* magazine fostered an ideology that the future was *now* and created a style to match.

As early as the late thirties and forties Herbert Dhlomo had begun consciously to create a coherent national myth — contemporary politicians and writers were reincarnations of the past heroes and ancestors: Professor D D T Jabavu, in his role as president of the All-Africa Convention (founded in 1935), was

Cetshwayo; B W Vilakazi was Bambatha, A J Luthuli
was Shaka. Similarly, men of the fifties have become
heroes of the seventies and eighties: Henry Nxumalo,
Can Themba, Luthuli, Sobukwe. But it would be
wrong merely to consign the men of the fifties to the
past. Many South Africans who rose to prominence in
that decade (Mandela, Sisulu, Tambo, Mphahlele,
Brutus, Rive, Pieterse, etc) are as much figures of the
eighties as they are of the fifties. They are of the
present generation.

With the fifties (and after) came the destruction of
many townships (Sophiatown being the most famous)
and with their disappearance coincided the vanishing
of much of black urban culture (see Can Themba's
'Ballad to the Coffee Cart'.) But not only did *famous*
national heroes emerge — the *Drum* writers also began
to make heroes from everyday life, and to plot not only
national resistance but day to day resistance (see, for
instance, Kolisang's poem 'A Game of Guessing'). Jazz
musicians, miners, shebeen queens, newspaper sellers,
even criminals, became new heroes of the community,
often anonymous, a democracy of the streets. Also, a
small but courageous tradition of workers' literature
emerged (signalled, perhaps, by Gaur Radebe's poem
of 1945 and continued by his colleague Modikwe
Dikobe into the sixties, seventies and eighties — in his
poetry and in his brilliant novel *The Marabi Dance*.
Both Radebe and Dikobe were involved in the
Alexandra squatters' movement of 1946.)

1960 brought Sharpeville, the bannings of the
African National Congress and the Pan Africanist
Congress and the beginnings of armed struggle.
Numerous people went into exile; some were writers;
some became writers. The theme and condition of
exile, begun in the nineteenth century with the

deportation of leaders to Robben Island, and inter-
mittently continued throughout the twentieth century
(see, for instance, Plaatje's famous words that, with
the 1913 Natives Land Act, the South African black
'found himself, not actually a slave, but a pariah in
the land of his birth') became endemic. There have
been many facets to exile — the seemingly-permanent
condition of many writers in foreign countries; the
temporary exile as reflected in James Matthews's 'Trip
to Botswana'; the amputation felt by both 'home' and
'exile' writers cut off from each other; the exile of
people banished to 'homelands' — exiles within their
own country; and the exile within, alienated from his
own life. In the words of Amelia House:

> Exile
> is not leaving
> cape town
> or coming to
> kentucky
> or being in london
> paris or rome
> but knowing
> there is no easy going
> back

This selection does not aim at any comprehensiveness,
particularly in the field of exile poetry: that must be
left for other specific collections; here the idea can
only be hinted at.

The sixties is the lost decade: many critics have
gone so far as to imply that, as far as black South
African writing is concerned, writing hardly existed
(outside of the exile writers) for this period. This is
not true and a good deal more research is needed to

uncover the writings of this time. There is little doubt
that there *is* a continuity. Oswald Mtshali's book
Sounds of a Cowhide Drum, published in 1972, was
not a new beginning: but it has also been excessively
criticised as well as praised because it was misplaced
in terms of South African literary history. It would
be sad if Mtshali's later poetry were dismissed in
terms of his early now-unpopular success.

Comparatively, the sheer volume of poetry during
the sixties is greater than the fifties. This is indicative
of the fact that after Sharpeville there was much
writing taking place in South Africa; though much of
it was only published later. Mtshali's first poems
appeared in *The Classic* and *New Coin.* A year later
The Classic published poems by Ndebele, Patel,
Serote and five poems by Gwala. One can safely
conclude that many of the poems published in the
early seventies were largely written in the late sixties.

In 1971 Renoster Books published Mtshali's
Sounds of a Cowhide Drum and a year later Serote's
Yakhal'Inkomo. This was the poetry of black aware-
ness and black experience. In 1972 Spro-Cas, the
forerunner of Ravan Press, published James Matthews's
and Gladys Thomas's *Cry Rage* (banned). Some
critics wrote it off as sheer *protest.* But James
Matthews, the short story writer of the fifties and
sixties, emerged as a black consciousness poet
declaring black assertiveness. These were followed
by two anthologies *To Whom It May Concern* (1973)
and *Black Voices Shout!* (1974) (banned). By the
mid-seventies black poetry was regularly appearing in
Izwi, Ophir, Bolt, Donga (banned) and occasionally
in *Contrast.* Much of what was published was selected
by non-black editors.

In 1970 Nat Nakasa's *The Classic* was put to bed, to

give birth in 1975 to *The New Classic* under the editorship of Sipho Sepamla, who wrote that 'it is about time new and old voices were heard, about time growth was exhibited at these points from which waves of sound are sent. The beat of the heart is too strong for our silence to be true and real . . . we are tired of being spoken for, thought about and wheeled around.'

In this period preceding the 1976 Soweto uprising black poetry written by members of SASO and BPC appeared in the docks of the courts in Pretoria. Black poetry was on trial. Much research is needed in this area of black poetry because in historical terms it clothed old ideas with new and forceful imageries. Historically the poetry of the black consciousness movement is one of awareness and assertion of 'the black experience'.

After Soweto, came *Staffrider*. Much of what has been published there has been criticised as mere rhetoric, but in essence it continues to provide a 'workshop' for black writers and so much care must be taken to analyse the standpoint of the criticisms. In 1980 two issues of *Wietie* appeared but owing to lack of funds the editors could not continue. At the moment the only publication which publishes a substantial amount of black poetry is *Staffrider*.

In the seventies we saw not only the polarization of the people, but also the polarization of literature.

In the eighties the forces at play have been the Zimbabwean desire to create a truly non-racial state on South African borders, the potential independence of Namibia and the increased armed struggle. These forces will influence much of South African writing in the decade.

But it is not really useful to categorize history or

literature in the arbitrary and artificial terms of decades. A more meaningful period-division would be from Sharpeville 1960 to Soweto 1976. While poems like Dhlomo's in the forties through to Bessie Head's 'Things I Don't Like' in 1962 reveal that the idea and usage of 'blackness' was nothing new, it is true to say that from the early seventies the terminology of black consciousness began to dominate literary language — becoming almost hegemonic. During this period too, the young writers were adamant in their rejection of the view that art must be self-contained, responsible only to itself, acceptable only if up to certain 'standards'. 'Let art be life,' wrote Matsemela Manaka.

With the uprising in Soweto in 1976 life strangely gave content to literary metaphor. Africa, the 'child' of the future, suddenly became *real* children. Confronted by the magnitude of the event, some writers have genuinely responded to it, others have unhesitatingly *used* it. But it must be remembered that for some writers the image of the child is more than mere metaphor: they saw real children, sometimes close friends, being shot in the streets.

Other interesting issues are raised by many poems in this selection: there are the hints and influences of Pan-Africanism and negritude; there is the fact that the majority of poems are statements and questions rather than illustrative stories (exceptions are poems like those of Themba, Dikobe, Mbali and Mtshali); there are a few visual or ' concrete' poems where the form visually reflects the theme (see, for instance, the poem 'A Cry from the Cells', tortured in its form, or Borolong Seboni's 'Punch-U-Ation' where the African continent is seen as a question mark.)

Furthermore, not all the poems published here are

'political'. If this is a disappointment to some they should bear in mind the words of the painter J K Mohl in 1943, who said, in reply to a criticism that he should give up painting landscapes and concentrate on portraits of his people in poverty and misery, 'But I am an African and when God made Africa, He also created beautiful landscapes for Africans to admire and paint.' Incidentally as far as the editors know, at least one of the poets in the selection is white, but the ideology expressed in his poetry is indistinguishable from contemporary beliefs among blacks.

Certain criticisms of the poetry contained in the selection can be anticipated. For instance, images of the birth of Africa and Mother Africa are sometimes empty; some writers are too quick to say 'we'; some language, as we have already noted, has a tendency to become hegemonic. Though for some writers future 'freedom' holds more promise than it may be possible to deliver, in the words of Richard Rive the effect of liberation for all is

> . . . going to be a sad song, brother,
> 'Cause we don't know the time
> And it's a difficult time to learn
> But we can learn it, brother,
> You and I . . .

But when some writers seem to cut corners in their haste to identify with workers, and write of the oppressed as a single universal class, it must be remembered that the creation of the ghettoes has concertina'd the classes so that the links are close in home-life if not always at the workplace. And a small but healthy Islamic tradition provides at least one variant in language idiom. Perhaps most unfortunately

— but significantly — male writers far outnumber female writers, which one can hope will change in the future.

Over the years a number of black writers have come close to attempting to write a national epic: Jolobe's *Thuthula,* Dhlomo's *Valley of a Thousand Hills,* Serote's longer poems, Dikobe's *Dispossessed,* Madingoane's *Black Trial,* Mazisi Kunene's *Emperor Shaka The Great.* In a sense this book is a collective epic. If it is read carefully, there is a story to it, a unity of growth and composition, facets of a single people.

PART ONE :

Your Cattle are Gone : 1892–1949

Your cattle are gone,
My countrymen!
Go rescue them! Go rescue them!
Leave the breechloader alone
And turn to the pen.
Take paper and ink,
For that is your shield.

Your rights are going!
So pick up your pen,
Load it, load it with ink.
Sit in your chair —
Repair not to Hoho,
But fire with your pen.

I W W Citashe (written sometime in the nineteenth century, translation published in *Africa South* in 1961)

Chapter 1 :

Africa : My Native Land

TO US A SON IS BORN

To us a son is born,
We gladly blow the horn,
And bid our friends with us to scorn
The day of hopes forlorn!

On Sabbath night he came (10 − 4 − 92)
This man without a name;
With shouts and yells he made his claim
And that with might and main.

Some say his name is Bill,
But this is doubtful still;
Some Native name; fresh from the mill,
Would need no little skill.

And yet 'tis hard to tell
A name that will not sell,
Or one that rings so like a bell
As that of William Tell!

I must not keep you long,
This is no Easter song;
Yet all good gifts to him belong
Who never will do wrong.

Isaac W Wauchope   19 May 1892

NTSIKANA'S VISION

What 'thing', Ntsikana, was't that prompted thee
To preach to thy dark countrymen beneath your tree?
What sacred vision did that mind enthral
Whils't thou lay dormant in thy cattle kraal?

Was it the sun, uprising in his pride,
That struck with glittering sheen Hulushe's dappled
                                         side,
By Chumie's laughing fountain hastening merrily,
To meet strong Keisi's waters rolling to the sea?

A Vision? Yea! That presence once had shone
Upon the man of Tarshish, down from the heavenly
                                         throne,
And in the holy light of His mysterious Word
The proud Barbarian bows and worships God, the
                                         Lord!

Hark! 'Tis the sound of prayer, of savage melody —
Untutored voices raised to Him who sits on high;
Those hills and dales around fair Gwali's stream
Repeat again Ntsikana's sacred Hymn!

Wake, Gaika, wake! I see the gathering storm
By Debe's plains; Gcaleka's horse and Ndlambe's
                                         legions swarm;
Behold thy tribesmen scattered, thy warriors' doom is
                                         sealed —
The word of God rejected — by prophecy revealed.

A K Soga   28 October 1897

DEATH AND LIFE

Oh Death! Thou art an awful mystery:
Kings, potentates and people all must die;
Wisdom and knowledge own thy ruthless sway,
Light hides her eyes, and Glory fades away.
Before thy dreadful throne man stands alone,
Nor love, nor tenderness, nor virtue can atone.
Before thy withering glance life cannot live,
None can thine awful power or might deceive.
Within thy grasp none may thy hand restrain.
Pity stands mute, and mercy pleads in vain.
Enchained in dungeons dark are freedom, liberty,
What hope have we — poor weak and frail humanity?
'Oh death where is thy sting, O grave thy victory?' —
Thy gates wide open fling. The Soul can never die.

A K Soga   20 January 1898

SANTA CRUZ: THE HOLY CROSS

The Cross; a symbol of that faith
    That points to Calvary;
A living token of that Death
    That sets the guilty free.

Long hath it stood, so silently,
    Where Algoa's rock-bound shore
Beats back the waters of the sea
    With angry, sullen roar.

It tells of man's belief in God;
    Of Diaz and his band;
Who braved the waters and the flood

   At Christian King's command.

It speaks of Freedom's flag unfurled,
   For Christianity;
A beacon light, in this dark world,
   To God and liberty.

O Santa Cruz, long may it stand,
   As emblem, may it be
The cheer of Good Hope; in the land
   Peace and prosperity.

A K Soga   3 February 1898

TSHAKA'S DEATH

Awake—awake—Dukuza—wake! This day
Will I, thy lord, my conq'ring hosts prepare
To greet! Awake—awake—let my commands
Throughout thy huts resound; and with due haste
Be all thy people for the occasion clad!
Awake—awake! The conq'ring army comes!
Dense clouds of dust before them rise, who broke
The hateful Amapondo's pride and pow'r!
They come—they come—they come; and louder
                                                    sounds
The trampling of their feet; and denser rise
The clouds before their march! Awake—awake—
Dukuza—wake! Thy warriors now return!
Prepare both meat and drink, for they must feast
To strengthen their fatigued and weary limbs!

But stay! Why come yon hosts so silently
Along? Why sound they not the victor's cry?

They're vanquish'd! See how weary and outworn
They be! By heav'n and by the heav'nly pow'rs,
Both vengeance and destruction unto them
I vow, if they before their foes have fled!
Thy huts Dukuza, never—never more
Shall give them rest and food! Henceforth must they
Depart! My face must they behold no more!
They must depart! Mine eyes do loathe to look
On conquer'd men! Throughout my most illustrious
reign
I never bow'd, nor yielded to the pow'r
Of man; nor turned my back towards the foe!

They come! I mark defeat in ev'ry eye.
They bow in rev'rence unto me their lord,
With salutations which of wonted pride,
And dignity are void! Within my breast
Is kindled deep, unconquerable wrath,
Which soon must burst in ruin on their heads!
Dukuza, wake! Thy preparations all
Are vain! Give ear unto the frail response
Of these thy vanquish'd, and ill-fated sons!

Stay your advance, ye weary multitudes,
And render due account—ere thence ye move—
Of your success in Amapondoland,
According to these queries of your lord!

Tshaka's Questionings

1
'Wherefore lurks defeat in ev'ry eye?
    Wherefore silence 'mongst your ranks?
Wherefore raise ye not the victors' cry
    Round about Umvoti's banks?

2

Wherefore do your stabbing spear-blades gleam,
    Which from bloodshed have return'd?
Wherefore do your lines diminish'd seem,
    If defeat ye have not earn'd?

3

Wherefore have ye failed to bring me spoil—
    Proof that ye've the victors been?
Ruin will upon your heads recoil
    Such as mortals ne'er have seen!'

Dukuza, wake! Betwixt myself and these
Bear witness; and give ear to their response!

The Impi's Reply

1

'Stern lord, thy will have we obey'd!
    For thee we've nobly striv'n!
But victory, for which we pray'd,
    Unto our foes was given!

2

Thy rancour and thine anger spare,
    Thy pow'r is undefied!
A conq'ror dreaded everywhere
    For evermore abide!

3

Illustrious chieftain, stay thy hand!
    Let not Dukuza weep
For remnants of a luckless band
    Who must damnation reap!'

Awake—Dukuza—wake, and hear the doom
Which I'll pronounce on these thy coward sons
And if for them thou weep, I shall not spare
Thee, but consign thee to destruction's flames,
Together with these wretches trembling here!

Tshaka's Sentence On The Impi

1

'Ere vengeance dire on you I wreak,
    From out my sight go forth!
The south denied you luck; go seek
    Lost fortunes in the north!

2

And if disasters overtake
    You there, ne'er homewards turn!
Renounce me; and this land forsake
    And *these* for whom ye yearn!

3

And now betake yourselves from hence!
    Dukuza pities not
Frail men! Let death by violence
    With shame be your just lot!'

Dukuza—wake—awake! Thy dastard sons
In hunger and fatigue have onward pass'd
To meet their doom in yonder northern climes,
Where contumacious vassals mock my pow'r
Let them depart, and may they ne'er again
Return! Dukuza, weep not thou for them!
Thy habitations from disgrace are free,
And cowardice from thee is blotted out!

They're gone; they're gone, and ne'er shall see my
                                                        face
Again! Awake—Dukuza—wake—awake!
Prepare, with me, on human blood to feast!
Lead out the women of the vanquish'd band!
Before my presence let them be array'd!
Advance, ye executioners, and slay
Yon wretches, lest in time to come they bear
A race of children—dastards like their sires!
Upon them rush, and blot for ever out
The stigma of disgrace, and cowardice!
I've spoken. *Let the awful work be done!*

Awake, Dukuza; yet once more awake!
Behold these gifts which serfs have brought for me!
They be the presents that befit a king;
What lovely, lovely feathers are the crane's.
But stay. Who stabs me in the back? Alas!—
My day of doom has come! My sun must set!
Mahlangana can it be thou? Seek'st thou
To take my life by violence, and hurl
Me to destruction ere my prime? Alas
Mahlangana! And who is this that comes?
Dingana is it thou? Com'st thou to save
Me from a murd'rer's hands, or dost thou thirst
And crave with him for my life, and my blood?
Alas for me, the mightiest of all kings
Who've grac'd this empire's throne! *Alas for me,*
Whose kingdom knew no bounds! *Alas for me,*
Who conq'ring ever conquer'd; and who bow'd
To mortals none save you who are my own;
Who thus encompass me! *Alas for me,*
Who caprice hurl'd to gloom the shades of men
And women, and of babes innumerable.
Alas for me, who shook this earth with awe,

And sprinkled human blood where'er I pass'd—
That I should from celestial glory fall
To welter in this dust in sight of them
O'er whom I reign'd supreme! *Alas for me*
Who liv'd by fire and sword that I should meet
A doom akin to that which I pronounc'd
On women frail. 'Tis undisputed—*truth*—
That he who would by fire and sword exist
Must perish by the same! *Alas for me*—
Who shar'd the sunlight with the gods of heav'n—
That I should meet my doom by treachery
Of *you*—Dingana—*you*—Mahlangana!
Alas for me, who fell by intrigue foul
Thro' thee, Umbopu—servant, who had gain'd
My most implicit confidence, and love!
Alas, my brothers, ere my mutilated form
Be cast upon yon hill to rot, take heed
I pray the things which I shall now divine:—

Tshaka's Last Words

1

'Ye think that ye this land will rule
　　When I am dead and gone! Ye lie!
Ye'll bow before the white man's stool,
　　And him ye'll rev'rence by-and-by!

2

As I to you am yielding now
　　In shameful, shameful—death laid low,
So ye unto the sword must bow
　　And to destruction *all* must go!

3

Umbopu, for the trait'rous part

Which thou on me thy lord hast play'd
Dingana's sword will pierce thy heart,
 Whilst thou art pleading with my shade

4

For aid. Thy just reward is woe!
 Dingana spares thee not. Despair!—
For ere my blood has ceas'd to flow,
 Shalt thou like me—thy master—fare!

5

On thee, ill-fated brother mine—
 Mahlangana, the fates do frown!
No idle thing do I divine—
 Thou too must reap Damnation's crown!

6

Thy life-blood will Dingana seek,
 Ere my remains corruption see;
And with a wild despairing shriek
 To Spiritland thou'lt follow me!

7

Dingana, like a panting hound
 Before thy conq'ror's face thou'lt flee!
Where'er for safety thou shalt bound,
 The sword will overshadow thee!

8

Thy baseness, and thy treachery
 Will drive thee to a foeman's land!
And there thou'lt pay the penalty
 For deeds committed by thy hand!

9

Forgetful of thy cruelty
  Vain refuge at his feet thou'lt crave!
In manner as thou slayest me,
  Shalt thou be hurl'd into thy grave!'

Robert Grendon   1901

'ILANGA'

1

Thou splendour, whose gilt arrows pierce
  The mists that dim fair Embo's sky,
Advance the fiery, yet not fierce —
  Upon the vault of time to fly!

2

Arise, and shine upon our race,
  Since thou'rt interpreted — 'THE SUN':—
And with light's flood from us efface
  The blacken'd course which Night hath run.

3

And thou, Ohlange, whence this ring
  Of brightness hath aris'n this day,
And faith to thy awakening —
  Success will meet thee on thy way.

4

The truth seek ever to obey,
  Tho' thou to Falsehood foe must be;
At last thou shalt from out the fray
  Emerge, O SUN, triumphantly.

Vespertilio   *Ilanga Lase Natal* 15 May 1903

A GLIMPSE OF UMKOMAAS

The season of the year was Winter cold—
   The month was June when Nature's death-like rest
Was half-way overpast. With spirits bold
   I rose, the splendours of Natalia's west
To view. I plodded thither over hill
   And dale and brook; and brook and hill and dale,
Past scatter'd farms mid wattle groves until,
   Dark Nomandafu did mine advent hail.

And halting in the cool refreshing shade
   Of groves primeval, that the western flank
Of this proud mountain ornament, I made
   Surveys minute of landscapes, that would rank
Amongst the loveliest in this rugged land:
   And on the hills, which like sentries did round me
                           tow'r
And hold o'er all below supreme command,
   I traced the violence of dead volcanic pow'r.

Lo, there above—cleft—crevice—crag and cliff
   Their origin and history explain!
And there the everlasting wither'd—stiff—
   With brown and yellow flow'rs the frosts disdain!
Yet there Dombeya's foliage tinted red
   My faulty vision from afar deceives
And there Protea with black-burnt, flower-head,
   And forking trunk for evergreen with leaves.

My gaze arrests, and tempts me to declare
   That I have reach'd the limits of its range.
And there outstretch'd below me parch'd, and bare,
   Lies Deepdale-broad—grass-grown without a change
Save scatter'd farms, and fields of wither'd maize,

Where scatter'd herds of horses-oxen-swine
Upon the remnants of the harvest graze,
    In undisturbed leisure—line by line.

Now plodding on thro' shady bow'rs that lin'd
    The road, I often paus'd enrapt to gaze
Upon the vegetation that entwin'd
    The forest trees from root to topmost sprays
As often did I pause my heated brow
    To cool, and drink the woodland vapours chill;
Yea often—often did I pause to bow
    In wonder at the Arch-Creator's skill.

Here countless birds unseen of various tone
    Throughout this Sylvan paradise
O'er which the Autumn's yellow tints have blown
    Do sport and by their mirth as 'twere entice
The traveller, and steed outworn, and soil'd
    With dust from rosy dawn till silv'ry noon
To hasten on the way whereon he toil'd,
    And reach his home ere sets the crescent moon.

And blending with the warblings of the birds
    The crystal streamlets chatter over rocks
In ceaseless uninterpretable words;
    Which strange articulations Silence mocks.
And chattering incessantly thro' wood
    And over rock past Nomandafu's Pass,
These silv'ry waters flow in joyful mood
    On their meandering way to Umkomazi.

Gazania with its star-like golden head,
    And Aloe with its scarlet blossoms bright
Alone adorn the garb of Nature dead,
    And seem the only objects of delight.

And save the chattering of the silver stream
   And the sweet warblings of the feather'd race
The hazel wash'd mountain groves in silence dream,
   As tho' grim Death reign'd over this fair place.

Mahwaqa with his twice-cleft purple brow
   Doth heav'nwards tower silent and alone.
Whilst tiny Bulwer doth in rev'rence bow
   'Neath that majestic and stupendous throne
Beyond Kwahlamba with its snow-clad range
   The landscape decks with tints exceeding fair
And with a countenance that have a change
   Incessant seen, blows kisses to the air.

Below this wood which light can scarce penetrate
   Descend broad slopes attir'd in russet brown
And o'er thcm all in true majestic state
   Proud shaggy Nomandafu's splendour frown,
Now free from shade the slaty roadway glaz'd
   By constant wagon wheel-ruts gently winds
In its descent, and leads the hungry-craz'd,
   And thirsty blind to Deepdale, where he finds

Both meat, and drink to re-invigorate
   His weary body that he might away
So wearisome by speed precipitate
   Accomplish, ere the night-fall ends the day.
Then proudly leaps he to the saddle-tree.
   Then lightly tightens he the slacken'd rein,
Then away the steed and rider homewards flee
   And seldom thereafter are seen or met again.

From thence the roadway o'er a long white bridge
   Leads on thro' reddish-yellow soil and skirts

The 'Gatherer of Floods' and yonder ridge*
    Which countless ages with the river flirts—
This dire ascent in man fatigue instills!—
    Lo, further yet the tedious red track plays
Upon the traveller's eyes, till 'mongst the hills
    Beyond 'tis lost to view in cobalt haze.

And now on Deepdale's western side I stand
    To take my final and my farewell glance
Of scenes that I have left behind. How grand
    The vision proves! Oh how it doth entrance
My soul! Proud Nomandafu—hear!
    With yonder valley that doth 'neath thee lie,
And yonder 'Gatherer of Waters' clear
    Shalt thou upon my mind be stamped for aye.

*This hill is called Umkomazi, as is the river which it adjoins
and overlooks.

Robert Grendon   *Ipepa Lo Hlanga* 14 August 1903

TO YOU ABANTU
WHAT MAN'S ACCOMPLISH'D YE CAN DO

1

Put forth—*Abantu*—all the pow'rs
    Wherewith by Nature ye're endow'd,
The ignorance that round you tow'rs
    Encircling you in its black shroud
Dispel! There is no time for sleep,
    Or conversations that are vain—
No time to squat about and weep
    O'er privileges, and disdain
Facilities within your grasp.
    Awake!—This age demands not cries

'Gainst wrong, but veritable deeds.
   'Awake—no longer lag!—arise!'—
Thus all creation with you pleads.
   There's nothing in this world that's new,
Tho' knowledge often hides from view;
   When courage actuateth you,
What man's accomplish'd ye can do.

2
Awake!—arise!— this doctrine learn—
   That those who're fittest must survive;
That those, who by experience stern
   Are taught and led are those who strive;
That they who strive must toil and sweat;
   That they who toil ere long must reap;
That they who reap know no regret,
   And therefore do not squat and weep
Or yield, like you, to dull Despair.
   Awake!—arise!—go sweat, and toil,
By training hand and heart, and mind;
   By cultivation of the soil
And whatsoever task ye find.
   There's nothing in this world that's new,
Tho' knowledge often hides from view;
   When courage actuateth you,
What man's accomplish'd ye can do.

3
Arise! Go forth and take your place
   'Mongst them who daily toil, and spin!
Go forth, and strive in Labour's race,
   And deem not *Work* disgrace or sin.
Work is your heritage, your right,
   Your ladder to success, and fame,
Your sword and breastplate in the fight

'Gainst serfdom, penury, and shame,
And all that tends to tread you down.
   Arise! Go forth, and toil by brain,
Or manual pow'r! In all ye take
   In hand strive ever to maintain
Therein a cheerful love, and make
   No plaint when thorns beset your way.
If your intent be firm, succeed
   Ye must, and great will be the day
When what ye've sown puts forth its seed.
   There's nothing in this world that's new
Tho' knowledge often hides from view;
   When courage actuateth you
What man's accomplish'd ye shall do.

4

Awake!—arise!—go forth and do!
   Nor question *why* or *how* or *where,*
Or *when!* The world demands from you
   Of work a due proportionate share,
Be it accomplish'd by the mind,
   Or by the hand. The brilliant deeds
Of swarthy men must also find—
   Tho' often damned—the way that leads
To *Honour* and *Acknowledgement,*
   Press on! With courage all aflame
Strive ever *up* —forget the *down;*
   And then at length ye'll rise to fame,
Where Hate on you no more shall frown.
   There's nothing in this world that's new,
Tho' knowledge often hides from view;
   When courage actuateth you,
What man's accomplish'd ye shall do.

5

Press on! *No man is truly man,*
    Except his soul give full consent
To *all* that constitutes his plan;
    Nor will he ever know content.
The footprints of all great men trace,
    And strive to tread as they have trod,
All hardships, disappointments, face.
    Advance! E'en tho' ye're forced to plod,
Advance! The world from out your ranks
    A Shakespeare, Milton, Edison,
Expects, and such as have a name
    Inscrib'd in *golden deeds* that run
Forever thro' the Page of Fame.
    There's nothing in this world that's new,
Tho' knowledge often hides from view;
    When courage actuateth you
What man's accomplish'd ye shall do.

6

Press on! Your race has rear'd great sons,
    Who've thrill'd the human firmament
In days gone by. Let him who runs
    Recite achievements violent,
That stain'd the tracks of Bantu kings,
    Let him recall some mighty deeds
Whereof the Bantu minstrel sings:
    Of Jobe's son; of Nandi's seed;
Dingana, and the '*Vale of Tears*';
    Cetywayo and Sandhlwana's Tomb;
Moshesh and Carthcart of Crimea;
    Zilikazi's son, and Wilson's doom;
And so your drooping spirits cheer.
    There's nothing in this world that's new,
Tho' knowledge often hides from view;

When courage actuateth you,
What man's accomplish'd ye shall do.

7

Press onwards! Let your shields, and spears
   Tho' famous in some by-gone day
Be laid to rest. 'Mid floods of tears
   There let them rust, and *there* decay.
To you will Earth some day bequeath
   A race of sons, who will outshine
Yon stars, who did their spears unsheath
   For bloodshed, terror, and rapine
And wanton national suicide.
   Some *bloodless* Tshaka will arise
To vanquish *ignorance,* and strive
   By *bloodless* methods to devise
A plan whereby ye too shall thrive.
   There's nothing in this world that's new,
Tho' knowledge often hides from view;
   When courage actuateth you,
What man's accomplish'd ye shall do.

Robert Grendon *Ilange Lase Natal* 11 December 1903

AFRICA'S TEARS

Come to me, oh, ye children
For I am old and out of date;
Bring with you the wisdom
Whence it may be obtained;
Tell me not of Socrates and Plato
For their words are old and gray,
But your youngest infant State.

I have worried long without you
For a thousand years or so,
Come and put us 'in the know';
I have sat in the quiet cloister
My light behind a bush,
And I need your kind assistance
In the modern game of push.

J I Msikinya   *Koranta Ea Becoana* 7 September 1904

THE REGENERATION OF AFRICA

O Africa!
Like some great century plant that shall bloom
In ages hence, we watch thee; in our dream
See in thy swamps the Prospero of our stream;
Thy doors unlocked, where knowledge in her tomb
Hath lain innumerable years in gloom.
Then shalt thou, walking with that morning gleam
Shine as thy sister lands with equal beam.

P KaI Seme   *The African Abroad* 5 April 1906

AMAGUNYANA'S SOLILOQUY

I am a blackman: king of them forsooth;
And in these swarthy veins doth course the blood
Of ancient kings from Sheba until now.
Yea, at my feet doth bow a goodly score
Of lesser kings, nor dare one e'en so much
As gaze on me, save at my own behest.
And o'er this grand old Ethiopian veld,
High guarded on its farmost lines by you,

Blue mountain range, how oft, for countless moons
My kin hath chased the striped herd and slain
And roasted on the spit, and ate, and ate,
Till kings could eat no more.
                                        Once in my youth,
On yonder kopjie's chasm-rifted kloof
I came upon a lion fast asleep,
But in a flash awake. We grappled close,
He with his glistening teeth, long, strong and sharp
And shaped for tearing; and I with my wide
Blade, fresh whetted to its keenest edge. The strife
                    was brief. 'Tis true he left his dimples
In my flesh both here and there, but while the
Thundering roar still lingered in his throat,
The fire yet a flash within his royal eye,
Through a rich rent within his side, thrust through
By my right arm, his life gushed out, and I
Was left the winner.
                                        Until this day my
Foot hath never wandered to the limits
Of my father's heritage. My royal
Kraal rests on the mountain's side: my herds of
Lowing cattle graze in peace along the
Grassy banks of Umswalisa's cooling
Waters. A hundred thousand assegais
Are mine and will assemble at my call
Within a morning's sunrise.
                                        How fondly
I remember Mandlakaza's raid, when
That sly hyena thought to wrest a bone
Or two from meat the Lion's might still watched:
I let them enter well within my bounds
Clear on to Xikunguza's placid lake,
When with a mighty rush of men we came
Upon them unaware and charged them in

Our crescent form when in a trice our spears
Were drinking human gore, nor did a man
Escape. Their carrion carcass fouled the air
For months for miles around—a banquet fine
For many a foulest scavenger of night.
They came not more. One Lion's lesson taught
Enough.
                    These were the days when I was king
And had power to make and end a war.
And they were grand!
                    Then came the Whiteman with
That assegai of his, which hurls so fast
The hurtling iron ball, which will not cease
Nor rest till all is his, till foes there's none.
Before it human flesh however brave must
Melt like early dew. The goodly herds of
Choicest game which cropped the grass on yonder
Plain, he's run to earth and left me naught but
Grass to eat. He's sectioned out my choicest
Lands and placed his captains over them and me.
The very mountains he hath bored and crushed
And made havoc of and carted off to
Whiteman's home ten thousand manloads of their
Jewels and fine gold a precious lot of
Rubbish.
                    In yonder vale he's placed his
Kraal marked everywhere with all that never
Grew. I hate his most unnatural paths; his
Close right angled corners and hot walls. His
Den in which he lives is prison small. How
Little is his earth to me! I scorn his
Most effeminate ways, his fretful timecard.
His too fine food, his chafing raiment and
His eternal work. My home is all the
Vast horizon wide, my couch is earth, my

Blanket quilted stars; while as to raiment
Half a pelt is plenty for a lifetime.
I loathe his work. 'Tis only fit for slaves
Who fear the death. 'Tis woman's lot to work,
To till the soil to find the food to feed
Her offspring and her lord. 'Tis his to wield
The spear, to raid the enemy afar,
Nor suffer him to ever enter ours.

                      'Tis true the Whiteman brings
a Book which tells
Of many a vision yet unknown to mine.
I may not read the hazy mazes of
His much curved ink, but I read earth and sky
And men and should it all prove true in hours
Not yet arrived that his Eternal one
Is Great or greater than our own Great-Great,
Then will I do Him homage and serve Him,
And in the manner he had fashioned me.
But not in theirs.

Anon   *Ilanga Lase Natal* 18 May 1906

THE SPIRIT SONG OF MEHLOKAZULU

The crash of the rifle, the whizzing of spears.
No longer I hear their sweet sound in mine ears!
The war cry, 'Usutu' my warriors yelled
Like hounds, as they leapt from the leash where I
                            held
Them straining and eager, to fly at the foe;
All now is hushed in this Valley of Woe!

We thought in our fury with hate on the white,
Who lay in the darkness enveloped by night!

Each warrior clutching his spears and his shield.
Eager for daylight to rush to the field!
Yet, now we are vanquished! I gaze on the slain.
Who never shall brandish the war-axe again!

In the bush where we fell, our bodies do lie.
And faint from the Upper World, sounds the weird
cry

Of wailing and weeping! Our women are they
Who mourn for the fighters who fell in the fray!
Weep on, O, ye loved ones; yet tears are in vain!
We never shall march in the sunlight again!

As into the Shadows my warriors came,
Fording the river, I called each by name.
And now I've an impi of spirits to lead.
Yet nerveless our arms, and no valorous deed
In this Kraal of the Mist shall ever be wrought,
No war-cry be chanted, nor battle be fought!

O, Chaka! Where art thou? We call thee in vain!
Thy kraal of the Blest in this Valley of Pain?
The brave ones, our sires, who fell long ago.
Where are they, O Great One, thy children would
know?

O, take us, enrol us, we wait, King, for thee!
To march in thine impis, 'thy warriors to be!

A E K   *Ilanga Lase Natal* 29 June 1906

WELCOME TO OUR SUPREME CHIEF

1
We welcome our Supreme Chief;

For your feet you have placed here,
On the hills of Ohlange
To open this our new School.

2
We thank and appreciate,
For this honour given us,
Sympathy we see in you,
Of our far away White King.

3
May this the beginning be
Of united sympathy;
United in loyalty,
To our King across the sea.

John L Dube   *Ilanga Lase Natal* 29 November 1907
*(As sung by the Ohlange Industrial School boys in
honour of the visit of His Excellency Sir Matthew
Nathan during the opening ceremonies for a new
building, 25 November 1907)*

OHLANGE

Above the Ohlange heights,
There hover ever glorious lights;
They glow, they gleam, they quiver
Ever, ever, ever;
As a flowing river,
From the mighty heart of God.

E M G   *Ilanga Lase Natal* 11 October 1912

AFRICA: MY NATIVE LAND

How beautiful are thy hills and thy dales!
I love thy very atmosphere so sweet,
Thy trees adorn the landscape rough and steep —
No other country in the whole world could with thee
                                        compare

It is here where our noble ancestors,
Experienced joys of dear ones and of home;
Where great and glorious kingdoms rose and fell
Where blood was shed to save thee, thou dearest Land
                                        ever known

But, Alas! their efforts were all in vain,
For today others claim thee as their own;
No longer can their off-spring cherish thee
No land to call their own — but outcasts in their own
                                        country.

Despair of thee I never, never will,
Struggle I must for freedom — God's great gift —
Till every drop of blood within my veins
Shall dry upon my troubled bones, oh thou Dearest
                                        Native Land.

Mrs A C Dube   *Ilanga Lase Natal* 31 October 1913

A TRIBUTE TO MISS HARRIET COLENSO
The staunchest friend of the Zulu Race

1

The sun is setting. Densely the clouds
Envelop the hills, and threaten a storm.
And fully ten thousand Zulu braves
Have stepp'd into line in half-circular form,

In yon spacious front of Nobamba kraal.
    But tho' dark be the heavens—darker yon throng,
That so vainly, so vainly thirsteth for blood,
    Whilst extolling dead kings in song after song
And the frequent freaks of the lightning's flash
    Back'd up by the thunderclap right o'erhead,
Arouse in Man's bosom deep reverence, yet
    O'er yon scene a dazzling brilliance shed.

2

But lo, as the tempest grows more fierce,
    And darkness deepens with stealthy pace,
Yon pageant encounters a brief delay,
    Thro' reluctance of yonder British 'grace'
To participate in the closing scene.
    But suasion renders her spirit so warm,
That she presently yields. Then out from retreat
    Steps forth the queen-like virgin form
Of Sobantu's daughter, and takes her stand
    In the midst of yonder spacious court,
Like an angel sent by the Lord above,
    With a message of hope to men distraught.

3

Then a tremendous shout goes up from the crowd!
    From right to left—and from left to right
It sways with the sway of yon warrior-forms,
    And the roaring rage of tempestuous 'Night'.
In the midst of the shout, me-thought I heard
    The mention of that white lady's name.
As my distant ears strove to hear the salute,
    An echo—'INKOSAZANA!'—came
With a swell and decline, like an organ's peal
    In its float from afar on the wings of the wind:
And again and again when the sound had ceas'd,

That echo seem'd to return to my mind.

4

When rememb'ring the part that her father play'd
    In the cause of the Zulu so hated and scorn'd,
And recounting the deeds—the deeds of a man!—
    That she wrought in defence of the king that is
                                                    mourn'd,
Need we marvel—I ask—why yon cultureless souls
    Are o'ercome with emotion—held by a spell!—
As she stands in their midst to receive
    A tribute—a tribute she merits so well?
'Tis a lie!—'tis a damnable lie!—
    That the savage with virtue is not imbued;
For yon full deep-throated salute to her
    Bespeaketh intensest gratitude!

5

She alone—she alone—of the White Man's race
    Hath cleav'd unto you thro' thick and thin!
She is verily—verily more than a friend!
    There be few like her, that have censur'd sin
In the strong, who trample the weaker down!
    There be few like her, that have parried so well
The thrusts of detractors ever on watch
    To further the vile intentions of Hell,
By exciting strife betwixt Man and Man!
    There be few like her, that have splinter'd the fangs
Of Natalia's mamba, and its venom excis'd,
    And depriv'd of its swiftly fatal pangs!

6

Then revere her, ye Zulus, yea revere
    Ye her for her own and her father's sake!
Since Heaven bequeath'd her to Zululand,

Your contact with her shall no man unmake!
Revere her, for none—yea none have toil'd
    In your behalf as she! And behold!—
Your debt to her—which she claimeth not—
    Ye can never repay!—'Tiṣ not valued in gold!
But the heart of Man in a moment may change!
    So if friendship t'ward others become defil'd
Let it never be said, O 'Race of the Heav'ns',
    That you turn'd your back on Sobantu's child!

Robert Grendon   *Izwe Le Kiti* 4 February 1914

Chapter 2 :

My Country

SONG

Yes, keep and feed the sprite,
Especially the hairy sprite;
   Yebo! yebo!
He'll show us how to crack magic out of poles
So that we'll scatter and slay our enemies,
Then nobody will do us harm
While we use this wonderful charm;
   Yebo! yebo!
Let the hairy spirit live
Let him live, let him live.
   Yebo! yebo!
   Yebo! yebo!

Sol T Plaatje   From *Mhudi* 1920

MZILIKAZI'S SONG

Sing on, sing on! Mzilikazi's a youth today,
   For since we left the bewitched valley —
I never did feel so great before,
   Sing on, sing on!
I never did feel so young before;
   The pillar of my house is here,
I never did feel so glad before,

Cheer on, cheer on!
Not since we left the vale bewitched
    Inzwinyani, the place of sorcery.
I never did feel so strong before.
    Dance on, dance on!

Sol T Plaatje   From *Mhudi* 1920

SONG OF THE BACA

Who did it, aye, who did it?
They say the water did it
Who did it, eh, who did it?
Some say the Baca did it
Tell us, tell us, who crushed Chaka?
Why not, why not a Baca?

Sol T Plaatje

EMAKHAYA

Go, let us go my friends, go home.
Go, let us go to see our little hills.
We've long been working on the mines,
We long have left our homes for this, the place of gold.

When we get home they will be waiting there,
Our Mothers happy when we come inside,
At Mazandekeni, home, my home.

Return my brother, from the place of gold.
Reject the town.
Cherish your mother, children and your own.

They'll clap their hands for joy
When you come home,
At home where they are waiting.
Come, come home.

> From *A Hundred Zulu Lyrics* (ed Hugh Tracey)

DAUGHTERS OF AFRICA

Daughters of Afric, those voices are calling you,
Calling you now to be faithful and true—
True to yourselves, to your cause and your kindred,
True to your country to dare and to do.
Daughters of Afric, those voices are calling you,
Will you not lighten our burden of care?
Hands to the suffering, help to the perishing,
Hasten to answer the cry of despair.

A K Soga   1919

IN COMMEMORATION OF THE PASS SYSTEM MARTYRS (*Extract*)

1

When Israel groaned 'neath Pharaoh's yoke,
All Egypt took it for a joke.
When Belgians groaned 'neath Germany's laws,
The Germans' laughter cracked their jaws.
When Bantu women, great with child,
Lie, trampled down 'neath horses wild
The firmament is rent with cheers,
Of them that joy when 'kaffir' tears.

2

Tell me what was old Egypt's fate,
And her reward for Israel's hate!
How needless 'tis for one to tell,
What's known to old and young as well.
What then has Germany's laughter brought?
It open'd her mouth like a figure 'O'—
Shall then these cheers be changed to tears,
And these our tears be turned to cheers?

3

Whilst here, like neutrals they intern
Your flesh, your minds dare ne'er unlearn
The courage of those souls now gone
As heralds to the judgement throne.
In prayers, we ask the judge divine,
'Is this Pass System law of Thine,
That caused our men untimely death,
And still may cause more woes on earth?'

4

Pile heavier still the fetters,
Our blood make run like waters,
While heaven smiles on you!
You'll one day get your due;
For, as sure as dewdrops can remove,
A boulder which strong winds defies,
So sure can tears make God reprove
The tyrants who our cries despise.

M Mphahlele   1919

IN PRAISE OF LANGA

Come, let us sing!
  Mzilikazi has a son.
Come, let us sing!
  Langa is the name of his son.
Come, let us dance!
Langa has a spear.
Come, let us prance!
  His sword is a sharp pointed spear.
Go forth and summon the girls of Soduza
  To the dance;
Go call the maidens to the Puza,
  And the dance;
For Mzilikazi has a son!
Langa, the Fighter, is his son!

Sol T Plaatje   From *Mhudi* 1920

SWEET MHUDI AND I

I long for the solitude of the woods,
Far away from the quarrels of men,
Their intrigues and vicissitudes;
Away, where the air was clean,
And the morning dew
Made all things new;
Where nobody was by
Save Mhudi and I.

Speak not to me of the comforts of home,
Tell me of the Valleys where the antelopes roam;
Give me my hunting sticks and snares
In the gloaming of the wilderness;

Give back the palmy day of our early felicity
Away from the hurly-burly of your city,
And we'll be young again — aye:
Sweet Mhudi and I.

Sol T Plaatje   From *Mhudi* 1920

BARS

There are Bars of diverse sorts!
Judged by what their text imports.
Some high there are, and some are low,
As we do purpose here to show.

First, the Bar of Courts Supreme,
Where the barristers do seem
By using arguments most strong
To prove wrong right, and right the wrong.

Then there is the great Side Bar
With its members near and far,
The 'Land-sharks' they are often called
Because some pluck their clients bald.

And the Bar at river mouth,
Barring ships from North and South.
And 'Bars' in ostrich feathers too
Diminishing their value true.

There are Bars in all the pubs,
And a pub in self-styled clubs,
Where fools imbibe, and get so drunk
In degradation they are sunk.

But the lowest Bar of all!
This the 'Colour Bar' men call.
It strives to keep those races back,
Whose skins are either brown or black.

Lo! this Bar is now removed,
Since the Courts have clearly proved
In well considered judgement trite
That it is 'Ultra vires' quite.

So the natives will rejoice,
With one heart, and soul, and voice,
At this small crumb of liberty,
Conferred by long deferred decree.

Alpha Beta   *Umteteli Wa Bantu* 24 November 1923

A GAME OF CHESS

'Neither will win,' the watchers say
    Now that the contest starts.
'For Black men move without their heads,
    And White without their hearts.

'And if one shall advance,' they said,
    So much as one short pace,
His fellow-men will shun him then
    A traitor to the race.

'You wooden men give up the game,
    For what are all these squares
But black and white and black again,
    The pattern of your cares?'

The Chessmen quiver into life,
  For love has conquered pride,
Those that were angry face to face
  Are quiet side by side.

P Q R   *Ilanga Lase Natal* 15 February 1924

AN AFRICAN STAR — R T CALUZA

'Midst Afric's host of sons and daughters,
A nation full of power and honour,
Whose darkness, light has sworn to conquer,
There lives a son whose colour and talent
Set Afric's great and true distinction.

Afric's traditions, and modes of old,
Her cries, and passion, her appeal for light,
In strains of sweet, patriotic songs,
Shall now and ever live.

Of whom do Afric's old and young pride?
The name CALUZA, 'The African Star'.
His love for man, his BANTU airs,
LOVE, FAME, and PRIDE for him have found.

For those of Afric's host whose eyes have seen
His mode of tread on AFRICAN STAGE,
Have had his name translated.
HONOUR! LONG LIFE! PEACE! to the African Star.

N G M   *Ilanga Lase Natal* 29 February 1924

POST MORTEM

'I'm an educated man,
I can read and write, I can.
Even when I was a scholar
No one wore a harder collar.
Don't believe that there was ever
Anybody quite so clever—'

(Listen, just for want of thinking
This poor fellow died of drinking.
Doctors cut him when he died
So that they could see inside;
He had thought himself so smart,
But they found he had NO HEART.)

P Q R   *Ilanga Lase Natal* 7 March 1924

THREE FOLK POEMS*

A New Disciple

In beaded skins,
With sticks and shields,
The heathen roams
His native fields.

*[Author's Note: It is my hope that these simple verses may
help to serve an early movement towards our own literature. A
national literature can only be built up of many parts, and
with infinite pains, but if we can plainly express now some of
the true feelings of our people, however simple, we may be able
to lay a sure foundation. Here I attempt to give you the intense
Christian joy of the newly-converted.]

But if he yields
To Christ his sins,
He loses less
Than what he wins;

For hearts and homes
Our Lord will bless,
Dissolving sins
In happiness.

Gifts To God

See an African,
Lord, before you stand,
With a heavy heart
And an open hand,
As my gifts to God
Who gave me a wife,
His Mercy and Love,
And my very life.

A Stranger At The Wedding

Shall soul and sense unite
Now, at the beginning?
Or those two find delight,
Bloom slowly, winning
Their spiritual home
Like honey from the comb?

That is for them to know.
But (bell with bell ringing)
I must gladly bestow
(O hear the singing!)
A kiss of peace, in prayer,

Upon the bridal pair.

P Q R   *Ilanga Lase Natal* 14 March 1924

THE DEATH OF A ZULU

The weather is mild
At the house of one of the dead.
There is fruit in the hands of his child,
With flowers on its head.

Smoke rises up from the floor,
And the hands of a ghost
(No shadow darkens the door)
Caress the door-post.

The woman inside cannot sleep,
Too wild to weep:
Food lies uncooked at her feet, and is taken
By scavenging fowls.

Outside with a sudden fear shaken
The little one howls.

P Q R   *Ilanga Lase Natal* 16 May 1924

OHLANGE IS OUR SHIELD

1
Throughout the world the hills are known.
    The Hills of Ohlange,
Where seeds of sound learning are sown.
    By beac'ning Ohlange.

2

These hills lay low under the sod,
    Then gloomy Ohlange
Till like a soldier with a sword,
    Debe called Ohlange.

3

The once unknown Hills of our Land
    Now famous Ohlange,
Stand lofty in the Christmas Land,
    The learned Ohlange.

4

Zulus, Basutos and Xhosas
    Gather at Ohlange;
Their voices blend in the Chorus!
    'John Dube's Ohlange!'

5

Like the shining rays of the sun,
    Boys move from Ohlange,
Illuminating like the sun,
    Our world from Ohlange.

6

Live long Ohlange, Hills of Fame,
    And education shield
Till all races chant the name
    'Ohlange is our shield!'

A F Matibela   *Ilanga Lase Natal* 24 October 1924

MY COUNTRY

My Dear Country — I love you well.
In my heart your welfare is uppermost;
Thoughts of thee, make my heart to swell
With zeal, and this thought foremost
   To serve you well.

Land of charms and gladness,
Land of mountains and plains.
Why is it, my heart is full of sadness
And tears gush like drops of rains?
   Oh, to serve you well.

Is it because my country is no longer mine,
Is it because days of freedom are over;
Is it through this, then, my heart doth pine?
Ah! that such days should pass for ever!
   Still I love you well.

Each corner and nook was dear to me,
Each rivulet and hill-top a pleasing sight,
These were echoes of innocence to me,
These which, today, are a sorrowful plight.
   Can this quench my love?

Sorrowful! aye — sorrowful and dreary,
Because no longer a black man's country,
Natal, my country, my heart is aweary,
Tears scar my cheeks because of my country.
   I love you well.

Here and there poor whites claim you,
My country — leaving Natives helpless.
Here and there cotton planters claim you,

My country — leaving Natives hopeless.
  All appear to love you.

My country, I love, I love you well,
In my heart you'll ever be dear,
Thoughts of thee make my heart to swell.
To you let all our hearts be near.
  We love you well.

'Rollie Reggie'   *Ilanga Lase Natal* 12 February 1926

TO SATAN

Curse you, hell's Satanic Majesty,
Preventer of the Truth — you bug!
Voetsak, and never let me see
You, you hoary-headed humbug,
Vamoose, you lying, skulking cad.
Your doctrine is to me taboo;
To hell with you, you stiff — you're mad,
You make me see red, white and blue.

You teach mankind to make the dop —
That fiery drink of different hues —
And when the bloomin' stuff is op,
They see green snakes and get the blues.
You teach Muntu the skokian,
Which lands him in the tronk;
You tell him — lying baviaan —
The stuff does not make dronk.

You coax the damsel from her home
And land here in the soup,
Then in a very different tone

You tell her that her number's 'oop'.
You think you're wise, you demon freak,
And you call your followers legion;
But wacht-een-beetjie, beastly sneak,
With you they'll stew like devilled pigeon.

Apollyon, you've got the sack
Forever from this coon,
So, vat jou goed and with you trek
To hell, you cracked buffoon.
And, cloven-footed Beeskop Nick,
Stay where I've relegated you;
With you I've no more bones to pick,
Your heart is full of demons blue.

Beelzebub, you silly twat,
Beelzebub, you've broken,
My word's my bond — so that's that —
Beelzebub, I've spoken.

H D T   *The Worker's Herald* 15 November 1926

TEACHERS' MEETING

The Heralds sound the bugle call;
One hundred souls roll up to answer.
You can see the male and female teachers
Filing into a gorgeous hall.

They have not come to regulate
Their own defensive battle;
Their rule is to sit up late
To watch the procedure of its mettle.

Someone throws dust on the crowd!
They clap and applaud significantly,
Even it be sweet or bitter food,
They rush to snatch it gleefully.

That's just when the cup becomes full
By all the babies droll,
They fear to bikker with the bull,
Which makes one's belly boil.

An earnest speaker takes Theology,
The next one explains Physiology,
Nobody seeks to raise their finances,
Not a single soul receives their grievances.

What's the use of becoming amused
In attending the teachers' meeting?
Because there's very much money abused,
And yet you'd gain absolutely nothing.

I have had innumerable debates at College
History, Geography, and Nature Studies;
But now I have grown to an older age,
I solve domestic commodities.

I must confess I'd feel ashamed
Of quarrelling over nonentities,
Because very many teachers are accused
Of failing to adjust their destinies.

'Zulu'   *Ilanga Lase Natal* 22 April 1927

OUR DYING SPEECH

The funeral bells are tolling at a distance
On the summits of the Lebombo Mountains,
They speak about the dying of our speech,
Which once was predominant in Zululand.

The gentlemen of the good old age
Were fond of their mother-tongue,
You would have liked to hear our braves
Rendering it through their powerful lungs.

On the memorable eve at that famous meeting
'Twas on a hill-top near Isandhlwana,
When the brave Induna spoke solemnly
About the sad tales of Inyezana.

His baritone voice and impressive eloquence
Produced the sweetest harmonic semibreves,
He then spoke about fire and blood
Which wiped our heroes to their graves.

The last of the proper Zulu language
Was spoken by fugitives at Ulundi;
Today Mammie speaks foreign idioms,
Which predicts ill-luck to our Idhlozi.

If Shaka were to rise from the dead
He would not be welcomed by the guards;
Nor would he be proud of the honour
Of ruling over a hundred thousand bastards.

Our customs are condemned by our pastors
And our language neglected by the teachers,
The uneducated Natives are bereaved and depressed

By the sad loss sustained by their brothers.

An appeal to our educated brethren
Is made even in the heathen kraal,
Remember your traditions, your very existence
Lie safely preserved in the Zulu Taal.

'Zulu'   *Ilanga Lase Natal* 1 July 1927

THE THREE ABORIGINES

A Plea To Africa

Oh Africa, sweet sunny Africa!
Behold thy dusky sons and daughters!
Hearken to the prayers of your children;
And forsake not the offerings of our mothers.
Why do we cast such dark shadows o'er thee,
By producing discordance and irrational innovation?
Shall we ever be happy and gay,
And be redeemed from such awful confusion?

A Poor Race

The inadequacy of my means is quite enough
To imperil my dignity in public society,
Imagine poor Jim, the Kafir, just a Nigger boy
Emerging from savagery unto doctrines of Christianity.
Have ye not begotten us to live peacefully,
Contentedly, and free to reverence our Creator?
Oh, Africa land of my Hope!
Listen to the untiring prayers of our leaders.

A Divided House

You refuse to offer us your ingenious Commentary
Which develops nations magnificently;
You refuse to lend us your powerful machinery
Which unites each nation solidly.
You have not replied to our Congress meetings
For nothing there can be achieved unanimously;
We become lunatics at political gatherings:
Each barks a little louder o'er a bare rotten bone.

Census

Yet our birthrate becomes lower and lower.
And I'm afraid our numbers are slowly diminishing.
Nothing can recover such irreparable losses
Which gradually exterminate the living.
Our women have hopelessly become barren,
Through liquor and poverty begetting immorality.
All these lead up to a wide, a very wide road
Trodden by the Bushmen and Hottentot races.

Bushmen and Hottentots

Those aboriginals and Zuid Afrikaners
Could not withstand the evil vice of civilization,
They completely lost the land of their ancestors,
Their traditions, language, and ultimately their
                                            existence.
They too were landlords and inhabitants of this
                                            land;
Splendidly they flourished under the sway of their
                                            chiefs,
Yet they dwindled from well organised tribes to
                                            scattered bands,

Wretched homeless wanderers and poverty-stricken
                                              beggars.

'Zulu'   *Ilanga Lase Natal* 29 July 1927

THE WAILINGS OF ROLFES R R DHLOMO

Now I know why my heart is sad
And the joy of my soul has fled;
I know why this world seems dreary
And my heart is heavy and weary.

Now I know why I cannot help sighing,
Why I cannot help moaning and pining;
I know why I wail and sigh in vain,
And madness seems to assail my brain.

Now I know why daylight seems to be night,
And my joy is in a sorrowful plight
I know — can I help knowing
That ahead of Natives oppressive winds are blowing?

I know why Natives seem to be slaves
They — the offspring of the braves!
I know because my heart is cringing
And all my hopes are fast sinking.

Now I know, verily I know this,
That all our former bliss
Has fled to return no more,
Freedom of speech we'll enjoy no more.

Now I know why I seem to tread the rugged road
And my heart groans under a heavy load

I know why my eyes are dim with tears.
And I am weary as a man with many years.

Now I know why clouds of impending sorrow
Seem to warn the Natives of a gloomy morrow
I know this, because my heart misgives me
When I think what the Natives' future will be.

The Black man's way is long and dreary,
Travel he must, though his feet be weary;
Travel he must, since it is his gate,
He, the victim of opposition, prejudice and Hate.

To God he should bow and implore
Strength and faith to love Him more,
Since here on earth he has no rest,
Sorrow, fear, premonition fill his breast.

I know that as long as Natives are sure of unity,
The dark future they can easily endure;
That although by some whites they may be disowned
Yet by Unity to future advantages they may be
                                        enthroned.

Unity will ultimately drive away our fears,
United Leaders can wipe away people's tears
And lead the masses to glorious ends.
Only in this way may our leaders be called people's
                                        friends.

   Here endeth my wailing which came pouring from
my heart during the night, and when I awoke —
behold it was a dream.

R R R Dhlomo   *Ilanga Lase Natal* 12 August 1927

THE FIRM HAND
AN UNFINISHED STORY

How oft had he repeated when his laws they took to
task;
There's one only way to govern, one must wear the
tyrant's mask,
If with subjects inarticulate you condescend to reason
You will certainly discover long premeditated treason.

Poor comrades these who drooping sat with scarcely
veiled alarm
At this latest proclamation. Let them trust in his right
arm!
It would not be the first time he had showed them
might was right,
With the strength at his command he would woo, not
dread, a fight.

Consultation of opinion was the ruin of the state,
Turn a blind eye to discretion if you wished to
dominate,
Spear and broadsword were the weapons that would
teach the populace.
If his subjects did not know, it was time they learnt,
their place.

Disturbances and rioting were agitators' game,
And popular complaints were planned to mud the
royal name,
But these he had long knowledge of, and never failed
to quell,
He held the reins with firmest hand and rode his
horse full well.

What was this latest measure he had of late pro-
                                              claimed?
At man's most sacred treasure its clauses subtly aimed
For brutes and beasts and simplest folk are kings in
                                              one domain:
Who touches man's own womankind will do so at his
                                              pain.

The edict was deliberate; it deemed it politic
That wives should stay at home at night, sedately
                                              domestic;
So curfew should ring out the rule, and at a stroke of
                                              pen
Women should be right virtuous and be indoors by
                                              ten.

This doughty stalwart king, alas! one thing he did not
                                              reck
That patience in the mutest breast too often pressed
                                              will break.
Resentment black the simplest soul with thoughts of
                                              vengeance tears,
The bravest lion on forest path the wounded leopard
                                              'wares.

The king his hobby horse astride (were this tale told
                                              in jest)
Sad lady's ride on tiger's back in Riga would suggest
But the story's never been writ, I think, of the fate of
                                              this brave lord,
If ever again the royal steed's hoofs at the palace
                                              gates were heard.

J M   *Umteteli Wa Bantu* 18 July 1931

DESPAIR

The Star of day that shines forever bright
And spreads o'er all the world its ray of light
That all may live in happiness and joy
Means not a jot to Black Mother's Boy —
The Queen of night and all the host of Stars
That rally round her as in time of wars,
The gentle winds that to and fro do move
Unseen through pits below and hills above,
The Sea whose deepness is alike the thought
Of this weak heart, envenomed and o'er wrought
By biased minds that break and then command.
The greedy selfish men whose word must stand
Heedless of its base and false conceit
Mean not a rap to me, but sure deceit.
Great things have come and gone just like a squall,
Some men have lived and died at Nature's call;
Why then have I been left behind, dear Death,
A poor white-livered cub, the curse of earth,
Enslaved and mocked with all my Bantu Race
By those who see the black touch of my face,
The colour of my skin and woolly hair?
I'm through, come take me now, I must despair!
O Death, I ask for liberty and peace,
Instead I get oppression and disgrace.
O cursed crime and thou, O reverie,
Shall I not hope that chains of slavery
That bind me hand and foot and render me
A hopeless creature, child of woe and shame,
May someday be removed, the bondman freed?
Or shall I fight to break these chains indeed,
That those who after me may come to life
May never feel the pains of bondage's strife
And never curse me who before them lived?

Nay, I will not fight, I have resolved:
Neither pen nor sword would be of use.
But now I'm through! I want Death's little pause
For I'm just like the undesired weed
That must be rooted out for swine to feed.
Some thing I am, worse than dogs that howl at
                                                 night,
They sneer and kick and chase me out of sight,
But one or two good men, the true Godsends
Are fighting tooth and nail to make amends.
I've fed their children from my very hand,
And carried them about, d'you understand?
The food that builds their bodies and their brains
Is cooked and served by me, not without pains,
But when they meet me in the street, great swells,
They shout, take Jim away from here, he smells!
Fond little things, you're not the ones to blame;
I've heard the tale of men who die through shame
And step by step have passed o'er filth and mire,
And having reached the climax they desire,
They look with scorn upon the stepping stones
Of their success and rise to lofty zones.
O, let me eat and drink and then be done,
I cannot merry make with anyone,
For fear of plots and stratagems to heed
Behind the smile and kiss of a friend indeed.
Was it not Brutus who great Caesar stabbed
And made th' unkindest cut so that he sobbed?
Was it not Judas who betrayed our Lord?
Beware of friends and foes, they bring discord.
I've lost all hope, all faith, and cling to Fate:
Let good or ill come nigh, and not too late.
Make all your laws and hang me by the rope,
Or lead me to a stony mountain slope,
Thence drag me to hell's door: do not refuse.

Shoot me or mutilate this muddy house
Which is the earthly home of Man sublime.
Send me to jail, the public school of crime
Or banish me for spite or pangs of hate,
All will not alter things; that is my Fate.
Through all these years my life shall nothing fear,
I'll pass without a smile, nay not a tear,
Until at last sweet death shall come my way
To lead me through the dread grave away
Into the land I've always longed to see,
The promised land where all are ever free,
Where colour prejudice is all unknown
And man is never reckoned by his gown:
No rate to pay nor taxes to collect,
That is the place for all of God's Elect.
Therefore get out, thou wretched melancholy,
For nothing shall I have that is unholy;
Fie! I have been cursed right down to shame,
Now I must die, this is no place for me.
I bid you all fair farewell, this is the time.

E C Jali   *Bantu World* 21 May 1932

'CIVILISED' LABOUR POLICY

Hertzog is my shepherd; I am in want.
He maketh me to lie down on park benches,
He leadeth me beside still factories,
He arouseth my doubt of his intention.
He leadeth me in the path of destruction for his
                              Party's sake.
Yea, I walk through the valley of the shadow of
                                   destruction
And I fear evil, for thou art with me.

The Politicians and the Profiteers, they frighten me;
Thou preparest a reduction in my salary before me,
In the presence of mine enemies.
Thou anointest mine income with taxes,
My expense runneth over.
Surely unemployment and poverty will follow me
All the days of this Administration,
And I shall dwell in a mortgaged house forever.

L R   *Umteteli Wa Bantu* 29 October 1932

THE POET'S DEFIANCE

The Orbs and Constellations of the Heav'ns
May give me health, wealth, grief or pains;
The winds may blow or may not blow at all —
O, damn it all, I'm ready, ready for the call.
And Jupiter may poise and bring great dearth,
Destroy both plants and animals on Earth,
Great plagues may come and leave me woe behind —
What do I care? I'll neither shriek nor mind.
Black Diamond of Africa I am;
Nor other man can boast of this, O Mam:
The diamond proof my Bantu race unmatched,
Who though ill-treated yet they pass unscratched.
I hate a joke and have no faith in a friend;
Behind a smile or a kiss there hides a fiend.
As singly as I came so I'll proceed
And neither pity nor your tears I need.
Great plagues, wind and fire change not my face,
This land's injustices leave not a trace;
I pass with a cheery smile through thick and thin
My life, death and fate is upon my skin.
When death shall come, I'll say goodbye to none

Lament not my departure woebegone;
My corpse may feed the Ants or deck the Hearth —
And damn it all, there's nothing good on earth.

E C Jali   *Bantu World* 4 February 1933

A BANTU LAMENT

Black folk, kindred of Africa,
'Mongst folk who live in light we dwell:
Behind we are in deeds—But ah!
Do we endeavour to do well?

Their intellect we've got to seek:
In culture they excel us far.
Of enterprise we need not speak,
For lackadaisical we are.

But to endeavours let us turn
Which give our race what it most needs,
And by them we will surely earn
A history of worldly deeds.

For inspiration we may reach
Beyond the seas to Negro soil
In schools our children let us teach
Of Carver, Garvey and Dubois.

And aye in reverence we pause,
When Aggrey's deeds our minds imprint,
Their hero-worship then must cause
Them to be proud of their dark tint.

We little know what life can hold,

In vain we strive accomplishment,
For riches, fame and power loaned
To them who seek advancement.

Oh Spirit! Thou who knowest all,
Do wake us children from our doze.
That we may noble deeds recall,
And in them find a safe repose.

Hasten Black folk, time now arrives,
Let unity our ideal be.
Union our destiny decides —
Endeavour for it, each colleague.
By fate or chance depressed we are.
Oh Spirit Great! we trust in Thee.

Simon McD Lekhela *Umteteli Wa Bantu* 10 June 1933

'WHAT IS IN A NAME?'
In Memory of Sol T Plaatje

A question asked so frequently,
Yet seldom it receives reply.
Read carefully the lines below!
They're sure to satisfy.

A year has passed since we interred
Remains of one we least could spare.
Defender, Fighter, Champion,
Sleep, you have done your share!

The shock was felt by multitudes!
The blow severe turned hearts to ice!
For the demise of noble Sol,

Was a great sacrifice.

One who for others strived to live;
His people's rights his foremost thought;
Discouraged often in his toils,
Great battles though he fought.

A lot has he achieved. But Ah!
A lot has he left incomplete.
It is for those he left behind,
To further and complete.

His pen he wielded forcibly.
His weapon always was the Press.
Speaking from public platforms too,
The people to address.

And though his earnings were but scant,
Strife won for him fame and reward.
For here was one devoid of wealth,
But buried like a Lord.

Author, Translator, Orator,
In you we've lost a precious prize!
Your death, occurred a year ago,
Today we solemnize.

Your ready smile and kindly word,
Career, endeavour, intellect,
Humour and generosity,
We aye will recollect.

A word of heartfelt gratitude,
To all who joined in sympathy,
And were responsible to cheer

The mourning family.

Came Indian, Coloured, White and Black,
And others, miles, to join in Grace,
Homage to pay around the grave
Of one who served his race.

Came from Inland and Overseas
Letters and telegrams — a stream,
And gen'rous aid for which is thanked
All friends who well did mean.

The papers far and wide are thanked,
For kindly answering the call,
Distributing lengthy reports
Of noble deeds of Sol.

Your struggles have been very hard —
Sleep on and take your well-earned rest!
Your efforts we appreciate,·
May you be ever blest.

V N Plaatje   *Bantu World* 24 June 1933

BE OF GOOD CHEER

Hark, hark, be up ye Afric's sons;
Be up and bear your weight.
There is no time for you for funs,
The time is getting late.

See yonder hills you have to pass,
They are still far away.
You dare not stay, you on must march,

No time for a delay.

The weight press hard upon your back
—It's from across the sea,
That selfish weight you soon will sack,
And settle proud and free.

Be heedless of your burden sons,
Your flag you soon will hoist.
Not far away there rests your chance;
March on without a noise.

White clouds of darkness overhead,
Are threatening to your course—
The clouds which Afric's waters fed!
You'll ride them as a horse.

Cheer up, cheer up, ye Afric' sons;
Cheer up, and bear your weight.
There's no time for you for funs,
The time is getting late.

Aug B Swarts   *Bantu World* 8 July 1933

BASUTO MOTHER'S PRAYER

Son of my blood and womb,
You of my love and tears,
List' of my heart to thee
You of our race and forebears.

Know of the race we are,
Learn of the whence ye came,
Build for the coming day,

Honour to your name

You, my son, a mother's pride,
Give of your best to all,
Noble your hip and work—
Lest ye forget and fall.

Render to them our masters,
Honour for all they've done;
Leading us up and onward
To a day of days, its dawn.

Makinidan   *Bantu World* 8 July 1933

A ZULU THOUGHT

Not in the word we choose,
Is there the meaning wished,
The soul and heart possess,
The word unsung, unheard.

Be in the prayer we voice
To God for good to live,
Be of the thing we need,
To know, to do and brave.

Friendship true we seek,
Amid life's stony way,
Its gift of facts true
We pray for day by day.

Anon   *Bantu World* 8 July 1933

FAREWELL MY LADY

Four years of loving
Have all come to nil
Four years of loving
Will always appeal
Why did you tell me
That we'd never part
It's now I can see
You were false at heart

Each little hour
Now that I'm alone
Seems to devour
The day of its tone
My life is now sadness
And laughter has gone
And yet in that sadness
You still linger on

Farewell my Lady
The parting has come
You cannot blame me
For soon I'll succumb
When you are greying
And old age has come
Still I'll be hoping
That some day you'll come

Farewell my Lady, my love, my heart
My fond recollections you cannot destroy,
They're fond souvenirs that are locked in my heart
For though we're apart, they still bring me joy.
Yes! I'll remember with wonderful bliss,
The wonderful joy of that first lover's kiss

Appearances come, when enraptured by your love
Were that you're an angel sent from above
For I thought there was bliss when I look'd in your
                                                    eyes
And that there was Heaven in your wonderful lies,
But now I find in my recollections
With tears in my eyes and a pain in my Heart
That yours were stories full of deceptions.
Farewell my Lady, my love, my heart.

Shep H Maloy   *Bantu World* 13 April 1935

REMEMBER

Hallow the day when your children
Are sitting at home around you;
Cherish this day and remember,
That Life or Death may soon call them.

Will call and never return them
To the places they once occupied;
When the echo of their sweet youthful voices
Will have died to return never more

Remember my friend to do good
Do good while breath yet existeth,
Be kind to the aged and sorrowing.
And He whose eye never dimmeth,

Who never sleepeth nor slumbereth.
Will write it down in His mem'ry,
Will remember, preserve and keep you,
Appoint you a place in His glory,

Remember my friend, the last hour;
When the beat of your heart will fail you;
The dateless, mysterious hour,
When you must go forth alone.

Advance then my friend, go bravely.
Be ready to answer the call,
Unfearing, unmoved, unwavery;
When the final shadows fall.

L H P   *Bantu World* 20 April 1935

COMPENSATION

Because I had been a wandering sheep
Because I would not be controlled
God in His anger, holy and deep,
Gave me pain and hunger and cold.
Because I had been a gentle sheep
Because I loved the sacred fold
God in His love, tender and deep,
Made me strong and wise and bold.

S M Stanley Silwana   *Bantu World* 19 October 1935

BLACK AND WHITE

To be so black is curse you say,
For God has deigned it so;
A greater lie ne'er came man's way,
To toss him to and fro.

The blackness of the changing night,

Is part of shining day,
For God did make creation right
With black and white to stay.

M G   *Bantu World* 21 March 1936

ODE TO DR W B RUBUSANA, PH D

The Star that shone with glare
Through storms and wintry nights
Shall breathe no more nor share
Our joys and our delights

The hand that wrote with might
Unchecked by earthly fear
Though withered, cold and light
Is honoured far and near.

The lips that moved with words
Of wisdom and of love
Thought shrunk like aged chords
Have said when none dare move

The eyes that gleamed with tears
Of love, for Afric's sake
In bitter days or years
Are dimmed at Life's noon brake.

O Death thou cruel king
We dare not curse thy name
Despite our hearts that sting
For Life's a passing game.

Men of Afric' young and old

Be bold and fearless as he
For there he lieth stiff and cold
He died to make us good and free.

Souls of Afric' here and there
Be honest and truthful as he
Maids of Afric' sweet and fair
Be loving and godly as he.

S M Stanley Silwana   *Bantu World* 2 May 1936

I SING OF AFRICA*

I sing of Afric' my Native land.
Let England hear if she hath ears.
Ethiopia yet shall stretch her hand
To vanquish all who caused her tears.
Then swarthy bards shall tell her fame
In rhymes that swell and soothe the heart.
And all who curse her sacred name
Shall honour yet her craft and art.
Land of my birth my hope my love,
Fair home of the kind and the brave,
Thy Sceptre yet shall rise above
Ere hills be sunk beneath the wave.
I sing of Afric' my land of birth.
Let Ireland hear if she hath ears.
Ethiopia yet shall prove her worth.
No, not by hate or poisoned spears.
I envy not the sons of Poland;
Nor care to rhyme of ancient Rome
Where cursed pontiffs formed their band

*A response to the Italo-Abyssinian war.

And bloody warriors made their home.
How wonderous are her crystal rills
That wind and wind so very well!
How beauteous are her rugged hills
Whose age no man shall ever tell!
Land of my heart I pledge to thee
My faith and my strength and my all
And when I shall cease to be,
May it be for thy last freedom's call.
I sing of Afric' my Native land.
Let Europe hear if she hath ears.
Ethiopia yet shall stretch her hand
To banish all who caused her tears.

S M Stanley Silwana *Bantu World* 28 September 1936

THE STRUGGLE

Along my dreary life's path-way
There is no happiness, no game to play;
My steps are guided by enemies of peace,
By human wolves of envy and malice.

Each turn is a life's hard struggle,
Each motion a jump o'er a hurdle.
Shall life leave me so and helpless,
With none my life's bitterness to confess?

Ah, my life and soul are not mine,
They belong to the Creator of man and line.
Whose mercy flows down like the light
Of the silv'ry moon across the night.

What a struggle for existence!

What life's ripple and sweet cadence!
I look for favours from no man,
But, from Him that made me into a man.

My life is controll'd by that Star divine;
My future rests in its brilliant shine.
To make my life happy till I die
And leave the world with no grief or sigh.

L D R   *Bantu World* 28 November 1936

THE CALL OF THE SEA

Away lad, away
With the break of the day.
Nay lad, nay,
Sleep not under the hay.
Say lad, say
Would you like to stay?
Aye lad, aye,
Then I'm sure you may.

The world is calling me,
Over the sea.
I have no other plea,
Under the sea.
Away I must flee,
To the sea.
The ship is calling me
From the sea.

To the home of Drake and Raleigh,
Where the waters break and dally.
When they make a sudden sally,

On the great sea's angry belly.
Oh! for the sea—
It's calling me;
But just to flee,
To the sea.

Peter Abrahams   *Bantu World* 7 November 1936

THE NEGRO YOUTH

He stood alone,
A Negro youth.
What of his future?
His cap was worn,
This Negro youth.
Why was he born?
Born to lead an empty useless life,
Born to mar the record of his race,
Or born to lead his race?
Locked are the doors,
Locked—the doors of his future.
His burden to bear,
To suffer the pain of life's cruel ways,
That is why he was born.

Peter Abrahams   *Bantu World* 5 December 1936

THE REVOLUTION SONG

This revolution song travels wide;
'Tis constant as the flowing tide—
A murmuring distinct to all
Whose ears will listen to the call.

Hark, hear the strain, the melody,
It fills the listeners with glee,
It causes faint hearts to grow strong
And lend their voices to the throng.
So join the tune, ye black folk;
Someday 'twill remove the yoke.
O, chant it loud, you dusky braves,
Sing of the day your spirit craves.
Mix concrete and make roads, but softly croon,
On ancient talkin' drums beat loud the tune;
Go forth uniting every heart
In links no foe can ever part.
Go across the deserts and the sea,
And sing, 'Blackmen shall be free!'
Go everywhere beneath the sun
Join all black souls into one.

Walter M B Nhlapo   *Bantu World* 12 December 1936

UP! MY RACE, UP!

Up! My race, and be ye doing;
Be ye ever striking, brewing!
Wretched prejudice is brewing!
Brewing for to cast ye down!

Race antipathy is calling!
Segregation is appalling!
Endless insults ever mauling!
Trying to crush and daunt your soul!

But ye must keep ever plodding—
Stop! Stay, stop your duty dodging—
Cease your whining and your sobbing

And a dauntless spirit hold!

If your race name ye would treasure,
Each of you must give full measure;
This, of course, should give ye pleasure,
For it's up to each to build!

We must strive for truth and honour,
Faith and confidence to garner.
Then like jewels ye'll adorn her;
Racial rancour too ye'll kill.

Walter M B Nhlapo   *Bantu World* 12 December 1936

THE DEFEAT

Thy warfare is over,
Thy struggle is ended.
What thou hadst intended,
Has deluged the country o'er.

Now, Soldier, do rest!
Thy sword has no fame;
Shame doth shake thy fame
Deep into the palsied chest.

Soldier, the war is lost.
So let the victor reign,
And cause him no pain
Nor his steps mark with frost.

Peace is the one luxurious bed,
One magic bed of happiness,
That lights the shifting darkness.

Enter its precincts enchanted!

Thy warfare is over,
Thy struggle is ended.
What thou hadst intended,
Has deluged the country o'er.

L D R   *Bantu World* 19 December 1936

OUR FUTURE

The African Boys in the street,
Leap for joyous days to come.
In future, Batho shall defeat;
And at last days of rest will come.

Work on, press on, in unity,
Tribal feeling—bury it down,
One hope will lead to destiny,
Our race be freed from shame and scorn.

If we let loose, our leaders fall;
But unity will frustrate foes,
The concentration of us all
Will establish a race for us.

J Theodore Khunou   *Bantu World* 23 January 1937

WINTER AND OUR LITTLE POOR

It's sad to behold winter's approach,
And to see the poor gather, with fright,
What rags-sacks they can, wherein to crouch

When winter's bite and scourge loom up in might.

I seem to see our little Poor
Hop stiffly along in huddled forms
Chattering teeth and breathing that moans,
Dry parched skins, with rugged furrowed feet.

These are our poor that bid the close
Of each day 'good night', with groaning breath,
As they get bundled in search of cose;
A bite of porridge has been their bread.

They are the first to welcome sunrise,
With their sickly forms wound in blankets
That have long lost their claim as such.
They watch in earnest his rise, with fists.

The sun — the monarch of the long day,
Is father and mother to these folk,
Who have neither food nor hay—
Their bosses' bounty who live in bluff.

Then one after the other falls sick,
A victim of scanty clothes and cold,
Of starved system and fatal frictions
Born of the unfairness of Man's code.

It's painful to think how many lives,
Great, innocent beings each one of them,
Mown like the young grass, chopped like the leaves,
The morning glory of all Mankind!

W J Thabede   *Bantu World* 17 April 1937

BLACK AND WHITE BEFORE GOD

The history of the black race
Is full of tears and, oh, great pain;
But black and white see God's good grace,
Oppression goes on now and again.

Are you yellow or the white line?
Or are you in the race of Ham?
Christ died for all men—hope Divine—
God's one and only Paschal lamb.

Language and colour make no bar
Against the merciful God of grace:
How vain the thoughts of many are
Who boast of earthly strength and race.

The beautiful city, Zion—God's ark
For Africa and Europe has room,
But all righteous men can embark:
All ungodly find a dismal doom.

Walter M B Nhlapo   *Bantu World* 12 June 1937

THEY ARE GONE — GONE FOREVER MORE

With a book in hand, I peep through my window
When the hours of toiling are ended,
And evening shadows fall over the meadow,
And weary toilers come home by night
To rest their weary limbs, which aren't pretended,
To dream of morn, its celestial light,
Ere morning birds sweetly sing, and fires are lighted,
And sun's first gleam reflects on the wall

Revealin' photos of loved friends departed,
With whom in lovely days of yore
We played and schooled, and were true hearted;
But they are gone—gone forever more.

These no more flowerets, gay and bearded grains,
Were my friends with noble inspirations;
But what of those inspirations now remains?
Nothin', but the excitin' revelation
That they in life daringly faced the strife
Of which all men do greatly cherish
Along the dreary and weary march of life;
Are rewarded with nothin'—but to perish.
Poor souls, dear, hard working, that weren't weakly,
Who nev'r flinch'd, grumbl'd: but their burdens bore;
But now in the grave lie pale, but look meekly:
Oh, they're gone—O, gone forever more.

O world sinful, do you recall those footsteps
That on you walked and were divine!
On their tombs grow the rare inspirations, herbs
That aren't attractive as a cup of wine.
O world so sad, they gaze at you and me
With those longing, deep and tender eyes,
As they, foolish dear you and sinful me see
Wastin' precious time on nothing but dice!
O, poor, dear souls are depressed and lonely
To learn that nothin' pleases us, not even our land's
                                                    law;
But to gamble away with life and that only:
They sadly weep—gone forever more.

Walter M B Nhlapo   *Bantu World* 10 July 1937

Chapter 3 :
Rhymes of Solitude

SPRING

Carpet green with verdure laid,
Around the countryside displayed
From barren-brown to em'rald croft,
With temp'ring breezes kissing soft.

A subtle purity the air
Possessed—A rich refreshing flair;
That all the realm of Nature came
To celebrate in Nature's name;
The blue jacaranda all full clad,
Shed beauteous leaves for miry tread
Of peasant, lord—of all degree,
Pronouncing all how Nature's free.

The trees alive in comely bloom
They sough in rapture, not in gloom.
And blooming flowers with open buds
Suck life from Rain's life-giving floods.

E Fanele   *Bantu World* January 1938

THE SCOLLY

His hair is woolly, his face is brown,

His glance is furtive, his smile a sneer,
The backstreet hero of every town,
    The bully and the buccaneer!
He is the stepson of our nation,
    A menace to future bliss,
The product of civilisation,
    The scollyboy disturbing peace!
Get off the pavement as he staggers,
    And as by night he comes to life
He uses razors, or a dagger,
    Or in your side he sticks a knife!
When he is caught you never waver,
    You whip him as he burns with hate;
An oath escapes him not a prayer,
    He knows that it is too late.
Too late to change his mode of living,
    Or to forgive the human beings,
The dirty streets, the vice, the thieving
    Through hunger for a million things!
And as he stands defiant, foul,
    A man without God or shame,
Just listen to your own soul
    And hear him whisper—'You're to blame!'

S C Faber   *Cape Standard* 22 February 1938

MY MOTHER'S DREAM

Not long ago I dreamed a dream,
So short a dream to me did seem—
I heard a voice of mother dear,
A voice that made me shed a tear.

My mother spoke these words to me:

'No one my child who cares for thee,
No one to cook for you my boy.'
These words to me did not bring joy.

A tear, a sigh, a joy untold—
Intermingled with past recalled.
And ere the mess was made for me.
The dream did fade and where was she?

In heaven's paradise she dwells,
Where angels' voices always swell,
And came along the earth's footpath.
To see her suff'ring son on earth.

S P Maluleka   *Bantu World* 4 June 1938

FREEDOM

Where the highest peak of the tow'ring range soars
                                                free,
Where the rugged land goes forth to meet the sea;
And the little farmhouse, hidden by the hill,
Is met and env'loped in the ev'ning still;—
There the soul of freedom sallies forth by night.

Where fair brown children meet the morning sun,
Content to strive until the day is done;
To do and show the world what they are worth
To toil and suffer as He did on earth.

Oh, dear brown children — a laughter-ridden race:
For God, in sorrow gave you this one grace,
To welcome sunset with a smile. Laugh on
Until your mirth and freedom blend in one

To sweep away your pain with the dying sun!

Peter Abrahams   *Cape Standard* 28 June 1938

LATE QUEEN LOMAWA

O she has left us in tears and mourning;
To world intangible has flown;
She is now to her people a spirit;
Which tramps to land of dead alone!
O Ndhlovukazi, O Mighty spirit
Power's thine, the great to the grave.
This mat, blanket, earthen ware on earth ne'er,
See, take them with thee to the grave.
She's gone to the land we are bound for.
No Dante of it has e'er told,
It may have a tormenting furnace,
Or refrigerator where all freeze cold
The path she is treading to regions of dead,
Is for all, may soon be your own;
Each young and old soul gliding in shadow,
Unseen by beloveds travel alone.

Swazi ancestors gone, rulers of our fate.
For Lomawa the gateways unfold,
From sheen huts of joy and lyre and laughter,
Await to meet Lomawa, bright as gold.

Walter M B Nhlapo   *Bantu World* 8 October 1938

DEDICATION TO THE NEW OFFICES OF THE 'BANTU WORLD'

The harbinger of light
Our mouthpiece and our friend
Hath left her older site
To make somewhere her stand.
The mighty *Bantu World*
In new walls doth abide
She'll scatter now her word
To readers far and wide.
O! Father up in Heaven
Thine blessings we do ask
Upon the new place given
Do guide thy servants' task;
May the *Bantu World* be heard
In lands far off and near
May we by her be led
To know and not to fear
O keep her Lord of hosts
And give her goodly store
Against the foe that boasts
May she steer forevermore.

Obed Mooki   *Bantu World* 8 October 1938

LIBERTY TORCH

Up, Capetown Workers, up with the light
To blaze a trail in the people's fight,
Your blood the oil, your spirit the flame.

What is this flame which so steadfastly
You light today for your liberty?

It is the torch of truth—a burning
Which mankind has ever been yearning.

Hold high the Light, workers, hold it high,
That the beams can pierce the southern sky,
That in the glow the message we see—
The torch burns on till all men are free.

Deep from the sea in the mists of night,
Ghostly figures rise to beams of light.
In their rusted chains bleached bones of slaves,
Hopes uplifted from watery graves.

Afar in forests across the lands
Where slaves were beaten and hanged by hands.
On turning wheels broken bodies lie.
Beware, torturers, the light is nigh!

Workers of today who sweat and wet
Toil in mines, factories, farms, to get—
For the masters, luxury and ease,
Toilers, insecurity and disease.

The burning flame by the workers held
Over mountains, koppies, rivers, veld,
Is coming to free you, workers all.
Here is the message. Answer the call.

All workers who by sweat and by toil
Produce the wealth from the sea and soil,
No longer as the slaves will you stand,
For you will own the sea and the land.

J M   *Cape Standard* 6 December 1938

A PRAYER FOR AFRICA

Creator of heaven, Lord of lands,
Guide African shimmering sands
Through furnace of afternoon,
Through mystic light of the moon.
War-clouds above us are blowing,
Savagely world is growing,
O, mighty Lord of hosts
Be the bulwark of our coasts!

Thou gave us this land rich and good,
The sweet fountains and fields of food,
Where wave tall corn, and bloom of bean,
And the willow trees cool and green.
Save us from foes who for blood hunger
O'er nought for their friend bear anger;
O, mighty Lord of hosts
Be the bulwark of our coasts!

The many dictators all cast their eyes
On fields fertile and azure skies;
Their eyes make us shudder every day
And turn the raven-hairs to gray;
O, mighty Lord of hosts
Be the bulwark of our coasts!

We are weaklings, and our foes strong,
We're harmless, our foes mighty throng,
Doom their lust, blind bloodthirsty eyes
We pray Thee; Thou art great and wise;
O, mighty Lord of hosts
Be the bulwark of our coasts!

Walter M B Nhlapo   *Bantu World* 4 February 1939

DAWN ON AFRICA

The day has dawned on Africa,
Africa is dark no more,
The long dark days of Africa
Are like a dream of yore.

The savage drums of fighting
Pulsate no more of war;
They bring good news and tidings
Which ne'er were known before.

Spears have been replaced by pens,
The battle fields chang'd to towns,
The lions no longer have dens,
The farmers have captured the downs.

He looks at the distant horizon,
At the savage life he abhors;
With the new dawn, he too has a reason
To conquer all things without pause.

His home no more a rondhavel,
A thatch'd roof of sticks and mud,
His clothes—the watchman's marvel,
Elevate him beyond a dud.

No longer does he laze by a kraal
Cursing the troublesome fly;
His only 'sin'—the whiteman's scroll—
Whispers that time doth fly.

He sees today before him,
A future of hope and freedom;
Although he toils, he hums a hymn

Of Glory to God in His Kingdom.

The day has dawned on Africa,
Africa is dark no more,
The long dark days of Africa
Are but a dream of yore.

Shep H Maloy   *Bantu World* 4 February 1939

HERITAGE

Twine-tangled murky midnight bush,
The glow-worm, the hare and a hush—
White moon and the river beasts at play,
While the dusky slave moves on his way.

He sang 'neath the burden of his yoke,
Though with pain he groaned at the slaver's stroke.
The murky bush—the jungle vale,
And dusky slaves moving down its trail.

Out of a bent and slaving race
Proudly I can my fathers trace;
The leaf; it falls not far from the tree—
Silent and straight 'neath this load on me!

But I am not so savage in all,
And shame the greater if I fall;
A double heritage I guard—
My father's and my living God's—

But O, for the fair dark negro maids,
With swaying hips and flow'ry braids;
The tom-tom, the rushing long canoe!

These I claim as my heritage too—
                    In the dark and alone—!

Peter Abrahams   *Cape Standard* 7 March 1939

THE *MENDI*

Of many deeds of sacrifice worth a place in history,
Is sinking of the *Mendi* with Africa's dusky glory.
Awhile we remember, 'tis worth a souvenir lest it
                                    fall,
As years roll onward, tombs effac'd into oblivion's
                                    pall,
When brass monuments decay, still in our hearts ever
                                    be room.

Immortal is the *Mendi* until earth passeth in flaming
                                    doom,
If deeds obtain lasting record, what glory is in the name
Mendi and her noble contingent? Tell the ages their
                                    fame,
How in the sorest hour stood not to gaze and hold
                                    their breath,
Whilst in the fields of Flanders men charged fire and
                                    glaring death.

They repose on the breast of the British sea, ne'er
                                    tasted strife,
Which they longingly cherished when they left home,
                                    peaceful life!
That they were alive, never would write this poem,
                                    they are dead,
We dearly mourn for the blood of our blood, rivers of
                                    tears shed!

The tears that suffuse the eyes we cannot withhold
                                        from flowing,
When we see widowers and orphans prey to chilly
                                        winds blowing,
Nor can we forget when round the bowl of vanished
                                        years pass, by the fireside sing,
They're amiss, we sacrificed them as loyalty to our
                                        king.

When she sank the fog was dense, you and I were sad
                                        that day,
We felt something was wrong. That day we recall and
                                        kneel and say:
What if they sleep, when their duty be done. He,
                                        them ever guide,
He, them remember and know that lie concealed in
                                        the tide!
O, cruel sea! the day shall ripe when you the *Mendi*
                                        crew must yield,
And may we never forget the heroes in the sea
                                        sealed!

Walter M B Nhlapo   *Bantu World* 18 March 1939

LITTLE GREASE-MEN

These are they,
The fat of paunch
Living on the sweat of others
Glorying in their exploitation—
Pudgy fingers clutching coins.
Silhouette against the twilight

Creeping far—
Over city, veld and village
Stretch the victims of their rape:
This, then, sunset bear me witness,
Is the cause of people living hard.
Picture—
Gutter, early morning;
Picture—
Beggar lying dead.
Picture—mansions facing gutter;
Picture—filth in splendour set,
Filth in form of oily rapists,
Splendour made by beggar hands;
Picture hardness, picture hunger,
Picture stark death if you like.

Picture hands that keep a-movin',
Hands that make the world go round;
Picture beggars by the thousands
Dying . . .
Picture wealth and little grease-men
Built with hands of dying beggars!

Peter Abrahams   *Cape Standard* 4 April 1939

UPON THE DEALINGS OF MAN

O Lord, Divine Philosopher, give light
    To them who tread in dark polluted ways;
Unto the wrath to come whose crimson sight
    Upon them frowns, as Mars in battled days;
Show them the path to peace and saintly smile;
    Consider this my exhortation and
Reply in Thy uncopied Heav'nly style,

That unity may reign upon the land.
And oh, great Lord, convert the mind of Man
   To think not of black vice, but virtue pure;
Enlighten those that darken the fair land,
   And aid us our great burdens to endure.
Make pure the wicked ones who cause our woes,
   For what is wicked is but sin unclosed.

P J Maree   *Cape Standard* 2 May 1939

ONWARD, EVER ONWARD!

Onward ever onward!
   Be our racial cry,
Coloured men and women,
   'Tis to do or die.
And we'll surely die lads,
   Should we still conceal,
Colour, race, or mother:
   Seek the common weal.

There's a fair hereafter
   O'er the distant hills,
Where, with patience, labour,
   And determined wills,
With each man and woman,
   Whatsoever sphere,
Doing some small service,
   We'll at last appear.

Colour's not the lever.
   That exalteth race;
Spiritual power,
   Gains immortal place.

Quality's the measure,
  That's a nation's aim,
And it dwells in Coloureds
  Just the very same.

Join the march, good comrades,
  Ere they doom us West.
Once more prove the dubious,
  We can stand the test.
Other nations conquered,
  Let us battle through.
For the main essentials,
  We inherit too.

Then arise and labour,
  For the way is long.
Leave the little wranglings,
  Join the suffering throng.
Dark the road before us,
  All around the foe.
We are waiting on you—
  Will you let us go?

Onward, ever onward!
  Onward to our goal.
Strive with one endeavour,
  Strive with heart and soul.
Seek the common standards,
  Common aims and laws
Seek the racial concord,
  And the common cause.

J R S   *Cape Standard* 5 September 1939

MRS CHARLOTTE M MAXEKE, B SC

O lady great! Art thou gone
To where golden light of day is fair
No night to dull the perfumed air
Where with kins thou'll not be lone?

In the land of fadeless day
With lasting sights and perfumed breeze
Hills in tapestry and calm blue seas
O thou art gone there to stay.

Sleep! thou art happy and free
With radiant wings thou shalt e'er be
Thy people wait for thee in blue sky
And what is our grief to thee?

To fadeless daylight thou'rt gone
Where there's life and glory, dance and song
Of Africans and heavenly throng.
Go home! thou art not alone!

When thou art in land of sunshine
And we seem to hear thy voice once more
From those scented realms of glowing shore
Be spirit to this land which's thine.

Sleep lady! we shall meet again
Thine grave we bedeck with richest flowers
Which the sunny day rears in our bowers,
Thou wilt not be lur'd again.

Walter M B Nhlapo   *Bantu World* 2 December 1939

MOTHER MAXEKE, B SC

Sons of Afric' far and near,
We have lost a noble one;
Daughters fair and mothers dear,
Charlotte Manye's truly gone.

But she lives altho' not here
In a land of fadeless day,
Where no death, no pain, no care
Or distress doth come her way;

There she'll pave for us a place
As she did upon this earth;
And to her we'll surely pace,
If like her we strive till death.

Thus I pen this simple lay,
Calling Afric's gallant youth
Take up arms and boldly say:
'We shall follow in thy truth!'

Obed S D Mooki   *Bantu World* 2 December 1939

AMANZIMTOTI INSTITUTE, FAREWELL!*

Amanzimtoti Institute, farewell!
With a sigh, 'midst your cane fields, gum-tree lane
My days were spent, ne'er to return again.
Dead were I to love, sympathy that swell
The breast! The lanes, canes that whisper wave
My friends reared, nursed, now to the grave

*Amanzimtoti Institute was later known as Adams College.

Gone down; they lov'd your peaceful scenes and said,
Perhaps, as here we learned, 'Rise and Shine'
Ye buildings that shade great joy, seem divine.
Live, blooming and rejoice! And when dead
My friends will praise you and 'mid your bowers
Like many, find solutions to life's showers.

These thoughts, alma mater, ev'ry spot endear;
And whilst I think, with self-accusing pain,
New students shall walk in culture's domain.
In each low wind I seem thy voice to hear.
You are site for shaping Africa's brain
That now my heart alas can ill sustain:
Never will I forget thee—dear abode
Of light, where men learn to face life's end and odd,
Though from your rolls my name may be resign'd
When far your fame we'll bear an unalter'd mind.
Yet, hundred years old buildings, trees with shade,
Recall, when no more I see your fields green,
Where as a student, I walk'd, even play'd,
Was punish'd, for a girl dropp'd tears unseen.
Yes! my joys and sorrows you alone can tell.
They're dat'd on your walls, trees, ev'rything;
farewell!

Walter M B Nhlapo   *Bantu World* 10 February 1940

FIRST ROMANTIC NIGHT

There'll be other Saturdays
In the years to come,
When you're grown old and grey
And old tunes hum
Of love and blue skies

Love and dancing feet
And you'll hear the sky-lark sing
Plaintive and sweet
As on our first romantic day.

There'll be other moonlights
Other Novembers
Other crickets chirping,
But you'll remember
But there'll ne'er be to us again
That first romantic day
Nor another glad night
Quite like this.

Walter M B Nhlapo   *Bantu World* 2 March 1940

AFRICA IS CALLING

Africa has long been asleep,
    But she is now being awakened,
After a thousand years of a sleep so deep,
    In which her sons were to slavery taken.

Africa has long been oppressed,
    But things are now on the move;
Africa has long been suppressed,
    But her worth her sons are yet to prove.

Africa is my land of birth,
    Whose freedom I am yet to claim.
With neither swords nor poisoned spears,
    And liberty for my nation gain.

I sit alone by the hillside,

With the incentive thoughts of youth,
And my shadow only by my side,
Thinking of who shall ever find the fountain of
youth.

Africa doth plaintive call,
To thee her children so kind,
To wipe the tears that from her fall.
And again she surely shall be thine.

J W L Letsebe   *Bantu World* 18 May 1940

FREEDOM'S CHILD

The echoes are dying,
The whisper is gone,
But every tree seems to nod its head.
Is it its ghost . . . ?

1

I am China,
They call me Le-Yen,
The ricefields own me,
My best years are gone;
I have sweated,
Eaten opium,
And at last I died—
And now I'm going to die again.
But I've heard it, this whisper,
And I love its sound.
I'm China,
But they call me Le-Yen down here.

2

And I am a mother,
Some call me Japan.
I don't want an Empire,
Or a wonderful navy,
I don't care what rate I am—
I have no fight—
All I want
Is my son to return
And food for the children,
A dress for my daughter,
My afternoon tea.
And no uniforms.
I want peace, I want quiet
And my children's love.
That whisper—
What promise does it hold . . . ?

3

My name is Coolie. Untouchable.
I am a jewel
The brightest in a crown
Of a foreign king.
From my blood
Princes make gold to weight themselves.
I'm an Anna a day, I spit blood when I cough.
I am the floods
And a hundred million starving souls.
I am the droughts
And a hundred million dead.
I am Nehru
I languish in jail.
I am an Anand—
The tears of a tortured soul.
But I've heard this whisper,

My body grows
Bigger!
BIGGER!!
Now there's room for me only here—
No kings or princes,
And I cry:
'Inquilab Zindabad!'
I am India!

4

I am the gold mines,
Paying huge dividends;
I am the preacher—
Shining car, well fed;
My sermon is race purity,
And God was white and
White men must guard blacks.
I am the banker, Kipling,
And East and West
And the white man's burden.
I am the Institute of Race Relations,
And racial mixture is a crime . . .
I am a half-caste—
Racial mixture is a crime . . .
I am gold,
Fashioned out of beads of sweat of black men;
I am segregation and the pass-law;
I'm eight million slaves . . .
But somewhere, too,
I nurture a volcano,
And out of love
I shall cause a wild eruption
With an aftermath of laughter.

5

Slaves of masters, world without choice,
Serving those masters I still hear your voice;
The great lords who rule you are heading for death,
They suck in its vapour with every breath.
Bending your backs to tyranny's yoke,
Taking the full force of every stroke,
The master beasts are marching to death—
I heard it whispered in a dying breath.
The whisper was caught by the Proletarian breeze
And carried away across the seas.
And every sufferer heard the voice,
And in quiet I heard the wind rejoice.
And clear in the twilight the clouds burst wild,
Singing my song—'Freedom's Child!'

Peter Abrahams   1941

SELF

I am a shadow,
Restless,
Roving everywhere.
Dawn greets me
Sneaking from a park bench
And a rendezvous with cold and sky,
I'm a bum, hungry and lonely;
Milk vanishes from doorsteps at dawn
As I pass.

I'm a prostitute,
Seeking a pick-up from the street.
I have a kid and it cries for bread.
I'm a mother.

Just heard my son died at the Front—
A medal and an empty heart.

I'm a toiler, sweating all day,
But somehow I've more debts to pay.

I'm in the cold,
A youngster, hungry and thin,
My soul cries for love and laughter,
But I'm on this side of the window;
In there, there's fire and laughter
And the warmth of love.

I'm a poet,
And through hunger
And lust for love and laughter
I have turned myself into a voice,
Shouting the pain of the People
And the sunshine that is to be.

Peter Abrahams   1941

TO WHITE WORKERS

Now listen,
For you are my comrades.
Does a song sound sweeter
Being made by a white man?
When you listen to Robeson
Do you listen to his colour?

And so
When you think of freedom
Is it a white symphony

Or one of many colours?
And when you wish for laughter
Is it the laughter of all men?

I have a song to blend both hues,
I have a dream for you and you,
A symphony for black and white,
A love for all mankind!

Peter Abrahams   1941

SPRING IN A COLOURED WOMAN

Bruised lips lisped lingering love,
But mockery choked its embryonic soul.
You are seeped with life, pregnant woman,
Your full lips tell the tale of new creation,
The deep mystic rivers, reflected in your eyes,
Flashing the flushed self-satisfaction
Infuse your sensual lust with godly power.
The moon plays on the rivers,
Gliding over them with Merlin's transformation
                                        powers,
Gold planets rising wave of wave as many moons on a
                                    single river,
And each diffusing the gold of the other.
Rivers are strange in a woman's eyes—
In a pregnant woman's eyes.
The earth and the flesh and the sea and the sky,
They are one, pregnant woman. This is your Spring-
                                        time!

Gasp your breath through your parted lips,
Swollen and clammy with the touch of life!

What though death's breath may blow it away,
The hot breath of want suck the life from its soul—
Part your lips with that catch in your laugh,
Laugh long and free for Spring's in your blood!

A poet could not but share in your joy—
What of tomorrow's pain and want:
The tears of a poet and the joys of a poet
Are a mother's tears and a mother's joys.

You are godlike, pregnant woman,
With your bruised lips and torn dress;
You are the earth, fertile and productive in your
                                                Spring.
Though all the year round just a 'bastard wench.'

Peter Abrahams   1941

ON SOME WHITE 'FRIENDS'

He does not know of life
And need not prate of strife
Who has not felt and gone through this,
Till life for him becomes a hell bereft of peace,
And God and All becomes a mockery.
And he from life pleads to be free
To feel you're nothing, absolutely nothing!
Until from your gross wounds you conceive
                                                Something
Most beautiful and new,
And good, and strong and true!
And, having great things wrought, remain
Without a name, without a gain
Despised, hopeless,

Unsung, powerless!
Alas! Such is the fate of scores
Of the best souls, closing their doors,
Nibbling at their soul's core—
The fate of those who labour for
White 'gentlemen' fattening themselves,
Evil but sweet, artful as elves,
Pretending they are Bantu friends,
But working for their selfish ends
But Truth no man can always hide
In song and scroll their wrongs will bide.
The Lord will inspire a muse of fire
To avenge against those who conspire;
And groans which now fill gossip's hill,
And when the cheaters, cheated, are all bone,
The scrolls the truth will tell in naked epitaphs of
                                        living stone!
Will verberate through years God's purpose to fulfil.

ANON   *Bantu World* 1 February 1941

WAR DANCER

His bare feet slap hard on the ground. This man
Seems to hear the tom-tom, Afric' war gong.
And smell scent of enemy blood so strong;
And picture when after them in fury ran.
As he dances, throb of tom-tom beat in his blood.
Savage hate and blood thirst you see are there.
In such mood, it is safe to stand far aside.
He forgets himself when hearing blooming thud.
He jumps high from the ground and cleaves the air

With yells of anguished rage and ancient pride.

Walter M B Nhlapo   *Bantu World* 19 April 1941

AFRICA'S SONG OF FREEDOM

Sing songs ye children of Africa
Songs of mirth and songs of love,
Songs of praise for your native land;
For the Lord with His merciful right hand,
Hast blest us with freedom and love.
Forget ye sons, of slavery!
Ye daughters forget your orphanage!
Arise and show your bravery!
For lost are the days of strife with age,
And Liberty is at hand.
How long have we longed Oh Africa!
Have we longed for the joys of our land?
How long have we struggled with thee Oh Fate!
With thee Oh Fate! Thou cruel Fate.
'Gainst struggle, hate, and strife?
Let us with our banner unfurled,
March to the graves of our dead.
With hand overflowing with offering,
With hearts full of mirth and joy,
Then Oh then
Let us with one voice our prayers raise.

Rahab S Petje   *Bantu World* 14 March 1942

SWEET MANGO TREE*

1

When we were young, sweet mango tree,
We invaded you with virgin glee;
But now upon these shallow heights
Of Time and Test, sweet tree, what dights
Your scene is foliage of a mind
Burdened with life, wherein I find
Vicissitudes of all these years
Of smiles and tears . . . Life's vine which clears
One mind and gives it power and joy;
Another, makes its tool, its toy,
In youth and health, symbolic tree,
Your fruit we grabbed with greedy glee!
But now the wind mocks me and stings!
'O never, never, more!' it rings!
I hear its voice, and, fool, I weep!
For feelings strange through me doth seep:
Sweet pain, sad joy, thoughts vague but deep;
And craving sleep, I dare not sleep,
For now spite doubts and routs that throng
My soul, I know the path is long;
And I who crave for rest, must walk . . .
A lonely stalk that winters balk!

> Sweet mango tree,
> When we were young
> We climbed each rung
> Of life in glee.
> But now (O why?),
> My heart is wrung
> With pain when I

*Inspired by a visit to Adams College, his Alma Mater

Remember those
I stood among
Tried to outvie,
In brains defy,
Whose book now close,
Can never come
Again! But from
Afar once more
'O never more!'

2

In youth and triumph I bragged, 'I must
Be different!' Now mid storm and dust,
I pray to be like other men . . .
How different life today and then!
O call these faces back to me,
These fields who roamed with me in glee!
I find them not! They're gone! I hear
And see things ghostly—cold! A tear
Sprouts to my eye! And midst this crowd
Of youthful voices laughing loud,
I feel alone; stabbed to the core!
New features mock me everywhere!
Improvements! Progress! Rush and rest!
Their fair is better than our best!
But midst it all my soul, in quest
For hidden things, can find no rest.
Is sense of beauty, thought and wrong
Deeper than ours? Where is their Song?
I came back home wanting a song,
But now I ask: 'Do I belong . . . ?'
Back home at last I feel nowhere!
And hear 'O never, never more'
Again and yet again! I look
This way and that, but find no nook!

Knowing knowledge is a spur, I ask
'Why must philosophy of life
Forever be revealed in strife?'
Words come, 'To know, go, do your task.'

3

O Time! O Place! O Graves! I call
Bring back the souls, ideas, and all
Beliefs and Hope I held in days
Gone past! Once more those golden lays!
But 'Never, never more!' still I
Hear flouted back! I sink and sigh:
'O why do those who teach and lead,
Their trusting wards deceive and bleed?
They make us angels pure and good,
When life needs giants tough and crude;
Men who can work and dare, and sin!
Fail, fall and rise, but keep within
Them Hope, a vision clear of right
And wrong, love beauty, yet show—fight!
A genius is that soul who can
Defy the ways, conceits of Man;
The limitations of fell Fate,
And Time, and Place, to reach the gate
Of his ambitions, task and aim;
Get there, though damned, blood-soiled, and maim!
The world belongs not to the good,
The peaceful, gentle and the meek
(For the ineffectual good are weak,
And often reap wild deserts bleak!);
But to the souls who thirst and seek;
The casualties who, broken, stood!
Who out of woe and dirt wrought song,
And 'spite their weakness remained strong!
Immortals who deck history's pages,

Are souls who, struggling, took sin's wages
And used them to purchase new life,
Now all our glory is their strife!

4

So up and down the lanes I strode,
The lanes we strode in days of old,
With boys and girls who never never
Grow old to their old mates, however
Full grown or great! Those who were young
When we were young will e'er be young! —
Though old! The old man and his wife
Each other see in spring of life.
Here science, God, and philosophy,
Or love and sport with novice glee
We argued heatedly and long.
Or trilled with life we burst to song;
Proud of our intellectual powers;
Wasting our brains and precious hours
Mid sacred, sentimental bowers,
Shaping imagined saintly towers.
But now walked I alone in thought,
My mind in painful visions caught,
Alas! the stream, the flower, the tree,
All told of earthly life's futility;
The beauty of the kaffirboom!
But emphasised Man's mortal doom!
The 'boom, geranium, and the rose
Life's wretchedness seemed to expose!
Beauteous the gardens in the lawn!
But for my Race saw I no dawn
Or future if philosophy
Here taught is thought to set us free.

This trend of thought was broken by

A scene I saw as, passing by
A scarlet flower, I paused to think!
Cursed flower! to break the mental link!
And yet upon this self-same flower,
Saw I a sight that lent me power;
Here ants, beebawds, pied butterflies,
Yes, insects strange, and even flies,
To this whore flower, red as a flame,
To steal promiscuous sweets, all came!
Mid pistil, petal, in and out,
The insects toiled, buzzed, danced about.
There was no strife—there was no cause!
Here was full life—here was no pause!
I cried: Cannot humanity
Observe, take lesson and be free?
The insect world is perfect state
Which puts Man's states all out of date!
In things material, physical,
Novice is Man! The psychical
Is his divine, distinctive field;
To cultivate which Man would wield
Such power as would our minds invest
With strength to rise above all test;
Love, Beauty, Reason, Song—these four
Prerogatives will open the door
To that far-off dreamt of estate
When Man will tower above his fate.
But Gold and Flesh—World's gods—the door
Celestial bar! And 'Never more!'
We mumble in despair, and thus
Abandon paths still left to us.

5

Here, voices mocked: 'What have you done!
What laurels won, thou plaintive one

Since, years ago, you left this place?'
Then felt I like one in disgrace!
For no achievements brought I home
From travels wide beneath this dome;
Empty of gift back home I came!
And, looking back, I blushed in shame!
Not like those other brighter stars
Than I, adorned with tails behind
Them—glorious signs of their keen mind!
But, prodigal, I brought but scars,
Old weapons bent, besmeared with blood!
I cried, 'Forgive me, Mother dear!
All I have done is, I have stood!
No gifts bring I, I bring myself!
Yet I, even I, am of thyself!
Who stand not in the van but rear!'
New signs and faces young, 'Poor one,'
Jeered forth again, 'What have you done?'
Sad trees and fields, 'Let him alone!
We knew like us he stood like stone
When fallen, robbed and crucified,
He might have sunk—Fate he defied!'
I wondered who was it replied,
But felt a Presence by my side!

But now—'O never, never more!'
And in the Halls of Hope the door
Is shut! And from the glare of Light.
Stumbling, I go into deep night!

6

Neat, nestled 'neath rich scenes of green.
(Below sweet Manzimtoti stream
Glides past as lovely as a dream!)
The chapel stands, defying change!

Calm, hallowed, staid! Where all is strange,
Its breath is home! Ah! mark that paean!
O memories the chapel brings!
The choir that sang forever sings
Within my soul oft have I heard
Alone, in pain, those strains begird
My soul when all seemed lost and dark!
Imagination's healing spark!
Shall ever my life again
Come to my ears such magic strain?
Muse Mother of twin Wonders— Word and Song!—
                              our fervent souls you fired!
Dear lovely Bower of Faith and Strength,
Thy signs and truths we learn at length!

                    7
            Deep mystic tree,
            Charmed entity!
            Still I call thee!
            Speak thou to me!
            Where shall I flee,
            Where live and be,
            Where my Christ see,
            If not in thee,
            Sweet Mango tree?
            Behold and feel,
            Soothe me and heal
            And set me free!
            Bring back the days
            Faith, dreams, and ways
            I used to know
            Here years ago!

Thou emblem of the things I've seen!
Reminder of what might have been!

Help me forget the nagging Past!
To warm my hands o'er Faith's repast!

8

Sweet Mango tree! I ache! I die!
Hear thou my prayer and make reply!
I ask no more than what I've known!
The painful joys that are now flown!
Give back the things that I adore:
Love, Beauty, Laughter, Song—I implore!
Return but what I had before!
But hush! 'Accept the never more!
For once 'tis thus! Nothing
The dreams and songs of Youth can bring!
("O never, never more!") No force
Can from his Fate poor man divorce!
("O never, never more!") No power
In heaven and earth can turn one hour!
("O never, never more!") The door
Is shut! now and forever more!'

H I E Dhlomo   *Ilanga Lase Natal* 22 August 1942

SALANG KA KHOTSA
*(To the 624 Basuto who went down in a torpedoed
transport on the way to the Army of the North.)*

Ye are Basuto. In heroic pride
Ye bore aloft the banner of your name.
Your brothers fell upon the tawny tide
Of sandy deserts blooded with their fame;
Another tide of honour was aflow
When from your dragon hills ye marched away
Eager for victory, flashing eyes aglow

Keen as the morning of a snow-keened day.
Farewell ye brave! Our wounded hearts are proud
With tear-stained gladness that to you was given
Glory and spendour as your passing shroud
Dipped in the heart's blood of a nation riven.
Salang ka Khotso! On Bosiu's crown
Will burn the beacon of your high renown.

Anon   *Bantu World* 6 November 1943

'MAYBE'

I wonder, if I really know thee!
    Thou man I think I love.
I wonder if I really see thee,
    Read and know thy love's poise:
All I have to say is:
    'I wonder.'

Shadows are the depth of thine eyes
No human eyes can penetrate.
Will the strange feeling vanish
Or will it divide and separate.

Day in and out, in thine eyes I spy
Hovering shadow of awe
Creeping along and make thee shy
To yield a confession of no salvation.
That I embarrass thee, then,
    'I wonder.'

                    YET,
I adore thee
    And worship thee

To the core of my heart
   That confession melts:
      'I love thee.'

        FOR,
'Tis thou in thy worst,
And thou in thy best,
That destroys the best in me,
Thyself a shrine of cold
In the heaven of love I worship.

       THEN,
I do not wonder,
'Maybe' I'm only haunted.

Mavis M Kwankwa *Ilanga Lase Natal* 8 January 1944

HARK! MY LONELY HEART

Hark! my lonely heart;
Open wide the doors of your closed art.
List thou the winds of the South Seas,
Lest the swelling music cease.

Hark! over hills and vales,
That lovely sound that wails,
Whispering to you the Love it brings,
The soul it fills with faery wings!

To it the drooping flowers wake,
With joy they bloom and music make,
Like an angel-powered church bell chime,
Giving charmed praise to Nature and to Time

Then O my heart will you not stay
And listen to the heavenly sway,
While yet the wind is passing on,
Its message hold, before 'tis gone?

Zini Mfeka   *Ilanga Lase Natal* 22 January 1944

DRUM OF AFRICA

Sound the drum!
Sound the drum!
Boom!
Boom!
Beat! Beat! Beat!
Strive!
Fight!
Do or die!

    Praise ye, praise them!
    Praise the Spirits!
    Sing ye, sing them!
    Sing our Fathers!

The drum the voice of war!
A whole no parts doth mar!
One Tone without a jar!
O let it sound out far!
It stirs up all men's hearts!
'Tis king of battle arts!
O sacred oxen hide,
The drum will e'er abide.
It speaks of our great Past,
Of first things and of last.
Despite the oppressor's din,

The day the drum will win!
Brave soul, it calls, fight on!
Strive till the work is done—
The task to set us free;
No docile cowards we,
Souls who will win or die,
And will not cringe nor cry.
The Cause needs men will dare,
Hold fast and not despair!
Braves who will lead the masses
Through life's stiff, guarded passes,
And serve the Fatherland,
And gain the Chosen Land.
Though troubles envelope,
Warbling of Afric's Hope,
The drum will set us free!
The drum of unity.
The Drum of Life says, 'come!'
O men of might—the Drum!

Yea, 'tis the drum!
(Praise ye, praise it)
Yea, fight we will!
(Sing ye, sing them)
Strive!
Fight!
Save the people!
Rise!
March!
Who'll be there?

H I E Dhlomo   *Ilanga Lase Natal* 30 December 1944

IN THE GOLD MINES

Thunder away, machines of the mines,
Thunder away from dawn till sunset;
I will get up soon: do not pester me;
Thunder away, machines. Heed not
The groans of the black labourers
Writhing with the pains of their bodily wounds,
The air close and suffocating
With the dirt and sweat of their bodies
As they drain their hips till nothing is left.

Call aloud, old boy. It is far,
It is far away where you were moulded,
Where you roasted in the fire till you were strong;
The coal remained; you were sent away,
And we saw you cross the waters of the sea;
You were borne overland by the engines of fire
That puffed and glided to Goli here;
You screamed one day, and all at once there appeared,
There came rock-rabbits from all sides.

Those black rock-rabbits without tails
You caught and stowed away in holes
To own and milk as yielding cows
Whirl round and round, you wheels of iron;
It was for us they brought you here;
You were tied together against your will;
Today you thunder and strain unceasingly;
See how some of your kind, now rusty and old,
Have been cast away on the rubbish dumps.

As I pass along the road
I turn around and watch,
Wondering if you will ever give birth,

Perchance increase. But no!
Your brothers too go rusty
Within the mine compounds;
Their lungs go rusty and rusty,
And they cough and they lie down and they die.
But you irons, you never cough. I note and wonder
                                                    why.

I have heard it said that in the hole
There are tribes and tribes of the Black One;
It is they who raise the great white mounds
That astonish their black forebears
I have heard it said that on a certain day
A siren shrieked, and a black field-mouse
With mind all wrapped in darkness came;
He was caught and changed into a mole,
And he burrowed the earth and I saw the gold.

O yes, they burrowed, those burrowing moles,
And the great white mounds appeared.
Swelling from the ground and climbing and climbing
Till today they top iSandlwana Mountain.
I labour to the top, I wipe off the sweat,
And from on high I see the piles
Of fine white dust, fine dust arising
From below my feet. I look around
And I note that the piles block the earth around.

Thunder away, machines of the mines,
Thunder loud and loud,
Deafen with noise that we may not be heard
Though we cry out aloud and groan
As you eat away the joints of our bodies;
Giggle and snigger, you old machines;
It is well that you laugh and scorn our rage,

For great is your power and fearful;
You may do as you please: we succumb.

We agreed to leave our round-shaped huts,
To be herded here like castrated males;
We gave up our corn, *amasi* and milk,
To live here on pap and porridge;
All gone is our manhood: we are mere boys;
We see that the world is upside down;
We are woken at dawn, and we stand in a row;
Where was it ever done to bury a man
While he walks and sees with both his eyes?

Thunder away, machines of the mines,
I am getting up, not chameleon-like,
I will go beneath the earth,
I will strike the rock with the boring rod;
Even you above, though you hear not a sound,
Will know that I strike with the white man's rod
When you see the trucks coming laden high
With the stones that are white and blue.

My brother too will come with me,
The pick and the shovel on his shoulder,
His heavy boots on his feet;
He too will enter and follow me,
Swallowed by the earth, we will burrow away;
And if I should die right there beneath
What matters it? Who am I at all?
From dawn to dawn, O son of man;
I see them stumble and tumble and die.

When I went beneath the earth,
There were none of the giant mounds
Whereat now I gaze and wonder;

I carried my bundle to seek my home,
But was hit in the face by cropless stalks,
By empty huts and abandoned homes;
I paused and scratched my head, puzzled;
Where was my wife? My mothers-in-law?
I was told they had gone to the white man,
To the white man for whom I work.
I shut my mouth and spoke not a word.

Thunder away, machines of the mines,
Though reaching me from far-away Dukathole[1]
(The—place—where—the—calf—goes—astray),
Your voices stab deep into my soul,
Tinkling and tinkling in my ears
Like the startling sound of a bell far away.
They bring to my mind the lofty homes,
The riches, and the rich ones whom I raised
To the beautiful house on high, while I stay here
Dripping, sweating, a lean dying ox.

Rumble softly, O machines;
Because the white man feels not for others,
Must you treat me as heartlessly too?
Thunder not so loud in the mines;
Be pleased to hear what we have to say
Lest we have nought to say for you
On that far-off day, that unknown day,
When it shall be said of you irons
That you are the slaves of us, black men.

Wait just a while, for feeble as I seem,
From these same little arms one day
There flew some fierce long-bladed spears

[1] Germiston

Which I hurled till the sun was darkened,
And the great Cow-elephant's[2] kingdom stirred
And Phewula's[3] children dwindled. I was robbed.
But still do I go on dreaming, son of Iron,
Dreaming that the land of my fathers' fathers
Comes back to the hands of the homeless Blacks.

Today in the shadow of riches
I have nowhere to rest my body;
My fathers' fathers' land lies bare,
With no one to till it while I sit and stare;
What though I have the means to buy
And own once more my fathers' land,
I have no right to buy or own.
Look there, O Fathers above and below!
Can you not save me from such suffering?

They say deep down in the land of my fathers,
In the land of spirits and spirits,
You have powers that are not surpassed,
That when you speak to the Great-Great-One,
He does not regard the colour of the skin.
My blood keeps falling on the ground,
And cakes and clots in the burning sun.
I toil and toil and pray to you,
But no, you answer not a word.

Your land today and yesterday
Is plundered by bands of robbers;
It has fattened nations and nations,
But I and the Black House of my fathers
We have nothing, nothing.
We come out of the hole and see the grass

[2] Queen Victoria   [3] Paul Kruger

Fresh as the blue skies of heaven;
We look around and call out aloud,
Alas! You do not reply.

Thunder away, machines of the mines,
My hands are throbbing with pain,
My swollen feet are aching,
But I cannot relieve the pain
For the white man's cures call for money.
Thunder away, but wake me not,
Great things I have done for the whiteman chiefs,
And now my soul weighs heavy on me.
Rumble softly that I may sleep,
Close my eyes and sleep on and on,
Thinking no more of tomorrow and after,
Sleep and wake up far away,
Far away in the land of spirits and dreaming,
Sleep and never wake again,
But rest in the arms of my fathers' fathers
Down in the fresh-green pastures of heaven.

Dr B W Vilakazi   *Africa South* 1945
(Translated by A C Jordan)

AN AFRICAN TO HIS COUNTRY

   Oh, land of my birth
Full of green everywhere,
   Your gold, silver and diamonds
Feed the children of other lands;
   Mourn, you careless mother
Your breast is suckled by children not of your birth.

   Take your sickle to mow down
Those who cheat us even of your worthy breast.

Cursed be your womb, for therein lay
Your cheated sons and daughters.

Aye, you thieves, wherefore steal you
    My mother's love from me?
Wherefore hurt you the hand that feeds?

    Oh, land of my birth,
Full of green everywhere,
    Your gold, silver and diamonds
Feed the children of other lands.

    Your serene voice called,
Your house accommodated strangers—
    I, your noble child, who fought your wars,
Am left to die of hunger and disease;
    Mourn, you careless mother,
Your breast is suckled by children not of your birth.

    Green mountains and rivers full of flowers,
They are my natural enjoyment,
    But without accommodation my heart sticks to my
                                                ribs:
How can I have joy, you careless mother?
    Curse the stranger, and give me your breast to suck,
Then will I enjoy again
    Green mountains and rivers full of flowers.

    I am your child, natural heir to your throne;
When will you give me my rights?

Gaur Radebe   *Democrat* 19 May 1945

NOT FOR ME

Not for me the Victory celebrations!
Not for me,
Ah! not for me.
I who helped and slaved in the protection
Of their boasted great civilization;
Now sit I in tears 'mid celebrations
Of a war I won to lose,
Of a peace I may not choose.
Before me lies
Grim years of strife,
Who gave my life
To gain—what prize?
In land and sea my brothers buried lie;
The message came; they answered and they fell.
With blood and toil our rights they thought to buy,
And by their loyal stand Race fires to quell.
Now that the War is ended,
Begins my war!
I rise to fight unaided
The wrongs I abhor!
I see the flags of peace in joy unfurled,
And think of my position in the world
They say will come.
And I stand dumb
With wrath! Not victory in the battle field
Those precious things we crave for life will yield.
I see them gathered to decide on peace,
For War, they know, will lead to Man's surcease.
But, Lord I am not represented:
My presence there is still resented.
Yet where I'm not,
There Christ is not!
For Jesus died and lives for all;

To Him no race is great or small.
And if they meet without the Lord to guide,
They cannot build a Peace that will abide.
The cause of war are Greed, Race, Pride and Power,
Yet these impostors sway peace-talks this hour.
How long O Lord before they learn the art
Of peace demands a change in their own heart!
I'll fight! but pray, 'Forgive them Father,
Despite their boast and pomp they know not what
                                                                        they do.'

I hate them not; believe I rather
My battle will lead them to discover Christ anew.
This is the irony,
This is the agony:
As long as those in power repentance need,
I sit upon the spikes of Wrong and bleed!
Not for me,
Ah! not for me
The celebrations,
The peace orations.
Not for me,
Yes, not for me
Are victory
And liberty!
Of the Liberty I died to bring in need;
And this betrayal wounds and sears my soul. I bleed.

H I E Dhlomo   *Ilanga Lase Natal* 19 May 1945

THE HARLOT

I have no love for you,
You to whom my flower I give.
I need your aid . . . I don't care who . . .

For, though poor, I too must live.

You call me harlot,
Forget my cursed lot.
'Tis you, yes you
Proud Christian, greedy Boss, you apathetic citizen,
Didst me undo,
Though now my company you eschew . . .
For you retain a system that breeds me— despised
denizen.

Yet I am Queen,
I choose whom I would choose!
'Tis you, not I, who lose.
I form a chaining breeding link between
The black and white;
And in my way I fight
For racial harmony;
For in dire poverty
We are the same,
Play one grim game.
And colour counts for naught
When men in stark realities are caught;
Their eyes are open and they see
They are alike. For poverty,
Like Capital (or truth and works of art)
Reveals the naked aching human heart.

Call me unclean,
Yet am I Queen,
Your daughters, sons, wives, husbands, sweethearts
know
I reign! With tears and bleeding hearts they crown my
brow!

For I am Queen
Although unclean!

H I E Dhlomo   *Democrat* 4 August 1945

THE AFRICAN NATIONAL CONGRESS

Congress! Congress! precious name,
Thou art dear to us and all;
Congress! Congress! world fame,
Thou dost claim both great and small.
Thy brave sons did land o'er seas,
From Africa's sunny shores;
To make a stand and to pursue the peace,
To fight against oppressive laws.
When none for Africa did stand
In the days of long ago,
When the powers did take the land
Thou didst rise to say No! No!
Born of Seme and of Dube
The hardy sons of Africa,
Makgatho and Mahabane
Gumede and others far.

Thou wert small but thou art great
All men to thee do flow;
Thou dost strive to end all hate,
So that tribes all each should know.
And despite the burning Sun
Thou hast marched and marched with pow'r
Although the battle not yet won
We do watch from hour to hour
Congress! Congress! ever dear,
Fighting for freedom to gain;

Thou art honoured far and near,
From hill to hill, from plain to plain.
Sing to Xuma, sing to all
Who the ship doth forward steer;
Africa doth make a call,
Sing and let the world hear.
Congress! Congress! ever dear
Fighting for to make us free;
Congress! Congress! full of cheer
Thou dost fight to eternity.

Obed S D Mooki *Ilange Lase Natal* 29 September 1945

TO THE FALLEN

Out from the north, south, east and west they came
True men of every race, colour and creed.
Abroad is heard the clash of warring arms.
The arch-rogue fumes and threatens soon to fell
The tree of life and hope to sons of men.

With clubs in hand for fight full armed went out
The boys of Southern Africa our land.
Amid their ranks were dusky Bantu lads.
Beyond the Vaal, Tugela, Kei and from
Moshoeshoe's mountain slopes and Khama's plains
They came at gallop pace with challenge cry.

Was it on friendly rounds they sallied forth,
That we should look for all a safe return
And for the fallen weep unceasingly?
Was it to festal boards they heard the call
Where even coward hearts their steps do tread
To feast with no heroic feat to tell,

When men of worth repeat the glorious tale
Of battles waged, courageous deeds of yore?
Went they not out to track and slay the prime
Of foes—three-headed dragon, vicious snake
Whose grim defence some blood must mark the stand?

Weep not you mothers. See, this day of all
The days give proof you mothered worthy sons.
Dark days disclose the sparkling worth of men.
Uncommon times do bear uncommon sons.
Weep not you wives, take comfort and rejoice.
This hour reveals you wedded men of breed.
What refuge would there be for innocence
If they beside their kraals did idly lie,
And from the hills the trumpet called in vain?
Wipe you your tears you orphaned little ones.
Take heed, your brothers and your fathers dear
Were victims honoured for the sacrifice.
Forsooth your lovers, maidens sweet, went forth
As altar offering, pleasing first-fruit gifts.
Great is the loss to all the Bantu race
Of brawn and brain, of genius, skill, this wealth
Which has been ravaged by the cyclone wild,
The thirsty war whose drink is blood of men.

Let us not weep for them. Be comforted.
They made themselves a wall of strength around
The garden fair, thus shielding life, the plants,
Choicest of all the tree of life and hope
Meant for the health of nations tribes and tongues.
When driven is the foe the spoil will come,
The fatted cow and ox with hanging horns.
Behold at yon horizon dust appears
Which points to coming of this captive gift.
We ask not for the spoil from hostile camps.

Lean are their kine, diseased withal their stock.
What could a robber have to offer men
Since through his need his native land he left?
We look for spoil, for true reward from home,
From those defended with such cost of life:
The smooth fat cow—Impartiality
The ox—Full-opportunity-for-growth.
From tree of life we long for leaf to chew
That we may live like races of the world.
When once a lad is asked to arm for war,
That hour he wins the standing of a man.
Consideration, honour, all are his
In days of peace when men assess the past.
Are there no drops of blood or tribesmen brave
On Libyan plains beneath Egyptian skies?
Some drops gave scarlet hue to ocean waves.
Where'er these crimson drops have flowed, some
                                        buds
Will bloom whose scent borne on the wings of winds
Will give sweet temper to our land of birth,
Until its treasures also we enjoy,
Achieve the state which stature aids to grow,
Mankind to thrive. Weep not, wipe you your tears.

Did you not notice how they left their homes
With heads aloft, chests out, and marching well
With left and right step challenging the world?
Eternally they thus will ever be.
Did you not mark the flow of love the day
They left seen from sad looks of aged men?
The matrons sighed, the young wife's eye a tear
Did hold. The maidens wept, the children sobbed.
Their worth was plain and precious were they then
On that proud day of such departure sad.
When mountains are no more, forever thus

Will they remain, for love outlives all change.
Did you not hear how they made light, it seemed,
Of grievous things which pulled at your heart strings?
They laughed at danger and despised gaunt Death.
They looked beyond and saw the fruit, vast gains
To their own race, to mankind and the world.
All generations sure will pass, and change
Will circumstances of this world, but they
Shall never change. When these our hairs turn grey,
Forever black will theirs be, and when
Our backs are bent, with strength will they march on.
Their spirits, soul of all their brotherhood—
Heroic defenders of the tree of life and hope—
Shall never cease to march and conquer all.
Like a victorious warrior on crusade,
The spheres of life of nations and of man
Creating him anew and world afresh.
Sweet comfort, Heaven's gift, may mourners taste.
Divine Restorer, wipe away all tears.

James J R Jolobe

SHANTYTOWN

High on the veld upon that plain
And far from streets and lights and cars
And bare of trees, and bare of grass,
Jabavu sleeps beneath the stars.

Jabavu sleeps.
The children cough.
Cold creeps up, the hard night cold,
The earth is tight within its grasp,
The highveld cold without soft rain,

Dry as the sand, rough as a rasp.
The frost rimmed night invades the shacks.
Through dusty ground
Through rocky ground
Through freezing ground the night cold creeps.
In cotton blankets, rags and sacks
Beneath the stars Jabavu sleeps.

One day Jabavu will awake
To greet a new and shining day;
The sound of coughing will become
The childrens' laughter as they play
In parks with flowers where dust now swirls
In strong-walled homes with warmth and light.
But for tonight Jabavu sleeps.
Jabavu sleeps. The stars are bright.

Anon   *Inkululeko* July 1946

'THAT THEIR PRAISE MIGHT BE REPORTED'

Cetshwayo

O thou who kindled patriotic fires
To stem the enslaving fires of their desires
O thou who flared and flashed with flashings red!
Sandlwana wailed when troops you bred and led,
Poured down her ribs and painted her with blood.
You quenched the flames Ndondakusuka brewed;
From Indulinde, Menzi, to the sea,
Extended once your principality;
From dun Tugela, Intumeni heights,
Extended once thy might, thy light, our rights,
    Great scion of Mpande, hear

Our prayers, be ever near.

O thou who slew our Link, the 'Tuft-of-Hair',
To singe the which no man could ever dare;
Great Menzi's Laurie, Ndaba, blest with heart
Of lion's strength, skilled in fierce battle art.
Afright, whole nations bled, took to their heels
As, singing songs, thy arms smote their bastilles;
They ran and crossed the roaring Crocodile,
In scattered remnants crossed, file after file;
Plunged headlong to the Hippopotami,
The river sacred that swept them to the sea.

Great scion of Mpande, hear!
Succour thy seed; be near!

Battle Of Isandlwana

I tell you of a story sweet and fresh;
I tell you of a victory absolute!
'Twas in these silvan vales, Ulundi Kraal,
The Epic great began.
Upon the throne sat he our leader great
Who ruled the land with wisdom, peace and love,
According to traditions, ancient, pure,
Old customs, social sanctions, sacred laws
Of our Ancestral Spirits down Below.
The land was rich with maize, with freshness green
Yielding all kinds of food for living things;
And corn-fields brown their heads shook golden
                                                    ripe!

The trees sang peacefully of sweet content,
And music full the rivers warbled on.
All sight, all earth, man, life all seemed so young!
And cattle grazed in cushioned meadows sweet.
The hills that roar with battle's ire today,

Seemed far, far far away, mysterious, charmed!
Birds flew and sang beneath the heavenly dome,
Cloudless and free from smoke and dust of war;
The children laughed and lisped with virgin glee,
While the happy mothers proud all thrilled with love,
Their breasts felt they fill both with milk and joy
And children came and sucked love's strengthening
                                         food.

The maidens of the land in beauty bathed,
And Youth rejoiced in brawn, in skill in arms!
Men sat them down to drink and draw the snuff,
Or joined at hunt or met in Council court.
'Twas land of love and peace and planned content
And gods rejoiced and blessings rich endowed.

Then came the white man and a cold wind passed!
Then spoke the white man and a dark cloud came!
Then moved the white man and storm then blew!
Amazed the people saw—saw all too late!
Cheated the people knew, and raised their Voice!
And messengers of each ran up and down!
Harbingers they of tears and strife and toil!
What says the white man, 'gainst our army plans?
And drums and horns told men to gather all
At Ulundi Kraal, the Elephant's abode.
Behold the nation met, in Council grand!
List to the sound, the sparks, as speaks that Voice!
What says the white man 'gainst our being enrolled?
See messengers of evil and of good
Rush up and down, seeking or fame or name,
Helping to build or wreck—heroes and spies!
What now? Ah! 'Tis too late! Cast is the die.
'Arise! and cry, we fight!' the brave bulls cry!
'Arise! and offer strife!' echo the hills!
Now is all motion! All is action now!

Dabulamanzi, swift as eagles robbed,
Cool as a mountain, sour as souls wife-wronged
Prepares and trains and leads them all to battle.
Then see our spies, their spies, our scouts, their scouts;
Behold our plans, their schemes, their tricks, our
                                                   moves!

The rumble swift of feet, the clang of hoofs;
The thump of troops, the thrills of march and song!
Victoriously Dabulamanzi cries—
'The battle's ours! what fool dare say me nay!
Laager, there's none! Leaders and scouts all sleep!
Hear ye! Tomorrow we their blind camp storm!
This is my plan, attend ye all. First horn
Then wing, then breast, then body, and then—spears!
But as he spoke our spies returned and told—
Here comes the foe! a small detached group
Arise and lick them white, blind fools they are!'
Our warriors, mad with ichor's urge, sprang up,
Upon the enemy swept down like fire!
No man escaped or fought or gave a cry!
The enemy was singed like unto hair!
The warriors deep in rage and craft, dashed on
Down the mighty slopes of Isandlwana's hill,
Poured down upon the foe like eagles wild!
Dabulamanzi poised like a dart in flight,
Brave as a god, instructions wise gives forth:
'First fling the horns, then body, and then—spears!'
Him all who hear, his word pass forward swift.
Behold the panic midst the white man's camp!
These here dash there, those here! shouting! crying!
Some seize their guns, some horse! frightened!
                                                   fumbling!

Confusion and commotion rule the camp!
'Beat back the horns!' their brave ones cry — too late!
As ants robbed of their nest, confused and dazed,

Scatter this way and that, so in the camp,
As men afright our horns try to out-run,
We eat them up! We slash them down! the weaklings!
We stab them drunk! We chant them mad! the
                                        sucklings!
They reel! They twist! the ghostly pale-faced men!
Spear! Tear! Slash! Gash! Rail! Wail! Suspiration!

It is all over ere we have begun!
And is this all! O nay! it cannot be!
And this is all they so much told and sang!
And is this all they call the game of war!
And is this all Somseu told with boasts?
Ah! then, rejoice, O AmaZulu great!
It is all over ere we have begun!
Praise, honour, song, Dabulamanzi brave,
Thou owner of the day, Shield of your race!
Thou hast out-generalled, out-played, confused
The captains white our power who thought they
                                        knew!
It is all over ere we have begun!
O rest in glory, Seed of Zulu blood!
Your mighty song of battle you have sung;
(Your song of freedom still you have to sing,
And sing it will!)
The victory of Sandlwana's field is told!
Sandlwana's mighty Epic ever lives!

H I E Dhlomo   *Ilanga Lase Natal* 27 March 1948

BECAUSE I'M BLACK

Because I'm black
You think I lack

The talents, feelings and ambitions
That others have;
You do not think I crave positions
That others crave.

Psychology
And Zoology
Have proved that Race and blood are a fiction . . .
All men are Man;
Diversity means not disunion—
It is God's plan;
White blood and black in test transfusions
Answer the same.
They harbour childish vain delusions
Who better claim.

Because the people eat and sing
And mate,
You do not see their suffering.
You rate
Them fools
And tools
Of those with power and boastful show;
Not Fate, but chance, has made things so—
Beware! These people, struggling, hold
The winning card;
And when they strike they will be bold—
And will strike hard!

H I E Dhlomo   *Ilanga Lase Natal* 22 January 1949

AFRICA

My love is for thee! But words cannot tell

My thoughts, my heartaches and pains that swell.
Oh, had I not been born, known thy sky so clear
I would not curse nor sigh, I would not be here
                              To weep for thee!

O dear fatherland! What is in thy morrows
When others bleed us, and strengthen thy sorrows?
How can I laugh when strangers at me sneer
Knowing no pity for me in my land here?
                              I weep for thee!

Walter M B Nhlapo   *Ilanga Lase Natal* 12 March 1949

DROUGHT!

Lord, give us rain!
The cattle die,
The land is dry,
The children cry.
Desolation
And starvation!
Suspiration
And destruction!
What greater sin than all these guilt-drenched years
Has Mother Earth shown that these pangs this year
                              are hers?
To the skies in vain day after day we gaze.
The streams and birds lack song, the people maize.
The sky and air, the veld and paths, are fire!
And men, starvation strangled, death desire,
The deer all pant like mole hills . . . dry!
One cruel hymn is heard among
All men and beasts—the 'water' cry!
There is no colour and no song.

Their tongues drawn out, gaunt dogs loud howl their
                                                 plight;
And fish and dish lie dry; and every night
Each household meets to tell the tale of woe
Each eye has seen committed by the foe—
The foe invincible,
Fell drought invisible,
Except for signs
And foul designs.
Heat dances magic dances on the hills,
The drought our lives with evils countless fills.
If thou dost love, Thy mercy and Thy good
Now prove by giving Thine dependents food.
Lord, hear Thy humble children, stricken, pray;
Reply in vain if only for a day!
Ah! Water, water, water, water—life!
One shower, one drop would end the mis'ry rife!
Father stay Thy wrath and hear us;
Break the drought, send rain, and help us.
Sustain!
Maintain!
We cry!
We die!
Lord, send us rain!

H I E Dhlomo   *Ilanga Lase Natal* 13 August 1949

PART TWO :

Where The Rainbow Ends : 1950–1960

Where the rainbow ends,
There's going to be a place brother,
Where the world can sing all sorts of songs,
And we're going to sing together, brother,
You and I,
Though you're White and I'm not.
It's going to be a sad song, brother,
'Cause we don't know the tune,
And it's a difficult tune to learn,
But we can learn it, brother,
You and I,
There's no such tune as a Black tune,
There's no such tune as a White tune,
There's only music, brother,
And it's the music we're going to sing,
Where the rainbow ends.

Richard Rive (prologue to a short story published in
Drum May 1955)

Chapter 1:
From The Heights of
The Maluties

THE GOD OF FORMAL WAYS

I made a god,
And now he rules with iron rod;
I worship in his formal ways,
His name I praise.

I swear and lie
To them and my own self — to buy
A nod of favour and approval —
Still so formal!

He must implore,
While knocking at compassion's door;
I show him, yet within's despise —
Such form is vice!

My beaming smile
Is just to aid my flatt'ring style
The mirthless laugh a social stunt
Not to be blunt.

O God of Form,
You baffle reason, lull the storm
Of passion, and the pain of truth
You lie to soothe!

Made by me,
You split me into two, and see!
I sweat and chafe against your chains;
I've lost my brains!

You know it well —
I'd crush your power and break your spell,
You know I may not just decide —
There lies my pride!

Ezekiel Mphahlele   *The Voice* May 1950

COME, FREEDOM, COME!

Rising in the morn I cry,
    'Come Freedom today!'
At midday I sit and sigh,
    'When comes the great day?'

God! To Thee I bring my sorrow,
    Tears I daily weep;
Must they be my food tomorrow?
    If so, give me sleep!

Walter M B Nhlapo   *The Voice* July 1950

HOW LONG, O GOD!

Burst forth my heart complaining,
Yours can't be joyful song.
Sorrows you have been restraining
Within yourself for long!

Like flame let your feeling's flower
Cry aloud, let earth hear
Your mighty voice with all its power,
Tell the pains of many a year.

I'm black but kingly, and even
God knows; a slave I cry,
And for fatherland grieving;
And stars shed tears in the sky.

God! must my tears flow forever?
Hear me in my tears
Before I cross Lethe river
To land of no fears.

Walter M B Nhlapo   *The Voice* 14 August 1950

TOMORROW

Not with the moans of a damn slave
Shall my song resound;
Like white folks freedom I'll have,
And shall fly over the earth.

Not as a scorned 'Kaffir boy',
Continually kicked in life,
But free, heart full of joy,
Shall my song then be.

Walter M B Nhlapo   *The Voice Of Africa*
18 September 1950

THE BURLY SOP

One township lives a burly sop,
Who drinks and reels apace,
The quisling sold to reach the top,
White patrons him did place.

He writes and drinks and beats the air,
No sober light to show,
In councils with a mind all bare,
His masters does echo.

Men of sense and men of grit
The noble cause will steer:
No soulless cur, or void spirit
The purple cause will rear!

K V M   *The Voice Of Africa* 18 September 1950

LINDIWE LAUGHS

She laughs!
My lady laughs.
I sing
And feel a king!
Above
All arts comes love,
For when
We love 'tis then
We feel
Wings on Life's heel!
This morn
New life was born;
This night

All earth shone bright
When she
Smiled love to me.
We kissed!
The Devil hissed
In hate!
Tried to abate
Our joy
With false annoy.
He failed,
And raged and railed!
We smiled!
How reconciled
Seemed all
Things great and small;
That smile
Killed for a while
All darts
That pierced our hearts;
We felt
God-like one knelt
In prayer
Without stir!
I was
What no king has:
A soul
Who felt life whole;
Things all
Were I; I all!
Ah! Laugh,
My chosen staff;
Let's chaff
While life we quaff;
Your voice
I hear—how choice!

It ever
Rings; ceases never!

'They laugh!'
Our epitaph
Will be
When we both flee
This earth
You filled with mirth.

She laughs!
Lindiwe laughs!
I sing,
And am a king.

H I E Dhlomo   *Drum* June 1951

O MYSTIC LOVE

O mystic love! what life, when thou art gone!
Thy tender tendrils when O love, upon
The soul, like shattered dreams, can hold no sway?
When thou art gone, dark days will be my way!

H I E Dhlomo   1953

HOW SOON THEY PASS

So peaceful they lie, so dead.
A gloomy cell their bed.
But yet they live in me
Who now their course doth see—
The course by them begun

Beneath our Africa sun.
You sons of Africa
You are our guiding star.

Shall there be born a Vilakazi yet,
Who shall our hearts afire set?
Shall there live a Lembede still
Who shall our minds with peace instil?
Oh! who rise from Afric's sands a Dube
Who shall for Afric's children care.

But how they pass and quick
Who would through thin and thick
A nation worthy wake
Albeit their life at stake.

Their bodies though in dust
Repose, their spirit must
Linger in us still
To do what was their will.

Desmond Dhlomo   *Ilanga Lase Natal* 30 April 1955

RISE UP

Oh land of warrior bold and brave!
Where once you did your spearheads wield
Your own dear land you strove to save
Now crumpled down, and do you yield?

O Chaka great thy name I fear;
How like a god you strode this strand;
I praise you and this land once dear
Where once you strode with Black war band.

And I poor son, from your dust rise
And seek once more a once-dear land
— No assegais nor war-like cries —
But crave on earth a worthy stand.

Rise up! swarthy Chaka's train,
'Tis time that you should show in deed,
That you be brave, have evils slain
And love and peace you seek to breed.

Rise up! 'tis not by magic hand
You'll win a name in lands abroad
But through great toil and trusty stand
You'll live as all if time afford.

Desmond Dhlomo   *Ilanga Lase Natal* 13 August 1955

TO HERBERT DHLOMO

          H I E, H I E,
Me and all my brothers dark,
Those that mumble in the dust,
Without a hope, without a joy,
Streaked with tears for ravaged Africa
Have, with thy silence, ceased to live.

In vain we seek the lost dream to regain,
In vain the vision yet to capture:
The Destiny of a thousand million dark folk
Who seek, who yearn—
Alas! A fruitless toil.

          H I E, H I E,
Speak to us again;

Whisper thoughts yet to impower us
To live the Dream, to live the Vision
Of a free Africa over again.

Lewis Nkosi   *Ilanga Lase Natal* 22 October 1955

THE BEGGAR AND THE LADY

Do not pass me by —
My legless, armless trunk
My oily jacket — try
To remember me
On this pavement give
My empty hat
The benefit
Of your last
Coin.

Oh lady well-dressed
Shapely like a buoyant bird
Jewelled by jealousy
He will have you pressed
Between the leaves of his eyes
For you to gossip an eternity
To a might-have-been
Doyen.

Joshua Messan   *Purple Renoster* 1955

O GHANA

Bright with the souls of our fathers,
Beneath whose shade we live and die,

Red for the blood of the heroes in the fight,
Green for the precious farms of our birthright,
And linked with these the shining golden band
That marks the richness of our Fatherland,
We'll live and die for Ghana,
Our land of hope for ages to come!
Shout it aloud, O Ghana,
And beat it out upon the drum!
Come from the pine-lined shore, from the broad
                                    northern plain,
From the farm and the forest, the mountain and mine,
Your children sing with ancient minstrel lore:
Freedom for ever, for evermore!
This be our vow, O Ghana,
To live as one in unity,
And in your strength, O Ghana,
To build a new fraternity!
Africa waits in the night of the clouded years,
For the spreading light that now appears,
To give us all a place beneath the sun,
The destined ending of a task well done.

Can Themba   *Drum* June 1958

A GAME OF GUESSING

I adjusted my tie and put on my hat,
And walked out of my rusty shanty home.
I caught the 8.30 a.m. Booth Camp bus.
I heard the street clock strike nine,
Entered an elegant, stately shop.
'Yes, John. What do you want?'
Amiably said the lady behind the counter.

'How,' I asked, 'did you know my name, Madam?'
I in return, did courteously ask,
Thoroughly satisfied by her amazing ingenuity.
'Oh! of course I guessed it,' was her positive reply.
'Then, Madam, you are, I am convinced, surely
                                                  capable
Of guessing what it is I want.'

G M Kolisang   *Drum* December 1958

BALLAD TO THE COFFEE CART

A little tin shack on wheels,
Jars a Jo'burg pavement,
Like a busy ant the roadwife peels
Potatoes, stirs porridge, blind to enslavement.

It is the blackman's Coffee Cart,
Simpler, cheaper, nourisher,
And, oddly, so near to the heart
Of this Metropolis' chestnut worker.

Coffee is the least of its wares;
Sour milk, Mahewu, dumpling and meat —
Staples all — but I love most the democratic airs
Of the easy-smiling women who come to eat.

If only the guys with the burning meat,
And the slick restaurants where stomachs smart,
Did not agitate against that dinner on the street,
You'd meet me during lunch at the Coffee Cart.

Can Themba   *Drum* February 1959

Chapter 2:
Exile in Nigeria

EXILE IN NIGERIA

Northern Wind
sweeping down from the Sahara
flings a grey scarf round me on and off.
The car torpedoes through the smoky haze:
I wonder what you do to my interior—
burning dry the mucus
piercing
scouring
my lungs—
savage harmattan!

Northern Wind
filtering
through tree and grass and me,
you hear my windows open
with a creak of hinges—
windows that were shut so long,
oh, so long
in the painful south of the south,
and you laugh at me—
rollicking harmattan!

Northern Wind
smelling of what I cannot smell
reminding me of things I can't or daren't remember,

what is it you do to me?
If it's remaining embers your
wasted fingers
fumble for
or violence
you're whipping me into,
groping
among slumbering drives of long ago down
in the cellar of the brain—
ah, save your breath;
I feel a certain void
now my enemies are out of sight;
only distant sound of long-tongued hounds
I hear
across the Congo and Zambesi and Limpopo
down in the painful south of the south,
and my anger
is a sediment
in the pit of my stomach
waiting
for Time's purgative or agitation—
harrowing harmattan!

Northern wind
all I know
is that you numb and jolt me
lash the water off my flesh
and fill me with a sense of insufficiency,
vague longings and forlorn moments and
brittle promises—maddening!
Twelve months I heard of you
there in the humid side of your native sands
where heat oozed
from under me,
denuded

some of the lump of southern pain:
you did not come
I came so far to meet you.
Yesterday I watched the leaves
go fluttering
down
down
to kiss the ground before your majesty—
pretentious thing!

Northern wind
now whimpering
whining
now lisping
dead prophecies
collected from ruins of lost empires,
you weave
knotted fingers
through tree and grass and me
blowing down the serest:
stop,
tremble
when you see the savage green of us
beyond the touch of you!
Not like the lusty August winds
of the vibrant painful south of the south,
spinning us into
desperate tears and laughter
anger, hope—
blistering interlace—
still pushing us on to hell or heaven,
we running fighting running,
straining
like a universe of bending reeds.
Rather that,

northern wind,
than the long hours of sleep,
oh, so long,
that make a yawning descant
to your impotent howling,
the long mental sleep
that knows no longing
for even the now unattainable,
no unfulfilled urges
heartburns and lingering angers,
no fires kindled by wanton men
beaten out
in psychotic panic
left smouldering smouldering smouldering
in the Negro heart
in the agitated painful south of the south.
When will you stifle
this yawn of ancient languors
in the range of your compass—
indifferent harmattan?

Northern wind
while I've been talking
I've become aware of one thing
I had only surmised
since I left the
palpitating painful south of the south
they've done it to me—
taught me the violence,
revenge of Europe,
uncivilized me
by the law of
paper
gun
baton,

made me lie to them and smile,
made me think that
anger and bitterness
and running fighting running
were man's vital accessories.
Now here I fume and dig and paw the earth,
bellow
poised panting like a bull for the encounter and
ah, no visible foe,
resistance none,
no dazzling red;
Ah the aching void in me,
neutralized acidity of my slime!
Now you know
the unsteady fulcrum of an immigrant!
Tell me,
is this divine indolence
this
the horizontal sleep of the north?
the secret of the urge to be
only to be?
or just the great immensity of Northern Sleep?
Is it Tao's sweet narcotic wisdom—
spirit of harmattan?

Northern wind
you know nothing.
Only, since morning
I've ridden layer after layer of grey
my nose is dry
your load trapped in my hair,
You've followed me all day
relentlessly
into the catacomb of night
and still I feel

the unholy hounds of the
bleeding painful south of the south
chasing after me,
you flapping about my head
gyrating like a pack of idiots
in and out between the running wheels—
Enough!
I shan't be wooed:
Shelley's long long dead,
no messages thrown to the winds anymore
Enough
of dehydrated kisses,
barren maid,
no night club this!
But now I think of it
I'll stop at the roadhouse here
for a beer
just for a while—
the immigrant's journey's a long long one,
heavy.
He tunnels through
back again
beneath
pounding footsteps of three decades and more of hurt
on the beaten road above
weighing down
down on him.
When I burst into the dawn of brooding questions
I shall yet look at more butterflies, moths and leaves
you nailed
on my radiator
like a lover of curios who wants his picccs
dead and flat.
Morning!
New dawn tells me

that void can never last,
for the immigrant's journey's a long long road.
Over centuries
they scrambled
for my mother
from across the frontiers of snowbound boredom
decay
stale wines and bodies,
clawed down her green innocence
mauled her limbs
sold her shyness
planted
brass and wooden crosses
knocked them down at skittles
gaming for the land
while hungry eyes transfixed on a miracle
high on Calvary.
I'm a leopard
born of
a Mother
a God in torment,
converging point of centuries of change,
a continent of test-tubes.
My claws have poison:
only let me lie down a while,
bide my time,
rub my neck and whiskers,
file my claws and remember.
Then my mind can draw the line between
the hounds and hunted of the lot
in the blazing painful south of the south;
use their tools and brains—
thanks for once to ways of white folk.
And in yonder land of peace and calm,
you think I'll change my spots?

No matter,
no regrets:
the God of Africa
my Mother
will know her friends and persecutors, civilize the
                                                    world
and teach them the riddle of living and dying.
Meantime,
let them leave my heart alone!

Ezekiel Mphahlele   *Black Orpheus* November 1959

PART THREE:

From Sharpeville to Soweto: 1961—June 1976

The slender child is dying in the bush
And the mother beats the broken drum:
Boom! Boom! Spare the heart and take the sheep,
And the pot of grounded meal. Boom! Boom!
The slender child will sin no more.

Enver Docratt (poem titled *Slender Child* published in *The Classic* 1963)

Chapter 1:
Things I Don't Like

THINGS I DON'T LIKE

I am Black
Okay?
Hot sun and the geographical set-up
Made me Black;
And through my skin
A lot of things happen to me
THAT I DON'T LIKE
And I wake each morning
Red murder in my eyes
'Cause some crook's robbed me again,
Taken what little I had right out of my hands
With the whole world standing by
And doing nothing . . .
Okay?

Don't want your sympathy, brother,
Keep it. Keep it.
No, wait. Give it to my enemies,
They'll need it.
I'm Black so I don't want your sympathy,
Okay?

Don't care. I don't care.
But . . . this evening is kind of beautiful,
All soft and warm

And I feel mad lonely
Right in the hollow of the stomach.
And birds are flying home
With sunset on their wings
And everything's wrong with me
And I don't care,
And some bitch woman with dull brown eyes
Fries eggs and polony
For the fourth successive night,
Eggs and polony for supper,
And I don't know when last I had a woman.
The way I feel — so sick,
Never want a woman again
And I don't care
Lord, but the night is good
And the stars are hot green lights
Exploding and exploding
And everywhere there's kids and men and women
But I'm hanging around with nothing but hate,
Hate so bad that I don't want your sympathy,
Okay?

Why must they rob me,
Can't count the number that robbed me,
Why? They took all I got,
Even dignity.
Then they threw something at my feet
And I looked down. It was me.
My labour. My heart. My life
Shattered; and I was no more.
While the thieves walked on laughing
And no one said a word —
Okay?

But you don't know me,

The kind of man I am —
Enough for you to see I'm Black.
Poor boy, you say. He's so simple,
And sweet.
But you. It's you that robs me
And I don't know how to fight you,
A thousand million thieves;
Do you wonder I hate you? And say:
TO DAMN HELL WITH YOU ALL
Good, bad and sympathisers —
Okay?

Look at this crazy little kid,
Dirty face.
Grinning as though life is good.
Don't know nothing, kid. It's terrible.
Huh? Give you a penny. Get. Scram.
Don't look at me like that kid,
'Cause what I am is inside me,
A heart that loves fiercely, without hope,
'Cause tomorrow is the same as yesterday,
And signs all round say
NIE BLANKES: WHITES ONLY please.
And I go in back doors
And still I'm robbed.
Do you think I'm the kind of man
To stand around forever and be robbed?

Oh no.
Today is my day.
Going to get back, tit-for-tat,
All you stole.
Going to fight you till you or I
Lie smashed and bleeding dead
And don't care who dies,

You or I,
But going to fight —
OKAY?

Bessie Head   *The New African* July 1962

THE EFFICACY OF PRAYER

They called him Dan the Drunk.
The old people refuse to say how old he was.
Nobody knows where he came from — but they all
                              called him Dan the Drunk.
He was a drunk, but perhaps his name was not really
                              Dan.

Who knows, he might have been Sam.
But why bother, he's dead, poor Dan.
Gave him a pauper's funeral, they did.
Just dumped him into a hole to rest in eternal
                              drunkenness.
Somehow the old people are glad that Dan the Drunk
                              is dead.

Ghastly!
They say he was a bad influence on the children.
But the kids are sad that Dan the Drunk is no more.
No more will the kids frolic to the music that used to
flow out of his battered concertina. Or listen to the
                              tales
he used to tell. All followed him into that pauper's
                              hole.

How the kids used to worship Dan the Drunk!
He was just one of them grown older too soon.
'I'm going to be just like Dan the Drunk,'
A little girl said to her parents of a night cold
While they crowded around a sleepy brazier.

The parents looked at each other and their eyes
                                    prayed:
'God Almighty, save our little Sally.'
God heard their prayer.
He saved their Sally.
Prayer. It can work miracles.
Sally grew up to become a nanny . . .

Casey Motsisi   *The Classic* January 1963

DEAR GOD

God, you gave me colour,
Rich, sun-drenched, chocolate,
And you gave me valour,
Enough for Love, for Hate.

But, God, Understanding
And Patience, and gazelle
Acceptance of Suffering . . .
You rather gave me Hell.

It's in affectionate
Names that I daily curse
The modes how You create:
Of Love, Hate, so perverse

That but for the untold
Wisdom which, only Thine,
Silences my revolt,
A spark from The Divine.

I'd be like Thee in wrath,
In Life's demolition

Or creation, and pronounce
Supreme imprecation . . .

Dammit, God, I'm provoked
More than mortal or clod
Thy will at first evoked.
I'll thunder like you, God.

Can Themba   *The Classic* January 1963

A WORKER'S LAMENT

From five in the morning,
My lean body is crushed against the jostling crowd,
For pittance, I make my way among the passengers,
Swaying coaches make my heart jerk in fear,
That I may not my little ones see any more
Yet for food and rent I must work.

'SEBENZA'. The whole day long;
The foreman and the Induna scream.
They should because the boss explained:
                                        'productivity'.
Pale lips; hunger exposes my empty stomach;
Starch water only my stomach has breakfasted.
Hunger takes away pride from a man's self-respect.
But the burning heart for revenge vows:
'Kahle, a day will come; Me boss, you boy.'

The listless sun leaves to the night
To blanket the light,
Thousands of pattering feet homeward drag
And leave the Shops to the watchmen.
Again I join the jostling crowd,

Fifteen miles homeward journey to travel,
Crammed like Jeppe Station victims,
I stand on a bench to save myself
Being crushed to death.

Modikwe Dikobe   *New Day* January 1963

NOTHING UNUSUAL

Eyes like twin eagles confront the sky.
Under a vault of grey banked cloud
Rain silver-pins these flagstones down, by turns
Electric or velvety, froth-soft or lionroar-loud.

The courtyard, years-old, crackles and simmers:
Nothing unusual, except for the hunchback
Who turns to answer the verandah voice
With huge efforts not to seem taut or slack.

Strangely, this square supports no trees;
Wind touching the scene here you
By yourself must remember not to forget,
Since the mind turns only on what is new.

Then again sunbeams spike through cloud-gaps,
And light, by turns, gleams pale and strong.
Will the windows open once more? Or does doubt
Mesmerise us as usual for far too long?

Arthur Nortje   *Purple Renoster* 1963

THUMBING A LIFT

Emaciated sand-dunes and grease-black pylons
On afternoons teeming with impurities;
Brittle bitter-brown wire; the sky-blotching ravens
Must be September's electrified existences.

I live beside sap-fired willow striplings
Yet alien to their cause, spring-exultation.
Cars pass by the study of my brown thumb
Rhythmically beckoning in painful indignation.

Gnats swarm from scumcamps; above the asphalt
Shimmy-shaking witchdoctors gnarled like bluegums
Drunkenly perform their corrugated dazzle,
Leering through red heat with futile venom:

I scream in sad fury for movement home,
They ignore me, mama, they and their crazy
Machines, bright machines. Past this wheedling tramp
Cars swish and whizz in dust-whirling frenzy.

To be but a sliver of velocity pillioned,
Exquisitely frozen in form-rubber pose;
Or dreamily sculptured in lavish freedom
Trading vague pleasantries, parading poise . . .

There now: the lavender and beige discreteness
In a creamy atmosphere (cool man, relaxed).
Comes a smiling samaritan — ah but these bulging
Ogres palm me off on an incredible next!

Trafficking with me now in truces of poison
White flags of exhaust fumes envelop my person;
So I'm afterwards only OK when, chosen,

My hopes dimly chase a careering horizon.

Arthur Nortje   *Purple Renoster* 1963

IT IS NIGHT

It is night
It is a Johannesburg night
Stars mingle
With neon lights
All a merry twinkle
Of confusion
It is night in Johannesburg
And a jazz musician
Goes home.

It is a pitch black night
Pitch black and deep.
Noises cry out
In the depth
Of the darkness
Far out
In the distance
Of the night
Noises of Silence
And a jazz musician
Instrument in hand
Goes home.

There is a wind
That blows
Bitter and cold
It enhances
The loneliness

Of the night
It is the wind
That cleans the dirt
Of Johannesburg
The dirt
Of Johannesburg
by day
It is a lonely bitter wind
It drives the jazz man
Barely dressed
Home.

As he plods
His cold night home
Thoughts
Out of his head
Come and go.
A tear forms
To weep
Like a spring rain
A tear
Of thoughts
That come and go.

It is a long
Lonely way to art
A long weary way to jazz
When will it come
When will it be
There is no answer here
There is no answer there
The answer is
In a Johannesburg night

Half way

Down his cheek
The tear stops
As if in doubt
Then again
Its journey
Resumes
To burst
On his warm lip
But the jazzman
Is not content
With a bursting tear
He seeks a way
To fulfil
A burning life.

The night grows darker
He becomes smaller
The stars twinkle on
Against neon globes
But somewhere
At the end
Of his road
His horn will blow

The laments
Of the lonely
Johannesburg night
When this end comes
It will be like morning
Out of
A Johannesburg night

There will be
No more lonely nights
For him

No more a doubtful tear
Morning
Shall have dawned
Bitterness disappeared
The jazzman
In bitter smiles
of yesterday
His homeward way
Shall plod.

But now
It is night
It is a
Johannesburg night
Stars mingle
With neon lights
All a merry twinkle
of confusion
It is night in Johannesburg
And a jazz musician
Goes home.

Finn Pheto   *The Classic* 1965

DISCOVERY

The truth dawns. Or what can pass
as truth at pseudo-dusk in this room's limbo.
Rain-racks diffuse at evening:
half-sweet and semi-dust the street air smells.

Misted and arid atmosphere parallels
intricate self-searching cerebral processes:
the dry mind with these wet thoughts driving

vapours over walls of mirrors.

Recognition and reassurance
have become less automatic.
Truth is more grim to tell because
there are fewer celebrations.

Passing from this the secure
world to the insubstantial
mirrorless world my life moves
restless as waves in their surge for freedom.

The foam of weakness clings
to stones and other debris.
While thoughts strain to resolve themselves falls night
and right or wrong must be perhaps.

Because, considering all
has no finality.
We pass to opposite sides
of the same door, seeking each other.

Arthur Nortje   *New Coin* * March 1965
                                 *Published 1973

AND THE FLESH WAS MADE WORD

The knowledge of each other that we want
is telephoned and half-anonymous,
our voices are in wires, not each other's blood,
our letters reach each other poste restante.

(You must have seen a spider dying, moving
at last its long, thin, languid legs.)
Bind up our broken gestures, misted, dusked

behind the frosted mask of glass, however,
water our withered force
of pens and lips
and let it keep
for life, even lived deep, is only in discourse

and everything between us said and heard
bear testimony to the flesh made word.

Adam Small   *New Coin* July 1966

INNUENDO

I heard voices
and anguished songs
in those days
I said listen
to the voices listen
to the cries dying
you laughed at
the pulse of my mind
in those days
we took time
to look at deeds
in those days
when you had time to sleep
we took time to leap
in those days
when you laughed
we took time to know

K William Kgositsile   *Contrast* November 1966

AFRICA, MUSIC AND SHOW BUSINESS
An Analytical Survey in Twelve Tones Plus Finale

1

geography
    so many theories of east and west abound
    one thing is certain though
    this earth
    is round

2

slave bell
    slave
    master your bell
    your master ·
    like the cat
    was belled
    with time
    no clocks
    no clime
    stipulate
    late afternoon
    nor early mourning for the dead
    sombre tolls the very same bell that rings for joy
    bell
    slave
    time is your master

3

spiritual
    When i get to heaven gonna play on my harp
    gonna play all over god's heaven
    but only with the cats who can make the changes

4

western influence
  my baybee eesah cryink baa baa forra me
i geef her de mango
i geef her de banana
but she's stillah cryink baa baa forra me

5

rhythm afrique
  joey had the biggest feet
  so he played tenor

6

lues for district six
  early one new year's morning
  when the emerald bay waved its clear waters
      against the noisy dockyard
  a restless south easter skipped over slumbering
      lion's head
  danced up hanover street
  tenored a bawdy banjo
  strung an ancient cello
  bridged a host of guitars
  tambourined through a dingy alley
  into a scented cobwebbed room
  and crackled the sixth sensed district
  into a blazing swamp fire of satin sound

  early one new year's morning
  when the moaning bay mourned its murky water
      against the deserted dockyard
  a bloodthirsty south easter roared over hungry
      lion's head
  and ghosted its way up hanover street
  empty

forlorn
and cobwebbed with gloom

7

where loneliness' still waters meet nostalgia
and morning breaks the city sun and smoke
and towering grey the buildings murmur
grim subway rumblings in their roots
i scan the vacant faces and sad smiles
and long for home

the night my soul had herringed red
through raucous songs of childhood:
and friends and comic stories long forgotten
were whiskied out of memories dim
to function as narcotic
and silence cruel reality as it screamed
it's neither here nor there

i'm hemisphered
but three
the southern cross and libran scale
and god knows
he knows
where

8

ballet for tired sons and lovers
figure belt — is the tragedy of the illustrious son of
a suburban african chief who, disillusioned by the
apparent ineffectiveness of his magical work,
discards his girds and elopes with a fast-travelling-
northbound-salesgirl. After mesmerizing him with
her hypnotic, synthetic ornaments, she locks him
up in a fashion magazine and in order to keep him

amused, content and in her power, she clads him with so
many figure belts that he stifles and loses his voice
and in final desperation strangles himself and dies.

9

wind up
   the southern spring winds
   myself in two
   one wintered in cold steel northern city
   brittle eyed neon guards my empty stomach
   the other
   a dimming summer
   camera-ed in youth
   and matineed each minute of each dreary day

10

double cross
   in the afternoon came white dressed white men in
   a big white car they took him away

   in the afternoon came black dressed black men in
   a big black car they took him away

11

   the terrored dusk screams
   the land
   in the beginning
   love was
   the fuse igniting all
   clay
   and green leafed sun dynamoed my buck
   which now gallops petrified in the rumbling
      twilight
   through fields of empty stomachs' wide
      eyed plea

to where the midnight hides
dark robed three armed inevitable
one hand outstretched towards a pair of fleeing
    balances
one empty hour glassed
and last
a bloodied feather falling from a palsied palm

12

the harmonica
    it has been raining
    and in the gutter lies the harmonica
    gurgling incoherently

    the man stooped
    to retrieve the instrument
    and it obeyed and played

    the people heard and loved him

    he dwelt in skyscrapers and blew wind
    and soon his feet became unsteady

    one morning when he came down to dig his senses
    it was too late
    the pavement loomed up and cracked him violently
        in the head
    and the children ran away with bits of his brain

    and the harmonica rattled back into the gutter
        where it had fallen
    with the inauguration of time

FINALE

life in a national park/or — take five
    last night two monkeys stumbled onto an
    AMAZING
    COLOSSAL
    FANTASTIC
    secret
    on the outskirts of an african village
    where they had been sleeping off a drunken stupor
    they discovered an ancient clock
    ticking away in $1979\frac{1}{4}/35\frac{1}{2}$
    (they worked it out)

    they were jubilant
    after much deliberation
    as to who the rightful owner was
    (they even cast lots)
    they finally decided that the whole world should
    know of this amazing phenomenon and that by
    using their usual 'pay-while-you-hear' ritual, they
    could ensure themselves a life time of happiness
    and if it came to the push they would
    DISCOVER EXCAVATE and even
    INVENT
    more clocks

    this morning for some obscure reason (they thought)
    the clock decided to change to 4/4

    they were furious

    learned gorillas were called in on this appalling
        example of disobedience

    the suggestion that the clock's mechanism be
        studied was accepted, half-heartedly

but alas, it was too late
for when they touched the spring, there occurred a
terrifying explosion
and the whole monkey kingdom was blown to bits

the resultant itch woke up TIME
and she scratched vaguely under her armpit

Dollar Brand (Abdullah Ibrahim)   *The Classic* 1967

BODY

The brittleness of Life I know
how in the tongue
the lung
and palms of hands
the days break then we breathe
into the mind
O joy
pain
joy of living
loving
living
knowing pain of
knowing nailing its broken bits
bleeding through the fire, six, seven
senses of this cross

Adam Small   *Contrast* March 1967

NAKED THEY CAME

I have seen them come,

At break-neck speed,
Beheading wild flowers
With kicks from serrated edges
Of naked black feet,
As naked they come.

Pot-bellied, bow-legged,
They jump as they come,
A scourge on my conscience
For poverty is their blanket,
Bought from one common shop,
The shop of inheritance.

Naked they come,
With complete abandon,
All sizes all ages,
They stand and they gaze,
What a sight!
A tourist attraction.

Their lives insured,
Yes, unquestionably safe,
For soon they will join,
To work on the mines,
To work on the farms,
And soon more will come,
For naked they come.

Perhaps a crumb,
From my impoverished hand,
Will stem their hunger,
And crush their pride
Of people in their land,
The land of their birth,
For naked they come,

To their real homeland.

Basil Samhlahlo   *New Coin* 1967

TAKEN FOR A RIDE

I get my cue
from the glint in the cop's eyes.
I have seen it before.
So I have to find it.

I pull away from Mono
and hug myself in desperation.
Up, down, back, front, sides,
like a crazed tribal dancer.
I had to find it.

Without it I'm lost, with it I'm lost.
A cipher in Albert Street.
I hate it. I nurse it,
my pass, my everything.

Up, down, back, front, sides,
Mono's lip twitches,
She looks at me with all the love.
She shakes her head nervously.
Up, front, sides, back, down,
like a crazed tribal dancer.
Molimo!

The doors of the kwela-kwela gape,
I jabber at Mono.
The doors swing lazy, sadistic like Jonah's whale.
A baton pokes into my ribs.

I take the free ride.

Stanley Motjuwadi   *The Classic* 1968

WHITE LIES

Humming Maggie.
Hit by a virus,
the Caucasian Craze,
sees horror in the mirror.
Frantic and dutifully
she corrodes a sooty face,
braves a hot iron comb
on a shrubby scalp.
I look on.

I know pure white,
a white heart,
white, peace, ultimate virtue.
Angels are white,
angels are good.
Me I'm black,
black as sin stuffed in a snuff-tin.
Lord, I've been brainwhitewashed.

But for Heaven's sake God,
Just let me be.
Under cover of my darkness
let me crusade.
On a canvas stretching from here
To Dallas, Memphis, Belsen, Golgotha
I'll daub a white devil.
Let me teach black truth.
That dark clouds aren't a sign of Doom,

but hope. Rain. Life.
Let me unleash a volty bolt of black,
so all around may know black right.

Stanley Motjuwadi   *The Classic* 1968

AN AGONY

My head is heavy, my shoulders shrug,
because despite
all my eyes have seen
my head has said
my heart has felt,
I do not believe
that White, Black and Yellow
cannot talk, walk, eat, kiss and share.

It worries me to think
that only people of my colour
will liberate me.

You mustn't trust a White man
my grandfather used to tell me
when I was a child.
You mustn't think a White man cares for you
my people caution me.
You know when a White man wants to know you?
When you bring him money!

The Indian? He's black as you.
But, not as poor as you.
He knows his trade — cheating you.
He's happy to lend you money
just forgets to mention

the twenty per cent interest!
Until you have to pay it.

And the Coloured? I ask.
Ag! him, they say.
He doesn't know where he stands,
but, he prefers his skin whitest
and his hair straightest.
And somehow forgets the second names
of his black and kinky cousins!

I know of Whites, Coloureds and Indians
who are not like that, I say.
But, I'm told they are only a few.

Now, what about you my fellow African.
We are intimidated, they say,
Modimo, we're very very busy, they say,

not losing
our passes,
our birth certificates,
our train tickets,
our rent receipts,
our urban residential permits,
(not to mention our money, our husbands and our
                                            lives).

My head is heavy, my shoulders shrug,
because despite
all my eyes have seen
my head has said
my heart felt,
I do not believe
that White, Black and Yellow

cannot talk, walk, eat, kiss and share.

Joyce Nomafa Sikakane   *The Classic* 1968

REAPERS IN A MIELIEFIELD

Faces furrowed and wet with sweat,
Bags tied to their wasp waists
Women reapers bend mielie stalks
Break cobs in rustling sheaths
Toss them in the bags
and move through row upon row of maize.

Behind them, like a desert tanker,
a dust-raising tractor
pulls a trailer,
driven by a pipe-puffing man
flashing tobacco-stained teeth
as yellow as the harvested grain.

He stops to pick bags
loaded by thick-limbed labourers
in vests baked
brown with dust.

The sun lashes
the workers with
a red-hot rod;
they stop for a while
to wipe a brine-bathed brow
and drink from battered cans
bubbling with malty 'maheu'.

Thirst is slaked in seconds,

Men jerk bags like feather cushions
and women become prancing wild mares;
soon the day's work will be done
and the reapers will rest in their kraals.

Oswald Mbuyiseni Mtshali   *The Classic* 1968

THE WASHERWOMAN'S PRAYER

Look at her arthritis-riddled hands
Raw, rheumy and calloused.
Look at her sorrow-shrivelled face
Like a bean skin soaked in salty tears.

For countless years she has toiled
To wash her master's clothes
Soiled by a lord's luxuries.

Through bitter winters
Through broiling summers
In frost-freckled mornings
In sun-scorched afternoons
She has drudged a murmurless minion.

One day she fell and fainted
With weariness.
Her mouth a foaming spout
Gushing a gibberish.

'Good Lord! Dear Lord!' she shouted.
'Why am I so tormented?
How long have I lamented?
Tell me Lord, tell me O Lord.'

'My Child! Dear Child,' she heard.
'Suffer for those who live in gilded sin,
Toil for those who swim in a bowl of pink gin.'

'Thank you Lord! Thank you Lord.
Never again will I ask
Why must I carry this task.'

Oswald Mbuyiseni Mtshali   *The Classic* 1968

I WILL TELL IT TO MY WITCHDOCTOR

I will tell it all
to the witchdoctor,
as I sit on a mat
of woven grass and beads;
and dry monkey bones
shrink my head,
and rattle the eardrums.

I will listen to his voice
chanting incantations
like a priest giving a blessing
to a soul seeking solace.

I will ask him
to boil a pot of herbs,
and brew a Love potion
as strong as a mule's milk.

I will give it
to the world
whose eyes are myopic with misery;
and this world will wink a smile,

and dandle me like a devoted mother,
and smother me with affection
I have never known before.

Oswald Mbuyiseni Mtshali   *New Coin* June 1968

OUT

They came in droves
for your abandoned charms,
and I have watched the cup
passed under my nose
from hand to hand
conveying your assent.
I, who once held the cup in my hands
now turn my face from side to side
watching it pass from me
with eyes darkening
into pools of vitriol,
my sight blackened,
meditating the insult
in your averted face.
I am nothing
but my writhing jealousy
glowering in anger
watching anxiously
to see you say 'no',
but alas!
always you say 'yes'.

And so I ran into the night
jumping fences,
holding my ear close to doors
to hear where my name was spoken,

growling demanding entrance
and slinking away when refused.
The night is my eyes
blackened to meditate
the sins of the day.
I listen with the night
to hear my name
spoken in jest by all,
drifting from the cracking doors
with sounds of clinking glasses
when the toast is proposed in my name.
I briskly walked
and stood up against the window
commanding entrance,
my sight blackened.
I rapped the window,
'Voetsek!'
'O God, is this the end!
Let me explain.'
I ran to the corner,
then up again,
but got stuck at the window.
'Whore! whore!'
'Go! You're finished with.'
I rapped the pane
I struck the glass
but the darkness . . .
'Where are you, where are you?'
I took my feet
and placed them end to end
round the house till dawn,
and when the light came,
I kicked the dew with my feet
carried my heavy heart
slung over my shoulder

and passed my hand over my face
to welcome the day.

Mafika Mbuli   *The Classic* 1968

A DYING MAN

Poor father has passed a bridge,
His calendar long is due —
Life has played him well.
Today! This minute he'll die.

Children, grandchildren all around,
'Father, grandpa,' they all call.
His lips mumbling something but
Keen ears couldn't make it out.

Nurses running up and down,
All hurrying to help the helpless —
Father in need of something but
No earthly help can quench the thirst.

'I must! I must die!' he said,
'Call Mary, call her this minute.'
Mary was not there — she left while
Life was still with the now dying man.

He gasps with fumes white,
In colour coming out like a foam,
Death demanded its pay today,
His name appeared first today.

The bridge is crossed though,
The road is long and tiresome.

Too many tests, too many temptations!
'Oh life! Why should I suffer?' he said.

He was there in a white cloak —
His shroud snow-white and fastened,
So tied, but why should it be so?
A dying man fights you not, and nobody.

There are people crying touchingly,
Oh! What a pity! Let's pray
For those who lost him to Him.
The man's death was not a mistake.

He had to die! Yes he had to,
Did he make peace with Him?
Eternal rest, let him have that —
Peace that we all are waiting for.
His name was called yesternight,
His life-time is overdue,
He had to die — yes he had to.
'My Lord may he rest in peace.'

P M Mabyane   *New Coin* December 1968

BUT O . . .

You can stop me
drinking a pepsi-cola
at the cafe
in the Avenue
or goin' to
an Alhambra revue,
you can stop me doin'
some silly thing like that

but o
there's somethin' you can
never never do;
you can stop me
boarding a carriage
on the Bellville run
white class
or sittin' in front
of the X-line
on the Hout Bay bus,
you can stop me doin'
some silly thing like that
but o
there's somethin' you can
never never do;
you can stop me
goin' to Groote Schuur
in the same ambulance
as you
or tryin' to go to Heaven
from a Groote Kerk pew
you can stop me doin'
some silly thing like that
but o
there's somethin' you can
never never do;
true's God
you can stop me doin'
all silly things of that sort
and to think of it
if it comes to that
you can even stop me hatin'
but o
there's somethin' you can never
never never do —

you can't
ever
ever
ever stop me
loving
even you!

Adam Small   *Drum* September 1969

GAZAL II

My joy lies hidden in clouds of gloom,
Is it that fortune's stars are eclipsed?

My heart is restless, restless the world,
Some blithe maiden has loosened her hair.*

Ah fate! after weathering every storm,
My ship has struck a rock at the shore.

Oh sorrows of time, I will not weep,
I am pledged to smile at every turn.

The thorn saw the dew on the petal,
And asked : Is it for me that you weep?

So many friends at my funeral,
So great a crowd, yet I lie alone.

Bells strike joy on beauties' dancing feet,
Love sings its passion on the chord of love.

*The loosening of a woman's hair symbolises grief.

The darkness veils the light o' Unus*
This I know when night dawns into day.

*The Poet

Unus Meer   *Portrait of an Indian*
                                        South African 1969

MY COUNTRY

I love thee, my land Afrique!
I love the sea, that rolls on its coast
Love the rivers that flow through its veins
Love its every bird, every flower,
Every mountain, hill, rock, grain of dust
I love all of these and share with these
My love, my Africa, my land.

This land is wicked, evil they say —
Not the land, only some of its ways.
Is evil absent, ever? at all?
Evil and good, two sides of a coin.
Why blame the earth, the evil's in man,
The earth loves and nurtures all, the same.
I shall shed my blood for my country
I shall mix my body in her soil,
Oh Farooqi,* her gardens will bloom from my dust.

*The Poet

Farooqi Mather   *Portrait of an Indian*
                                        South African 1969

TO THIS DAY*

Trapped in the vice of memory
I remain unchanged to this day.
Hidden in veils of laughter
My tears gush forth to this day.

One gift remained when you left me,
Sorrow, unforgettable grief.
That grief of youth, keeps me in youth.
Keeps my life happy to this day.

An age has passed, I came away
Bearing the hope of a new day.
But the shadows of past laments
Pursue me closely to this day.

The gardeners have themselves sold out
To autumn the charms of gay spring.
Yet spring is treasured, spring remains,
Thorn and flower laugh to this day.

Heaven's envy, soil of my land,
Mixed in it the blood of my love.
How could I know, my life given,
I would be alien to this day.

*Translated from the Urdu in cooperation with Mrs Z Mayat.

Safee Sidique   *Portrait of an Indian*
                                        South African 1969

Chapter 2:
Beyond This Moment

I HID MY LOVE IN A SEWAGE ...

I hid my love in a sewage
Of a city; and when it was decayed,
I returned:
I returned to the old lands,
The old lands
Where old men old women
Laugh all day
Until their lungs are as dry as dust:
Where old men and old women
Talk all day
About the weather, about proverbs, about fields ...
About trivial things:
Where they talk all day
About trivial things ...

There was I in the wilderness,
Outlandish years dull
Like the rings of a rusted bell.
I stood aloof when the cows
Spread their moo across the rural greens,
I was king,
I was king of the bees,
I ruled over the honey,
I ruled over the milk pail
Full of white bubbles.

Ha! Ha! I held my hollow belly
In laughter when a hen dropped an egg.
My arms akimbo,
I knew the secrets of the world,
I knew the secret pleasures,
The better pleasures,
And God, let me lie on the grass
At the entrance of life — unwanted life.

Below the bottom of life,
My love lay drowned in the stench,
Of course I knew it
I knew my love was dead;
But oh no, let me lie unbothered
On the grass at the entrance of life,
Let me break the bonds that make me me,
Let me drift in the wilderness of callousness,
Let me drift an unidentified soul . . .

And when the fumes of decayed love
Were unfurled unto the winds,
And they covered the plains and the greens,
And their rot chewed by the trees,
And their rot sung
By choirs of drunken birds,
I knew I had lost;
God, I knew I had lost;
O who am I? Who am I?
I am the hoof that once
Grazed in silence upon the grass,
But now rings like a bell on tarred streets.

Njabulo Simakahle Ndebele   *The Classic* 1970

JERUSHA'S DANCE

It wasn't ready for our eyes,
while it didn't ask
to be born in a backyard
(of all places)

It took the sun for granted,
our way of life for the real thing
and the language of art and flowers
as the testament of truth.

(Nobody bothered to tell us it was a painting)

'Zuluboy' Molefe   *New Coin* April 1970

THE WIDOW

My husband lies dead.
What shall I do?
Nothing but poverty
Left to me.
No-one to tell,
Even at beer-parties.
My Ancestors' spirits
Look down on a louse.
My husband lies dead,
He left me no seed,
No-one to care for me.
I have eaten my heart.

Clifford Nhau   *New Coin* December 1970

ALEXANDRA

Were it possible to say,
'Mother I have seen more beautiful mothers,
A most loving mother,
And tell my mother there I will go,
Alexandra I would have long gone from you —
But just like we have no choice but to be born,
We can't choose mothers;
We fall out of them like we fall out of life to death.
And Alexandra,
My beginning was knotted to you,
Just like you knot my destiny.
You throb in my deepest silences
You are silent in the heartbeat that is loud to me
Alexandra often I have cried,
When, when I was thirsty and my tongue tasted dust,
Dust burdening your nipples.
I cry Alexandra when, when I am thirsty
Your breasts ooze the dirty waters of your dongas,
Water diluted with the blood of my brothers your
                                        children,
Who once chose dongas for death-beds.
Do you love me Alexandra?
What are you doing to me?
You frighten me Mama.
When I lie on your breast to rest, something tells me
You are bloody cruel;
Alexandra, hell
Alexandra what are you doing to me?
I see people but I feel like I'm not one.
I lie flat while others walk over me to far places.
I have gone from you, many so many times.
I come back;
When all these worlds become strange to me.

I come back
And amid the rubble I lie.
Simple and black.

Mongane Serote   *The Classic* 1971

MORE IMPRESSIVE ON THE MIND

more impressive on the mind
than the proffered smiles of babies
are the horrors of sunshine
(at least darkness is dark)
horrors
round which morning prayers coil
in pleading smoke
that merely settles on a dust of hearts
bleeding with laughter,
as children float in the sky
buoyed by bulging tummies
that echo with years
clamouring to be lived
o children!
o apparitions of children!
a child and a breast
a child wailing under a drunken breast
drip drip drip leaks the breast
drip drip drops the drink
on a new head.
a child and a breast;
a child and a breast and flies,
they make paths to nowhere from the nipple:
a warm child
fresh from the perfume of a decayed womb.
but hearts merely bleed with laughter,

pausing at some moment
to unload rich crumbs,
as a certain man
continues to park his car
in the shadows of a gum tree;
to brandish a note
and drive off with a certain maid.

it is then that old men
begin to lament
the death of those days.
a child and a breast, drip
a child and a breast, drip drip
drip drip drip . . .

Njabulo Simakahle Ndebele   *The Classic* 1971

LOST OR FOUND WORLD

Skies of truth are now scenes
At the mercy of my curtain eyes,
I wink often more often,
To draw the curtains
To cut and forget the skies.

The sea of identity is tears,
A too salty expression
Bleeding my blue veins that's my pen,
On the loose sand that shall sip,
And the wind shall help cover it,
From the needy arteries.

Mountains of hope are flowers,
Passes attracting cars like bees,

For the precious modern honey,
That is money.
This modern madness
Snaps flowers from their stems
Leaves dry dead bodies, walking up the street.

Old wishes is present deeds,
Bright with blinding for old
Dark with wonder for the new,
That's where we are
Lost or found world!

Mongane Serote   *Purple Renoster* 1971

THE SHADOW BEHIND ME
To E S Madima

A companion, an enemy
I see and feel him follow.
He followed yesterday and shall tomorrow.
Here we go, unseparable mother and baby.

Slowly and silently he comes,
Merciless a mother-tigress,
A monster but friend to the purse,
Yet nightly he watches me toss.

I hear and sometimes read
That his victims some suicide
When tired to abide,
Although another blood they hardly shed.

Someone told me yesterday
That for this Shadow Socrates boldly went

And Jesus followed, and the world wept.
Maybe all is but okay.

Tenda Robert Rachitanga   *Purple Renoster* 1972

CEMENT

An unprecedented abundance of cement
Below, above and all around
A notorious capacity to retain cold
Without an equal facility for warmth

Inside is captured a column of air
And a solid mass of human substance
A pertinent question poses itself:
Which loses heat to which?

As complete an enclosure as possible
Throwing its presence all around
Until recognised by all five senses
Achieving the results of refrigeration

Hovering relentlessly is the stubborn stillness
Permeating both solid and gas
A free play of winged imagination
And the inevitable introspection
Stretch themselves painfully over
The reluctant minutes of the marathon day.

Stanley Mogoba   *Purple Renoster* 1972

IT'S NOT THERE!

as i walk
i see
their faces — uncertain, yet hoping
their eyes — searching, but not finding it.

yes long ago
i also hoped
and i also searched
but i never found it

the truth is that it is knitted
into a garment of lies.

Ilva Mackay   *Blac Bulletin* 1972

JUST TO SAY . . .

There'll always be those
who'll want me to act
after their accepted fashions;
those who'll expect me to pull a smile
just to please their vanities;
those who'll wish I should agree
with their clawed existence;
those who'll say I'm not polite
jes because their grabby ways
ain't gonna be my stays,
and their swags don't fool me.

After a time, when we meet
our situations confronting
our reactions damning,

they will be shocked to find
the real people not there:
the walking public that jams
the street after 4.30 p. m.;
the mass that musters
the soccer stadium on Sunday;
the audience that is not given right
to listen to its own inner say.

The people will not be there —
Gone.
So gone there won't be
anywhere for the swags to go.
And I'll swerve at the nearest
corner of the street
and get into my first
genuine, private, laugh —
that will unfold itself. Into the people
For by then I'll be gone too
Real gone.

Mafika Pascal Gwala   *Ophir* December 1972

HANDCUFFS

Handcuffs
have steel fangs
whose bite is more painful
than a whole battalion
of fleas
Though the itch in my heart
grows deeper and deeper
I cannot scratch.

How can I?
my wrists
are manacled.
My mind
is caged.
My soul
is shackled.

I can only grimace at the etheral cloud,
a banner billowing in the sky, emblazoned,
'Have hope, brother,
despair is for the defeated.'

Oswald Mbuyiseni Mtshali   *Sounds of a Cowhide
Drum* 1971

SIR

Sir,
re: INDIGENOUS LANGUAGE [sic]
Alas, 1, 2, 3
the Bantu has, a, e, i . . .
to forsake his own
indigenous language
his beloved mother's
his old-fashioned forefathers'—
(What an unforgivable sacrilege)
for the sake of passing lily-white
a, b, c . . . exams!
gone, gone, gone
our true identity
'but this IS literacy'
or, whatever . . .
ModiMO! . . . thusa, tlhe.

Yours obediently,
Mothobi A Mutloatse.

Mothobi Mutloatse   *New Nation* January 1973

WA'RENG?

HE says I'm civilised
She echoes same
And they say they're Christian
We echo same
We think
we're Christian
Uh-huh!
They say we're uncircumcised
therefore unchaste, unpurgated
He says he's sociable
and they say he's unreliable
We think
we're humble
she mumbles
she's mad, isn't it sad?
Yea, we're all bad
nobody's ever glad
over anything, anytime
anywhere—ahem!
But—there's no tolerance . . .
only violence
wena wa'reng?
Bang! bang . . .!

Mothobi Mutloatse   *New Nation* January 1973

ON MARRIAGE
Such a careless subject!

If
death
is a bastard
like good old Themba says
then marriage
is an institution—
mental, like a crocodile
mind you,
a lewd
bed of false pretentions!
Halalalaaaa! !

Mothobi Mutloatse   *New Nation* January 1973

MAMELLANG
Or, Jumbled Thoughts

There are
times
bazalwana,
when men
I mean real he-men
who don't
indulge
in impure and ungodly
deeds
feel down at heart,
that their lives
are ill-spent
like the yearly rising rents
and would rather offer

their earthly souls
to mother nature
than be devoured
painstakingly by other cannibalistic ogres
and demons—
bipeds, with sound-boxes to reason,
called 'human beings'
the Almighty's creations—
some booze and wallow in splendour
and as you prick their skins, what!—
out oozes red wine!
aha!
(overlook the
exclamations!)
while others
(the poor souls)
languish in squalor
'cause
many value
life so cheaply
(God have mercy)
and yet only a chosen few
deem it
so dearly.

Mothobi Mutloatse   *New Nation* January 1973

A SAD CASE

He is ungracefully lean, big-foreheaded and weak,
he draws back his lips, showing his teeth and gums
like a dog in snarling, his distorted face is ashy and
                                        bleak.

Froth of saliva runs down his flabby lips, even when
                                                 he hums.
He twists his fingers painfully and squeaks like a
                                                 mouse.
He wets his trousers fully conscious and laughs aloud.
At times he assumes dimensions of a lunatic and
                                                 rouses
everyone in the neighbourhood, drawing a crowd
of ill-mannered children that follow him up and down
                                                 the streets.
Visitors seldom enjoy their brief stay,
to them he is a perfect nuisance, he keeps on asking
                                                 for sweets.
Only upon great request does he briefly go out to
                                                 play.

James Twala   *Izwi* October 1973

THE DURBAN INDIAN MARKET FIRE

i saw it;
crumbled to the ground,
pillars
standing for the
rain
        and
            wind
                    &
saw them too;
mooning up and down
hands deep in their pockets;
sniffing and keening
at the great loss

the crone leaned
against the pillar,
sadness in her face
as she looked at the charred
building before her eyes

the old cove was seated
on a tomato box; head
in hands as if suffering
from toothache,
concealing the unbearable pain
                    &
when i looked
at the durban tourists'
attraction, the indians'
life-giver that had turned
to ashes,
I turned away,
found a small alley
and snivelled.

Nkathazo kaMnyayiza   *Ophir* 1973

HOUSEWIVES

They gather here daily,
To wash their rags
And gossip.

Here, at the washing place,
The bricks greened with moss,
The women gather.

They sit in the shade of the house,

On the damp ground where sunshine never comes but
                              for a little while,
Cleaning the vegetables for the evening meal,
Or watching the children play,
Or just sitting carelessly,
But all the while talking,
Endlessly talking.

Kissoon Kunjbehari   *Ophir* June 1974

VULGAR NEIGHBOURS

Someone is sweeping the yard,
Her body bent,
Her arms moving with a monotonous regularity.

What is she saying?
That some son-of-a-bitch overturned the bin?
Did she not see her son do so just now?

Kissoon Kunjbehari   *Ophir* June 1974

CHILDREN PLAYING

You sit in the shade,
A cigarette forgotten between your lips,
Drunk,
Dead drunk,
Watching the children play,
Little children imitating adults
Blind children ravishing their innocence.

Kissoon Kunjbehari   *Ophir* June 1974

FEELING SMALL

They can take me
on a predawn ride
to an 8 a.m. hearing
they can cram me
into a people's coach
to ride
to their splendid offices
they can call me
boy
even as a retired pensioner
they can give me a yearly rise
and take it as fast as c.o.l.
I say they can move me
from slums
to a peachtree-lined Location
to squat temporarily
they can kick me
in the arse
just to ask me to shift a bit
they can be solemn
explaining the justness of their jury
protecting me from skelms and so on
I say they can beat their breast
a thousand, thousand times
to show
how they've made God listen at times
to rationalizations
But brother!
they can never, never be so large-hearted
to free themselves of fear
'Strue's living God!

Sipho Sepamla   *New Nation* 1974

GOD, PLEASE . . .

god, please . . .

do not let them turn me into a shop
to be opened at six in the morning
and closed at six in the evening
regulated in the thoughts i may
and may not display
advised on who i may
and may not welcome
in the sovereign territory of my being

remember that i've tried
to keep my books of account
as you've asked me to
crediting the right
and criticising the wrong
diligently, faithfully
honestly
because i know no other way

call back these self-appointed auditors
of my soul
who have declared me insolvent
and have condemned me
to a work-house
where i shall be fed
impoverished thoughts
for the best years of my life

god, please . . .

Shabbir Banoobhai   *New Coin* April 1974

PORTRAIT OF AN INTSHUMENTSHU*

I dwell in gaberdine trouser pockets.
My iniquity is honeysweet.

I'm smarter than a tsotsi's brandished dagger.
I do not smell of blood.
O, I suck no blood.

I kiss the vein
To freeze my prey
The cold kiss that exonerates me.

My work is clean!
I leave no blood on my track,
No blood under my soles!
*weapon made from a bicycle spoke, causing internal injuries
but leaving no external sign.

Paul Vilakazi   *Ophir* June 1974

THE START OF A REMOVAL

On a Monday morning

when some people were hailing taxis
others rushing to buses and trains

when teachers and school-children
were packing their books
peeping out of windows to see so-and-so
their time-keeper
was leaving for the factory or office-job

when the local businessman
eyes large and sleepy
like he was an owl
sat at the till
waiting for the early customer
to make his insomnia worthwhile

when the housewives started bending
their overused frames
raising dust on the pavement
in front of their yards
with home-made grassbrooms

when a midwife wearily flung
instructions at an old lady
whose daughter had just
given birth to her third child
by her third 'boyfriend'

the first five families
woke up
to the drone of bull-dozers
and the impatience of heavy-duty trucks

The removal had started!

Sipho Sepamla   *Ophir* June 1974

NIBBLING

there are people
who make truth
in their own light.
like i do

every time i say:
i don't like black people
who say to the whiteman
always:
to hell with you!
i say so myself
sometimes!

i don't like white people
who say
sometimes:
i am a liberal.
they make me think
of other liberals
always!

when i'm talking to a person
especially
a white lady
who hasn't said she's a liberal
it doesn't seem right to hear:
isn't he clever?
isn't he marvellous?
said of a black man
who is a success.

the expressions
sound tainted
with a tight-fisted
generosity
always!

i admire white people
who are perfect flatterers.
they leave me

with only one thing:
suspicion!

now, if i seem to accept
the separation of people
it is simply to work out
in my own good time
the phrases i'll use
to forgive others
for their many promises
turned grey on the sides!

i hate lies
one of which tries
to explain my bitterness
as anti-whiteness.
of course i do hate
some people —
i am in love
with mankind!

Sipho Sepamla   *Unisa English Studies Journal*
                                           June 1974

CARLETONVILLE

Black masks in the night,
Black faces invisible in the dark,
Black bodies blending with the pitch in the sky,
Black voices soft as sooty whispers in the wind.

Loud voices locked in deliberation,
voices becoming more and more strident
with home-brewed anger

that has been under timeless fermentation,
compounded by the complacency
lolling leisurely in White easy chairs.

Then . . .

Wham!

Rat . . . tat . . . tat . . . tat . . .
Tum . . . tum . . . tum . . . tum . . .

Groans in the dark,
rat . . . tat . . . tat . . . tat . . .
screams in the night bouncing
like black rubber balls . . .

yo . . . yo . . . yo . . . yo . . . yoo . . . yo . . . yo . . . yo

Hot molten lead pins flaming with fire
to puncture the black skins,
the bullets hit the bull's-eye
the bull is black,
the bull is enraged,
the black bull bellows in a big black voice . . .

The wind took to heel,
the night wrung its hands,
pleaded for mercy to no avail.

Rat . . . tat . . . tat . . . tat . . . tat . . . tat . . .

Echocs from the cracked skulls and broken bones
                                            reverberated
to the circumference of all compassionate hearts.
the earth shuddered

stunning Lesotho, Botswana, and Swaziland.

Headlines across the continents,
telex machines rattling the news
puncturing the ticker tapes of mining houses,
'11 Black miners shot dead'.

Again?
Again? Sharpeville?
the Stock Exchange hesitated,
undecided whether to rise in defiance
or sink in despair.

Rat . . . tat . . . tat . . . tat . . . tat . . . tat . . . tat.

An inquest was held,
after post-mortems had been performed:
the final verdict vindicated
the molten lead,
that had scythed the
'screaming and looting mob'.

For a moment the Black voice of the black bull is
                                                              silent
whilst the worms of discontent churn the gizzard
leaving a suppurating sore of silence.

But the Black voice is not dead.
Its echo is still there,
from Langa, Sharpeville, Cato Manor, Gelvandale,
When will it be X-ville?

Oswald Mbuyiseni Mtshali   *Ophir* June 1974

THE CROSS-BEARER

Anguish was there in his eyes
big red frantic marbles popping out
from their sockets.

He moved like a paper caught in a gust of wind
tossed by an unseen hand
through an unknown force into a vortex of death.

he scampered to the ledge of the fire escape,
he turned to look at us,
his mouth twitching unintelligible sounds;
we did not read his heart
otherwise we would have read the valedictory message.

He bounded over in one leap,
and he was gone,
for a moment we heard nothing;
then a distant thunderclap of breaking bones erupted
from the bowels of our volcanic heart.

The air stood still
caught in the grip of an eerie silence,
the city buildings swayed drunkenly,
even the sun seemed to whirl
and spin on the back of a top.

Then sirens tore the air,
Whistles shrilled,
bells clanged,
fire engines, police squad cars, ambulances,
the cacophony held us transfixed with helplessness.

We heard the din die down,
but he did not.

How could he?

Down below on the parapet he lay,
they had swathed his body in a refuse bag;
the White janitor stood next to the motionless form.

She meticulously went through his personal papers
and exclaimed angrily,

'I do not know this boy,
he wasn't one of my boys,
what did he want here?
He must have been a thief or a drunk,
he was not even supposed to be here in Johannesburg,
he is from Natal . . . look here.'

And there was the stamp on his dead Book of Life,
'Bearer to leave the Magisterial District
of Johannesburg within 72 hours.'

Seventy-two hours had not expired,
but the cross-bearer was gone.

Oswald Mbuyiseni Mtshali   *UNISA English Studies
Journal* June 1974

MY BROTHERS IN THE STREET

Oh you black boys,
You thin shadows who emerge like a chill in the night,
You whose heart-tearing footsteps sound in the night,

My brothers in the streets,
Who holiday in jails,
Who rest in hospitals,
Who smile at insults,
Who fear the whites,
Oh you black boys,
You horde-waters that sweep over black pastures,
You bloody bodies that dodge bullets,
My brothers in the streets,
Who booze and listen to records,
Who've tasted rape of mothers and sisters,
Who take alms from white hands,
Who grab bread from black mouths,
Oh you black boys,
Who spill blood as easy as saying 'Voetsek'
Listen!
Come my black brothers in the streets,
Listen,
It's black women who are crying.

Mongane Serote   From *Yakhal'inkomo*

LISTEN TO ME . . .

I'll pull out my hand and grab your hair
God;
Tell you to commit suicide.
And for every township church there is,
There I'll put a robot;
Green eternally.
Go black boy, uproot what you know and seek
                              what's new.
Then turn to your maker's God,
the self-styled gods.

I'll tell them, they are fuckin' liars,
Survival of the fittest was never a human principle,
You told me that's right
In your churches
You killed my ancestral souls
In your parliaments
You told me that I am wrong and deadly.
Did I believe you!
Then you told me that God is you.
A god armed with a gun and smiles that bit me
                                      mercilessly,
Daily through the centuries,
And made me, myself and I, my vitriol,
My scapegoat;
A thing to destroy.
You've been bloody cruel to me,
Now you must listen to me . . .

Mongane Serote   From *Tsetlo*

FOR DON M — BANNED

it is a dry white season
dark leaves don't last, their brief lives dry out
and with a broken heart they dive down gently
                            headed for the earth
not even bleeding.
it is a dry white season brother,
only the trees know the pain as they still stand erect
dry like steel, their branches dry like wire,
indeed, it is a dry white season
but seasons come to pass.

Mongane Serote   From *Tsetlo*

THE MINER

At the strike of the bell
he pops out of the hoist skip
like a pea shot from
the muzzle of a bazooka,
and shuffles from the shaft
on boots caked with mud,
that carry him and comrades
to the coir bed in the compound.

To stretch limbs
leaden with weariness;
to wash a face
daubed with gold tinted ochre,
and armpits mouldy
with sweat of the cocopan
refusing to run down the rails
of the ore-crushing mill.

He rises to kiss
the plastic 'skal'
foaming with food-filled beer,
and strike his chest
as a victor over a day's labour,
   'Brawn is mine, mine only
   and brain is yours, all yours.'

Oswald Mbuyiseni Mtshali   *New Coin* June 1974

DO THEY DESERVE IT?

Let them wake up at dawn
   to dig up endless trenches:

Let them pull out
    big rocks for roads and highways;
Let them make tea
    and stand from morning
    till evening.
Let them be crammed
    in self-closing-door township trains.
Let them sit or stand
    on open pavements
    eating fish and chips
    with three slices of white bread.
Let them build towns and cities
    where one day they'll be endorsed out
    'cos they don't belong there.

'Anyway they deserve it,
they're developing their
own country.'

Let them sell 'ijuba'
    for a living;
    for if they don't
    they'll starve.
Let them pay lobola
    but wed the white-style;
    for if they don't
    they'll be called heathens.
Let them wear a disguise
    of happiness and freedom;
    for if they don't
    they'll be fired.
Let them carry passbooks;
    for if they don't
    they'll be put in gaol.
Let them beg;

for if they don't
they'll throw cow-dung
in your eyes.

Nkathazo kaMnyayiza   *Ophir* June 1974

A MUM CALLS FOR HER CHILDREN

Children! Children!
Yes, mum
Where are you?
We are in the forest mum
Come back home
We are afraid
What are you afraid of
A big tiger mum
Where is it?
It's next to the big tree
What is it doing?
It's looking at us
Come, run home.

Alexander Mthombeni   *Izwi* June 1974

THE END OF THE DRAGON

Creche children made a big surprise
Their little hands killed the dragon
They cut it with table knives
Its skin was bought with a big sam
The flesh was sold to the circus.

Alexander Mthombeni   *Izwi* June 1974

THE HIGHWAY ROAD

Highway lies high from the ground
Just like a person sleeping in a second floor
It stretches further and further
Covered by the tar.
The stretch ends up in Durban.

Alexander Mthombeni   *Izwi* June 1974

MY FISHING VILLAGE IS

My fishing village is
                    hungry
my fishing village is
                    dying
my fishing village is
                    death
my fishing village is
denying me root.
Afrika said
look up to the mountain
                    and cry
and i must ask why
this fishing village is
                    denied.

Mike Dues   *Blac* 1974

MY TOWNSHIP

I hate the filth
that you spread

unashamedly
I hate the gutter
in the stony fjords
of your lips
the hungry echo
the sandy ugliness
the unwilling dead
you vomit
and yet I love you
for the me in me
the beautiful ugliness
within your playhouse
I love you
for you were not born
you were made

Christine Douts   *Blac* 1974

SOUTH OF THE BORDER

South of the border, Down Bantustan way
Develop along your own lines:
Invent, first, the wheel
Before you can ride in a car.
Television is not for you
But we can make concessions—
Use the gramophone.

Bathrooms, flush Toilets—
You need but very few
Since you've never been ashamed to wash
Proud and Naked,
In the village stream,
Or to hide your heels,

In the bush.

Whiteman's medicines
Are your herbs, liquified—
Stick to the herbs.
Agriculture is the basis of your economy,

Try to cultivate the desert.
And to this be as true
As night follows day
For greater is your reward in heaven.

Mbulelo Vizikhungo Mzamane *Izwi* December 1974

TO PAINT A BLACK WOMAN

clothe her in a black doek black pinafore
and a faded blouse
(forget her feet
she can be without shoes
for all we care!)

add
her look of resignation
with those sad eyes
which seem to be asking
that unspoken question —
'where have you been?'
or
'what have i done now?'

'Zuluboy' Molefe   *Contrast* December 1974

BABY THEMBISA

The charge sheet read:
  State v. Baby Thembisa,
  one   adult   Bantu   male
  of   no   fixed   address,
  charged under the *Abuse*
  of Dependence-producing
  Substances et cetera *Act,*
  No.   41   of   1971,   for
  being   in   possession   of
  20   dagga   cigarettes   on
  Republic   Day,   31st May,
  1974.

I entered the cement cold
underbelly of Joburg's
magistrates court,
for consultation
with my client,
the said Baby Thembisa,
regarding the aforementioned
allegation
made by the Drug Squad.

I saw my client naked,
sitting on the concrete floor
like a lotus flower,
reading CRIME & PUNISHMENT.
He said,
  'Justice is a white goddess
  to which we blacks are wise.'

Essop Patel   *Ophir* July 1975

GHOST

He was rich and old.

He died the death of an ordinary servant.
The night after planting him,
old men waited in the dark,
sitting in front of his hut,
facing toward the cattle kraal.
After a long wait,
before midnight,
HE came, he came acting visible,
wearing invisible legs.
Before he entered the hut,
a brave voice said: 'Thobela,'
and asked him what he wanted,
'cause he was supposed to be in his
everlasting bed.
He told us how to divide his
cows and belongings,
among his children.

Motshile Nthodi   *Ophir* July 1975

NOTES FROM AN AFRIKAN CALABASH

Sound power is an inter-eruption
That protrudes at once
An atomic cloud
Of feeling
A unit emotion
Killing with one blow
This is music's witchcraft;

Audience formation turning into an exorcised Babel
                                        nucleus
Purity gushing into the core of everybody within this
                                        Jazz radius
A few hours of heaven descension
As Black-notes from an Afrikan calabash cleanse us
With a BOLD BLACK HERITAGE.

Lefifi Tladi   *Ophir* July 1975

THE BORDER

the border

is as far
as the black man
who walks alongside you

as secure
as your door
against the unwanted knock

Shabbir Banoobhai   *Ophir* July 1975

DARKNESS

yes sir i have arrived
walk the night if you dare
there i reign over death
'swonder you legislate the night
i walk erect in the night
you crouch in retreat
crowding each nook in fear

of the stench of my blackness
agitated by a darkness

Sipho Sepamla   From *Hurry Up To It!* 1975

AGRARIAN REFORM

I saw a black man
shake a beseeching voice-box
at whites
crying for coins

And have you heard
of a place called 'Zombie'
where people scream
like poltergeists
crying 'bread!'
and 'water!'
oh I have

But I have also seen
bullets soak into the heart
of a Soweto boy. Saw him
cleave fractured African soil
resuscitate it making loam
of long-eroded Azanian earth

And I know now
the rigor mortis
has not set in
There is still time

Christopher van Wyk   From *It Is Time To Go Home*

NOW WE SHALL STAND

now we shall stand
not cowering
not fearing

now we shall stand
as strong as the colour
of our blood

now we shall stand
as bold as the birth
of the sun
now we shall stand.

John Samuel   *New Classic* 1975

SIGNIFICANT CHANGE

Apricot blossoms
        here
                in ordered rows man-made
                burnt winter's lawns dropping back
        against the rising-new bud-green of hedges
        there
                profuse, branched in trees
                scarred rough, sullen skies climbing high
        against the dusty earth's still holding firmness
        abruptly
                snatching the corners of rheumy eyes
        unsuspecting
suddenly everywhere blowing gustily
these captivating promises offer the season

Apricot blossoms
                    sprays of beauty
      lace the air
                    wild clustering tendernesses
      delicately pink
                    the frilly froths of snow
                    reflecting more subtle, deeper
                    pink fragilities, purpling blues
                    as spunky petals
      tremble free

Apricot blossoms
                    unexpectedly undetained
      This Spring's released the accommodating earth
      to an eternal
      natural
      significant change
                    Its seeds not celled behind
                    bottled prison doors of terror

Claude Noble   *New Classic* 1975

MY ORGANS

My heart pounds
Limbs interpret the sounds.

My vein is an angry
                    river
              for a hungry
                    container.

There's jazz in my intestines
You might think bra Hugh blows nostalgia.

A tapeworm is a terrorist lying in ambush.

My nose is a twin chimney
for a charred cigarette —
an exit for rejected perfumes.

My lung is a concertina —
Crescendo when I see Christina!

Oh my lithe tongue
You are under house arrest!
A saliva pool for you!
Be bogged by Babalaaz!

My lips are sheets
Pap kay-bee lipstick
tobacco and blood
are dabblers.

Microscopic people in the skull
are voluble in dark hours:
'We want freedom! Sex! Booze!'
Folding like a tortoise at dawn!

Nape 'a Motana   *New Classic* 1975

APARTHEID FALLING

They tell me,
my educated brothers do,
that the colour bar in South Africa
is coming down
I'm not impressed.

They show me signs
that are no longer there
on park benches and on lift doors
those signs, they used to say
whites only — blankes alleen.

They point out to me
black men and black women
khakhi-clad office boys and
overall-wearing street diggers
and they say
don't you see
all those people
sitting on those benches
where only whites were allowed
to sit all these years?
we tell you, man,
apartheid is dying
I'm not impressed.

They tell me
my educated brothers do
about other educated brothers
who eat and sleep
in hotels
where only whites were allowed before.
they say to me,
you see, the whites are changing
everything is changing.
we tell you, man,
the colour bar is going.
but I'm not impressed.

I will sit up and take note
when the whites say to me,

black man, no more pass for you
black man, you are free now
       to work and live where you will
black man, the soil on which your township house
       stands you are now free to own
black man, the education of your children
       shall be free and compulsory
black man, you shall be paid
according to your skill and worth
       no longer according to the colour of your skin
and I will believe it
when the whites say to me
black man, you shall elect
men and women from your race group
who will sit and talk with us
in Pretoria and in Cape Town
and together we will decide
how our beautiful, bountiful country
should be run.

Obed Kunene   *New Classic* 1975

SISTER SING THE BLUES

Sister dish it out, go on give it,
sing, sing, sing my black sister
stir the atlantic with your soulful tunes,
fill us with determination,
rejuvenate the lost manhood in us,
sing like our forefathers faced battle,
icho ntombi, icho sungoyiki
khuthaza amadoda, ukhuthaze nawo amagwala.

Azania has no more men

men die drunk and half-mad
in the dusty ghetto streets
sikhuthaze ntombi kaMakeba
sister go on sing the blues.

You renounced your country unwillingly,
because you wanted to live
you wanted to belt it out,
to tell whitey he's doing shit,
you're doing it baby,
your words inflict deep wounds
wounds that haunt and taunt
every sane black man.
sikhuthaze ntombi kaMakeba
sister go on sing the blues.

Black sister your sweet voice
that awakens the dead
and inspires the living,
when your voice reaches the ghetto
black men look at themselves.

Lebona Mosia   *Ophir* December 1975

THE STREET LAMP

Towering on isolated corner,
beam falls only on white spot
where privileged combat summer heat
with watermelon and ice cream.

Master clad in Safari with eyes
stuck in Newspaper headlining
terrorist and landmines on the

border of Zambezi.

Far around white beam
there's naked darkness,
where hunger,
death,
rape,
assaults are glittering stars of Township night
where legislatively drowned father has sunk for five
                                              years for
complaining of Street Lamp.

Leonard Koza   *Ophir* December 1975

EXTRA

Swivelling on the corner
the paper waving in the air
like a rag on a washline
his anxious whistle low
cupped between his hoarse cries
his beseeching
compelling demand that you buy
the paper
his striped skipper
awkward pants
heeled tackies
his angry ebony skin
his bangle that spun on his wrist
and his desolate humility
that he should sell
news of a life
that always

passed him by . . .

Fhazel Johennesse   *New Classic* 1975

DOORNFONTEIN

Doornfontein
ek sê
is not like it was

Rollicking full of life
you met all the manne
everywhere

Those ous from Corrie
or the Ville musn't
come make shit here
we Doorie owens
won't take their kak.

Throbbing and bursting
shebeens and brothels,
Ou Cecil Rhodes and
Barney Barnato must
shit
in their graves
to check what
is happening in their
old koeksters.

Nay there's no shit here,
the lanies we get on with
they are just like us.

And now they are
bulldozing the place down
there's hardly anyone left;
except the whores and oere
and of course all
the Mac Fuggers
looking for meat.
Sometime we going to
bulldoze down their
homes ek sê
and send them to a
township and see
how they like it.

hey man, all the
High Bucks come
from Doorie.

What High Bucks ek sê?

No mfo, Doorie
was the place
there were play-whites
and there still are,
but just like Sophiatown,
and Jeppe and so on . . .
they moving us all out
of town
making scars on our
lives and in Josie
but Doorie will
always be Doorie
ek sê.

Colin 'Jiggs' Smuts   *New Classic* 1975

THE BULLFIGHT

Snorting furiously
Bellowing incoherently
Pawing the dirt in
Uncontrolled rage

The matador flutters the cape confidently
To the quivering mass of anger: The bull
Then . . . the mad rush, the matador
Twirls a ballet step-hop, skip and clear!
The bull hurtles towards the cape
Thru' it, past it.

Now be careful about your role
For the matador is experienced and armed
Put down your spear, and lift the pointed horns
And think before you rush at him
For he merely represents what you hate — captivity

This is no time for hysterics —
It's 363 years too late.

Fhazel Johennesse   *New Classic* 1975

THE ANONYMOUS HOUSEBOY

The madam won't worry about shoes for me
no genuine cowhide needed
the soles of my feet are hard and sturdy
so why bother
but for a vintage collection
let me write home for Izimbadada.
The white tennis shoes

neat and slightly oversized
are my everyday footwear.
In them,
and inside my incredible
kitchen boy suit
that never fits too well,
(I prefer mine white
it makes me
look like a circus clown.)
But all the same I'm happy,
a free suit from the missus
it's as good as
a well earned bonsella.
I bathe poodles
and take fox terriers
for a walk in white suburbia.
Nobody knows me.
I occasionally meet
homeboys emptying the ashes
into dustbins.
It's a usual salutation:
'How's home?
Has your heifer yielded
anything this year?'
I stick to my strict duties.
Then there's a big fight at the flat
and the white Baas fires me.
I'll do the mine or
become a night watchman.
I'm satisfied
my children will not starve.

Sol Rachilo   *New Classic* 1975

ALWAYS MY PEOPLE

Always my people i see
looking at the northern region stark
like christian fanatics
at a dangling crucifixion

but beaks of malice-carved vultures
bite their eyes away with croaking propaganda

and their hands dangle
rusting
entranced
waiting for a sermon from Mt Drakensberg
to chill away the hated species
with defeating history

they wait
breeding leaders to supervise the tears
of oppression
these frustrated doves
cooing hoarse in a hot deserted bush
calling for rain from a cloudless sky

these people
whose heavens are dreams
of bigger vultures with weaker beaks
that fry themselves to benefit the slave

so they wait

and i say to myself
blessed are the weak in mind
for they shall crawl into their beds

with a hope of a better dream . . .

Zinjiva Winston Nkondo   *Ophir* December 1975

AFRICA

Africa . . .
you stood deformed
burdened with the fruit of your blood
and your huge heart filled the air
with the eminence of hardship

as i lay crumbled . . . half moon
in the warm watery spray of your womb
prepared for exit
frail wriggles gave you hope of my life

when you dropped me
my birth cry was a crying relief
a sought after pain
and you adorned this wasteland with a smile
that broke and hung on your face
like a ripened fruit

then full-throated ululations bathed the mud hut
perforated out into my father's heart
who buried his grave in the palpitations of my heart

Africa . . .
here i stand
the hope of your labours
against the wall at the abysmal end of patience
and when i'm supposed to sing
i croak curses

Africa . . .
I know you want to nurse me
to embrace me
you want me to scratch-ease the inthings
of your insulted heart
but tut . . . the struggle is over-due
my appetite is whetted against barriers
so i needs must face the wall
when i turn back
i'll either be on heroic shoulders
or in a black hearse

then Africa know that my heart
is a haven of love
bigger than seasons . . .

Zinjiva Winston Nkondo   *Ophir* December 1975

BEYOND THIS MOMENT

I've begun to count yesterdays
spent with you
when you would pinch at love
in your little box
your face wrinkled with sneers

there's for me a memory
I seek to cancel
of fallen heroes
and forever trembling hopes

I must go beyond this moment
that seems to ensnare footfalls
in shifting sands

I want to build a monument
to house what remains
of a fragmented legacy

for too long
I've strained to obey a wish
in my guts
the terribleness of a memory
that waylays all days
like a drunk living today
on yesterdays

there's a leap beckoning
I only hesitate
the thought of an unknown chasm
that hugs two moments
and with you here
you gaze so harsh
I feel an impotence
I can face in dreams
of many moments beyond this

Sipho Sepamla   From *The Blues Is You In Me* 1976

A DAY IN OUR LIFE

1. What is pain?

ask any black man
he'll tell you
without looking it up in a dictionary
how's to be picked up
booted in the back,
fly in — head first

knocking yourself against the spare-wheel
and to be driven around town
buckshee!
ask any black man
he'll tell you
without looking it up in a dictionary
how's to be picked up
to talk about 'things'
to a friend who always urges you
about your opinion of the mpla
frelimo fnla and umkhonto kashaka
who knows?
he might be dangerous
have you ever seen
an sb wearing a uniform?
ask any black man
he'll tell you
without looking it up in a dictionary
how painful it is
sitting and writing in a cold candle-lit room
till the wee hours of the following day
to have your work banned
and ruin the future of your publisher . . .
ask any black man
he'll tell you
without looking it up in a dictionary
how bad it is
to be promised a better wage in ten years' time
while inflation and col soars.
ask any black man
he'll tell you
without looking it up in a dictionary
what pain is —
go on, ask him.

2. *Roadblock*

I really don't know
why they always do it in the morning
when we haven't a minute to spare
when all are rushing to work
to be stopped and told to walk
because our vehicle is not roadworthy.

3. *'The food is bad'*

'the food is bad
and our tea is served
in enamel bowls!'
that's how they shouted
proposing to down their
tools or leave the machines running.
'pick some men
who'll take your complaints to the management,'
he said, trying to force his voice
among the angry black swarm. His eyes
told his fear as he waited patiently
for the answer.
it came
terse and straight,
'it's no use,
they'll give them curry and rice
and they'll forget us.'

4. *Adjmeri Arcade (Durban)*

hey man!
slow down.
you'll knock the people over
if you move so fast

this place is crammed
damn crazy with people
people who are music crazy.
swing man!
the music is tops
from the Record King.

watch your wallet, gentleman!
watch your purse, lady!
pickpockets are rife here
you can be mugged any time.

ah! look at the gals!
ain't they beautiful?
loosen your tongue man
you may get your
till death us do part here.

Nkathazo kaMnyayiza   *Ophir* 1976

I REMEMBER SHARPEVILLE

On the 21st March 1960
on a wrath-wrecked
ruined-raked morning
a black sea surged onward
its might ahead
mind behind
it had downed centuries-old containment
one goal fed its dazed loyalty
to shed debris
on an unwilling shore
like a sponge
it sucked into its core

the aged and the young
school-children fell helter-skelter
into its body-might
as it rolled over
crushing the cream
and the scum of its make-up
into a solid compound
of black oozing energy

in a flash
of the eye
of gun-fire
like spray flayed
they fled they fell
the air fouled
the minute fucked
and life fobbed

our heads bowed
our shame aflame
our faith shaken
we buried them for what they were
our fallen heroes and our history

for orations we had the religious
for gun-carriers we had a string of hearses
for flags half-mast tear-soaked hankies

we craned necks to raise voices higher still
for them that lay row upon row crammed
a regiment under the blazing bloodied sun
they had lain deserted around and upon their original
                                                    graves
left alone to bleed and plead for forgiveness
like the mangled bodies of their warrior forbears

the dust grit we ground as we gnashed teeth
the mournful wail of salt-stained faces
the groan and grouse of aggrieved relations
shall be our pledge to the dead

a monument in our hearts we shall mount
their unheard-of names to engrave
on time's sturdy wings their ideals we shall pin
Africa's priceless heritage to mankind.

Sipho Sepamla   *New Classic* 1976

Chapter 3:
'In Exile'

LONELY ROAD

Lonely road,
Not a star;
Lonely road,
Shadows far
And quiet,
Still as a dying heart.
Softly falling,
Sadly dropping
Lonely road and you.
Shadows,
Strange dim shadows,
Creeping shadows,
Beat on the prison'd soul.
Sadness—sadness,
Bitter sadness,
That's the road I go.

Peter Abrahams   1961

LONELY

It gets awful lonely,
lonely;
like screaming lonely;

screaming down dream alley,
screaming blues, like none can hear;
but you hear clear and loud:
echoing loud;
like it's for you.
I talk to myself when I write,
shout, scream to myself;
then back to myself
scream and shout,
shouting a prayer,
screaming noises,
knowing this way I tell
the world about what still lives;
even maybe
just to scream and shout.
is it I lack the musician's contact
direct?
the smell of human bodies?
or, is it true, the writer
creates
(except the trinity with God
the machine and He)
incestuous silhouettes
to each other scream and shout,
to me shout and scream
pray and mate;
inbred deformities of loneliness?

Bloke Modisane   1961

IN AIR

Five gleaming crows
Are
Big, black forms

Five black crows
Are
Creatures floating

Five black creatures
Floating
On wide-stretched air

Five gleaming forms
Are
Blackly floating

Five gleaming crows
Float blackly
On wide-stretched air.

Peter Clarke   1961

IN EXILE

Open skies flare wide enough
to make me vaguely anxious.
Nimbus wisps
trace patterns of the past.

Wind sweeps between the towers
through tunnels, old and new.
My heart is

hollowed with the boots passing through.

Garments gather and play about
my limbs: they tremble to a return
gust. Leaves and transient
streetscape conjure up that southern

blue sky and wind-beautiful
day, creating paradise.
Otherwise:
the soul decays in exile.

But wrong pigment has no scope,
so clot the blue channel of memory.
On a sand slope
I build a picture of the sea.

The grains that slide away
are wind-breathed, are stirred by finger.
Benign, a cloud
obscures the sun, this hunger.

Arthur Nortje   *New Coin* 1966

FOR MELBA

Morning smiles
In your eye
Like a coy moment
Captured by an eternal
Noon and from yesterdays
I emerge naked
Like a Kimberley diamond
Full like Limpopo after rain

Singing your unnumbered charms.

K William Kgositsile   1967

TO BE PROUD

In the twirling mountains overhung with mist
Foretell Nodongo the proud name of the subsequent
                                              hours
Since, when you beat the loud music of your wings,
The secret night creeps underneath the measured time.

When you behold the fixed bulk of the sun
Jubilant in its uncertain festivals
Know that the symbol on which you stand shall
                                              vanish
Now that the dawning awaits us with her illusions.

Assemble the little hum of your pealing boast
For the sake of the reward meted to Somndeni
Who sat abundantly pride-flowing
Till the passer-by vultures of heaven overtook him.

We who stood by you poverty-stricken
Shall abandon you to the insanity of licence
And follow the winding path
Where the wisdom granaries hold increase.

Then shall your nakedness show
Teasing you before the unashamed sun.
Itching you shall unfurl the night
But we the sons of Time shall be our parents' race.

Mazisi Kunene   *Presence Africaine*

THE ECHOES

Over the vast summer hills
I shall commission the maternal sun
To fetch you with her long tilted rays,

The slow heave of the valleys
Will once again roll the hymns of accompaniment
Scattering the glitter of the milky way over the bare fields.

You will meet me
Underneath the shadow of the timeless earth
Where I lie weaving the seasons.

You will indulge in the sway dances of your kin
To the time of symphonic flutes
Ravishing the identity of water lilies.

I have opened the mountain gates
So that the imposing rim
Of the Ruwenzori shall steal your image.

Even the bubbling lips of continents
(To the shy palms of Libya)
Shall awake the long-forgotten age.

The quivering waters of the Zambezi river
Will bear on a silvery blanket your name
Leading it to the echoing of the sea.

Let me not love you alone
Lest the essence of your being
Lies heavy on my tongue
When you count so many to praise.

Mazisi Kunene   *Presence Africaine*

FAREWELL

O beloved farewell . . .
Hold these leaping dreams of fire
With the skeletal hands of death
So that when hungry night encroaches
You defy her stubborn intrigues.

Do not look to where we turn and seethe
We pale humanity, like worms
(The ululations might bind you to our grief)
Whose feet carry the duty of life.

Farewell beloved
Even the hush that haunts the afternoon
Will sing the ding-dong drum of your ultimate joy
Where we sit by the fireside tossing the memories
Making the parts fit into each day complete;
Yet knowing ours is a return of emptiness
Farewell, yewu . . . ye.

Mazisi Kunene   *Presence Africaine*

AS LONG AS I LIVE

When I still can remember
When I still have eyes to see
When I still have hands to hold
When I still have feet to drag
So long shall I bear your name with all the days
So long shall I stare at you with all the stars of heaven
Though you lead me to their sadistic beast
I shall find a way to give my burden-love
Blaming your careless truths on yesterdays.

Because I swear by life herself
When you still live, so shall I live
Turning the night into day, forcing her
To make you lie pompous on its pathways.
So shall I wander around the rim of the sun
Till her being attains your fullness
As long as I live . . .

Mazisi Kunene   *Presence Africaine*

Light, green-yellow luminescent, tender
seeps through these deep-foliaged weeping willows
to filter streams and runnels of soft glow
suffusing enclaves of green and sombre gloom,

and all my frantic and frustrated sorrow
dribbles from me in a pith-central tenderness
extracted by awareness of the charm
that graces this distraught and mourning land.

Oh lacerating land that pulps out anger's
rancid ooze from my resisting heart
now, with this loveliness, you distil in me
a balm that eases and erases all my hurt.

John Bruin   1970

I might be a better lover I believe
my own, if you could truly be my own:
trafficked and raddled as you are by gross
undiscerning, occupying feet,
how can I, the dispossessed, achieve
the absolute possession that we seek?

How can we speak of infidelity
when, forced apart, we guess each other's woe?
My land, my love, be generous to forgive
my nomad rovings down the vagrant streets:
return to me, sometime be wholly my own
so you secure me entire, entirely your own.

John Bruin   1970

DEAD FREEDOM-FIGHTER

Dear brother,
My blood is jarred with grains:
The gritty grains of chilling guilt.
For where was I?
Oh, where was I?
When those slinking cowards
Fell upon you
In a mass?
The only thing I have wherewith
To staunch
Your fresh bleeding wounds
Is the tattered cloth
Of my torn conscience
And the searing breath
Of my futile chagrin,
Futile, did I say?
Not the least, comrade brother,
Oh, no, not the least.
You fought
For mother Africa
And your atrocious death
Is the keen lash wherewith
She'll whip her enemies

To cowering shame
And her sons to redeem her name.

Mongameli Mabona   *Presence Africaine* 1970

POEM: SOUTH AFRICAN

        And at last then the nostalgia
palliates itself
so I can rise
            midmorningmute
and sing through its shroud
having looked
        on shattered faces dark with terror
                    drugged with clouded sunshine
come from
        scarred landscapes
        earth
        raped
                Goldrich once the world was
                far away
                        for me in my home rain
                which grew rainbows
Now love is long
            distanced in
    a telephone call
and passengers
            crowd the ports
bound out
            by sea and air
and land
the wind guillotines
                    your correspondences
But these broken sentences

stumble to heaven on the hill despite
the man with the whip who beats my
emaciated words back

They die but
        at last
get us all together as a vision
    incontrovertible, take me as evidence.

Arthur Nortje   *New Coin* April 1970

MY COUNTRY IS NOT

My country is not manicured
at the hot core:
My craft of polemic prevents that snow job,
sometimes necessarily through ambiguity
even should I say c'est la vie
purely to rob
some fervent foreigner of her virginity.

Do not therefore
with your suburban life,
smug like your southern cousins who cannot afford
to vote otherwise,
beef up on newspaper clippings
and buy me a brandy with obvious interest
because we seem to be slipping
in our endeavour to best
the boers.

I speak of my country in allusions:
the golden goose transmogrified
becomes the stormy petrel,

because, as sharpeville afternoons puissantly witness,
not at all am I tickled by a click song
from the knife-sharp jazzed-up townships
or a heart that unfortunately ticks wrong.

It is not folksy Miriam abroad
or Christiaan Barnard . . .
(the flesh lord)
that fluted our music through the wind, transplants
the lives seen in parentheses.

Arthur Nortje   *New Coin* September 1970

MY PEOPLE NO LONGER SING

Remember
  When my echo upsets
  The plastic windows of your mind
  And darkness invades its artificial light
  The pieces of your regrets hard to find
Remember
  I shall only be a sighing memory then
  Until you look in the fiery womb of sunrise
  Retrieving songs almost aborted
  On once battered black lips
Remember
  When you get sickandtired
  Of being sick and tired
  To remind the living
  That the dead cannot remember.

K William Kgositsile *Seven South African Poets* 1971

PROMISE

Clock and season march, each day more mellow,
since time must nourish youth beyond the blossoms:
the new furred power glints in early patterns,
brought with true focus to your beauty now.

Words drift in multitudes from your replies,
who've chosen foreign life: I ponder snatches.
We crossed like shadows, young and watchful insects.
My time has turned to life beyond this room.

All loves have love-songs, once a girl well thought of
set spinning a lugubrious Italian.
You, mermaid with your criss-cross rain of pale
hair, never had favourites, just friends.

That sweet detachment lingers rich in influence.
O day beyond the curtain swarms with rhythms.
My song to you is imminent: sky and glittering
sea and the grass of quick surprise, our world.

The luminous air presents its gifts of fragrance,
myself with its first taste in flowering spring.
The wind strays off the water with desire
among these leafing boughs to fork me open.

As I grow outward, what has held me shut,
unconscious of your vigil, you my swan?
I am as strong and fluid as a river
to give your empty spring its first fulfilment.

Arthur Nortje   *Seven South African Poets* 1971

LETTER TO MAMMA

Do not ask me
why we are here, mamma.
That is an irrelevancy.
We cannot tell
the difference
between the North,
the South.
Neither could grand-pa back home
A hundred years ago
when he was a child.
If it moves
we shoot
straight between the
slanty eyes.
That it is the enemy
of the ideal we are defending.
Do not ask me why.

Fred. You know Fred, mom.
Remember Fred. He is dead.
And Bill was killed on the hill.
Some others you know mom
are gone.
But we go on, and on, and on.
We are defending an ideal.
We know it does not sound real,
but here we see clear
the yellow peril in the green jungle
and the red peril in the green jungle,
the flies besides, and the mosquitoes,
the swamps, and the riverboats.
Then there are the bombs, booby traps, bazookas
and a sniper's bullet to stop you dead

in your tracks, mom. Remember Fred.
But we still stick fast, mamma
because we are defending
the Great Ideal.
But it is so far away from home, mamma,
so far from ideal.

I Choonara   *Seven South African Poets* 1971

SONG (FOR BEING)

For being forbearing
My darling and wearing
The mood of the morning
I love you I love you

For singing past sighing
And flying past winging

And caring past crying
For daring and dying

And seeing and hearing
For being, for bearing

I love you I love you

Cosmo Pieterse   From *Echo and Choruses* 1974

TWO SCENES: BOLAND AND CAPE TOWN
*Reconnaissance-Lear in the Windermere Slums
(Cape Town) and Sakkiesdorp (Worcester, Cape)*

I saw the first drops call, but pause
Before the hovels where their doors
Should be, and then, aslant, silently, sly.
They entered . . . ! Why?

I only knew after the storm had stilled
Its passion, wooed a child,
And left it, cold . . .
Those spies reported on the walls we build.

Cosmo Pieterse   From *Echo and Choruses* 1974

DISTRICT SIX (CAPE TOWN)

Nowadays its harbours converge their various oceans
The currents of warmth and western Benguella.
Some seamen are weary. The storm winds sigh.
The hips of the women are wide with labour.

As I enter this old city
The mild films of grey sleep as they ache to dawn and
                                                    spring,
And spring over some cobbles, macadam . . .
And even earth, with labouring breath, I greet
Its pain, my heart open and breaking
For the death that germinates in these streets,
And the buried birth waking:
Good land and morning —
Good morning, Cape Town, mother of pity,

Day, old lady of grace and rags and bones, I wish
　　　　　　　　　　　your morrow good, madam.

Cosmo   Pieterse   1974

SONG (WE SING)

We sing our sons who have died red
Crossing the sky where barbed wire passes
Bullets of white paper, nails of grey lead
And we sing the moon in its dying phases.

We sing the moon, nine blue moons of being
We sing the moon of barren blood
Blood of our daughters, waters fleeing
From bodiless eyes, that have stared and dried.

The seed of the land we sing, the flowers
Of manhood, of labour, of spring;
We sing the death that we welcome as ours
And the birth from the dust that is green we sing.

Cosmo   Pieterse   From *Echo and Choruses* 1974

PART FOUR:

Portrait of One's Life:
June 16, 1976—1981

Let us create and talk about life
Let us not admire the beauty
But peruse the meaning
Let art be life
Let us not eye the form
But read the content
Let creativity be a portrait of one's life

Matsemela Manaka (untitled poem *Staffrider* 1979)

Chapter 1:
Rustle in The Tall Dry Grass

THE VILLAGE RIVER

You love us,
for we belong to you,
Your water is our blood.
It is medicine
for budding witchdoctors,
who get ordained in you.

Father told us about you,
'Do not cross the river at night'
Unless our faces are mud-painted,
to trot on stepping stones homewards.

For sacrifice, take grandfather's brown ox,
Swallow it alone,
In return oil my feet with your waters
O, king of the underground world.

My age set group schooled in you,
They hunt and love there,
with faces smeared white
for your guards to see.

A G Nguza   *New Coin* April 1977

BLACK ART

I see our work of art
For it belongs to my ancestors,
They tell me what to do,
I always hear their whispers.

The dark colour of wood we like,
Roots can be snakes or medicine,
I listen to my old fathers and create
Whatever life form they want.

You say this is not it, they sigh
For you are not one of us,
We carve our experiences
Into simple sacred symbols.

See them living in our strange works,
Strong forms and colours newly old,
They live deep under the kraal's crust,
We love our art for it is the only one.

A G Nguza   *New Coin* April 1977

ANOTHER BLACK BOY

At a stokvel carnival
    he became a parasitic dot
His biological father
    is an ideological target
now tethered at a mud 'n thatch.

His spinster-mother boarded
    the sardine-train

When the sky whispered dew.

I fancied he needed
steel from sleep
But his eyes were vertical —
    glimpsing the nascent sun.

When next-door kids of matai-tai
    face the face of future with ablaze eyes
He groans under a Lanko carton
walking: 5 plus 5 plus 5 plus 5 plus 5
to swarming Tembisa Station
and squats with Indian eyes
behind 2 apple-pyramids
and sings a ditty for dough;
Hai zikwa apol! Hai zokwa apol!

Nape 'a Motana

LIMEHILL

budding flowers
    of discarded fruits
in the land of opulence
    miserably trapped
amidst white dongas.

dirt track dust
    choking
scavenging dogs
    aimlessly loiter
among weary children
    making armoured cars
out of barbed wire

     and carving guns
out of rotting planks.

Essop Patel   *New Classic* 1977

A CRY FROM THE CELLS

in the eerie chambers
i hear a voice scream
tearing my stomach

     i fear
          and grip, and clutch
my head
     between my legs
     my heart with fear
          kicking between my ribs
and the banging
     noise
          cell-door
          in the iron cell
i hear a voice scream
i hear the voice scream

     Baas!

     my ego sent to the devil
          heat pounding into my chest

and my nerves
     pulled
          the tear dropped into myself
          was hitting hard at me
i heard the screaming voice

. . . IJOO! . . .
   defenceless
   unprotected
binding his hands together
his hands ended on the cold bars

   and his finger prints
   left marks of blood

lasting impressions in the prison cell
12 mid-nite
when creeks spring
in the sweating night

   'JONG, HET JY HOM GESIEN?
   HOM GAT IS STUKKEND GESKEER!' his

pulse weak
   he fell on his head
   and the cold sweat
      rolled
      into his itching hands
they tore him
he fell
   and his collapse
   drowned by the hard floor
that is how his soul
escaped his body, bundled into a clumsy S

   on our cells
   his spirit hangs
   and his bold eyes
      i still see them
      they stare

and are full of tears

Ujebe Glenn Masokoane   *New Classic* 1977

THE VOICELESS ONES

In silence they have laboured,
Even to the bowels of the earth,
Where the wealth of Africa lies.
Black craggy hands
Scooping out the glittering wealth,
To pour it into white satchels,
Whose mouths are snapped shut
By avaricious Midasses,
For a Black eye never to see.
Three hundred years of silent toil,
With not a scrap of reward,
Beyond sustentation to keep on toiling.
Slave-driven to mop up all the effluent
Flowing from sordid affluence;
Gorged full of Black sweat.
Ebony physiques toiling in silence
For a stomach full of lead for a wage.
The ire pressure builds up
Like super-heated steam
In a flimsy tin boiler,
Strained to its limit of endurance,
Without a warning or a safety valve —
Doomed only to explode.

Fanyana Mazibuko   *New Classic* 1977

A RIOT POLICEMAN

The sun has gone down
with the last doused flame
Tonight's last bullet
has singed the day's last victim
an hour ago
It is time to go home

The hippo crawls
in a desultory air of triumph
through, around fluttering
shirts and shoes full of death
Teargas is simmering
Tears have been dried by heat
or cooled by death
Buckshot fills the space
between the maimed and the mourners
It is time to go home

A blackman surrenders
a stolen bottle of brandy
scurries away with his life
in his hands
The policeman rests the oasis
on his lips
wipes his mouth on a camouflaged
cuff
It is time to go home

Tonight he'll shed his uniform
Put on his pyjamas
Play with his children
Make love to his wife
Tomorrow is pay day

But it is time to go home now
It is time to go home

Christopher van Wyk   *Donga 8* 1977

THESE BLACK HANDS

Down in the bowels
Of the earth;
I've extracted wealth
That gives you comfort.

I've toiled hard
Complaining very little
Drilled rock
Sinking shafts,
Picked and shovelled
I am now obsolete
And useless.

My white brother
Has denied me
The right to defend myself
Turned me into his serf
    'No kaffir trade union'.

The bosses have combined:
Formed a chamber,
Recruitment of 'native' labour
Fixing of wages
And regulating it.

I am now useless
And obsolete

Suffering from lung disease
Coughing blood
And short of breath.

Modikwe Dikobe

COUNTER 14

Around Albert Street
Are faces pale, haggard and desperate
Lips cracked with cavities
Scrambling over job-seeking

In a yard
Twenty feet high
Bounded from sightseeing
    many more
Seated, shifting, yawning

Not even a bazaar
Would have so many customers
Queueing
Their fate
On a white face

'Escort'
72 hours grace
Out of the urban area
To starve, rob, steal
In own homeland.

Modikwe Dikobe

TIME

Time is not always money
Time is administration,
Coming in time,
    queueing
  Offering bribes
  Reaching a counter
  Documents stamped
That is time
Not always money
But patience.

Modikwe Dikobe

ASSEBLIEF BAAS

'Môre kom.' You've said, baas
Before cockcrow
I must be up
Plaas kom

I know, baas
If I fail
Ten lashes on my back
Ten lashes and trek pas

Asseblief, baas
My child is sick
Sick from bewitching
Die Kaffer doctor say so
Bones never lies
Die wit doctor know nothing

By night
Hy slaap nie, baas
Hy sien die spook
Die wit nooi
In die groot bonnet.

Ek vra baas
A day off
To consult my spirits
A white goat slaughter

Dankie, baas
Die picannin is up
Blood picannin drink
Die Kaffer dokter right
Die wit doctor
Know nothing.

Modikwe Dikobe

DISPOSSESSED

1

You were born in affluence
Land as vast as sea
Pegging, pegging each seasonal year
A plot for ploughing
Hundreds of livestock you possessed
Your dwellings a fortress
Your wives as many as your fingers
Each night, a different woman —
Not a word of grouse.

Someone arrived

Helmeted he was
Striding on a white horse.
Attention he demanded,
   'Get me fire kindled
   Draw me water
   Get one of your sons to look after my horse.'
In the open he chose to sleep
A gun by his side.

He was awake earlier than you
Inspecting everything on sight
Casting his face afar
Noting, Noting, Noting
Giving a scornful smile
As he looked at you
Turning his face in satisfaction
Murmuring: 'Blooming Kaffir.'

A year following
He returned
Accompanied by a troop of police
On a white horse he strode in front
   'Get tents ready, boys,'
He commanded his men.
In an hour a town is pitched
A flag hoisted
A bugle sounded
   'Fall in.' He lined up his men
Each a duty: tonight.
Your unlettered brain pronounced
ZARP! 'Mai-is-is'
Stupid you were
Not to say Zuid-Afrikaanse Polisie.

You were discontinued from trying cases.

'Call a pitso,'
You were ordered.
Head tax. Hut tax. Dip tax.
All piled on you
Hard cash. With Queen Victoria's head
A golden sovereign
Minted somewhere you don't know
I know you're hard put to part with a beast
Each is worth more than a sovereign
They resemble your gods
Only at your funeral
Shall some be slaughtered
To bedding you in cattle pen
A stick in hand.
Squatting. Conscious of duties.
Hover about your kraal
Day and night.

2

You were ordered to call a pitso
To Mai-is-is camp
You were told men are wanted
To dig. Diamonds out of the earth.
You cannot pay your tax by selling cattle.
Golden sovereign. Queen Victoria's Head.
You marked X against your name
You raised two fingers 'Modimo nthuse — God help
                                                    me.'
You bid farewell to your wives
None cried. Because your custom allows
No crying.
Soldiers to battle.

A long column. Day and night
You walked; tired, fatigued, thirsty, parched throat.

Feet sore. Some could go no longer
Died. By the wayside buried
'Lebitla la monna le tseleng — Man's grave is by the
wayside.'
Every night your stick never forgotten
Placed westwards
Path to be followed

Village, village built as your home
Insight
Happy hearts
Hearing human beings like yourself
Speaking your own dialect
Homes like your woman
'Morena-lord!' 'This is unbelievable
Unbelievable to see women like our own
Where are your men?'
    'KIMILIE.'
'How far is that place?'
'Two days. Two nights from here.'
Very hospitable are these women
Food. Locust nourishment for supper.
    'Spirits of our fathers
    You've travelled along with us.
    No cannibal has eaten us
    Nor a lion.
    Stay away evilness.'

Thirty men are sprawled within the enclosure
Soundless sleep
Unfelt in three full moons
Their flesh numbed
Flabby as liver

No sorcerer will touch you

For you look like witches yourselves
You resemble badikana
You resemble initiation boys
Blanketless sleeping
You terrify cats and dogs
You look like the bewitched

3

You arrive when working conditions are improved
Time past men worked hard
Worked by shoulder
Carrying buckets.
Now it's headgear. Ropes.
Dragging from the bottom.
'Sebenza. Turn the headgear. Dig.
The boss has made me boss-boy
You sebenza.
Forget your wife. Make extra money.
You're sexual as your sister.'

You're here to save money
To pay poll-tax
Twelve months of contract
Save your money in a syrup tin
Lock your box
Don't visit the native location
Oorlams they are
Forgotten their culture
Their language
'Kaffir' they shall say of you
A real 'oorlams'! Bushmen, Rolong, Thlaping,
Hottcntots
A league of Bantu tribes.

You can visit on week-ends

By the roadside, near the diggings
Is a meeting:
'Native Land Act, Pass-laws, Poll-tax.'
You will be urged to join the Native Union
A national organisation
Undoing your way of thinking
Unknotting your tribal affiliation
But look. Don't fall into beer dens
Prostitution is legalized
Legalized by concession
'Don't cohabit in public.'

Spare enough of your sperm
Three wives are not easy to satisfy
Each a night
Two nights to recuperate
But don't harbour venereal disease
Scc a compound doctor
Don't waste your money on herbal medicines.

Your contract is over
Pack your box
A roll of material
For your wives
A guinea piece for each
A three-legged pot
To cook on the way
    Farewell!

4

In your absence:
The Government has impounded some of your cattle;
    Dip taxation
    Tick sickness
    Mouth and foot disease

    Tsetse fly
    And culling
You're now poor as myself.

Look around:
    New dwellings
    Your 'fortress' dispersed
    Your junior wife gone.

The shopkeeper wants to see you
    Mealie meal credit
    Clothing material.
    Taken by your junior wife.

Your son is gone
    To Johannesburg
    Your seniority is usurped.
Nothing is left. Take another contract.

Modikwe Dikobe

MANCHILD

I'll always remember the year
the child sent greetings to his father
    how do you do out there
he yelled
only it was a coined word he used
power power
it reverberated up and down
the fortified walls of Modderbee
echoed across the salty sea
bouncing off the sunscorched island

I'll always remember the year
the child took on his father's garb
    how's this on me out there
he yelled
not waiting for his gingerly nod
he hurried telephone calls and machine guns
breaking the silence of sealed shrunken lips
he lopped off as with a sharpened sickle
stubborn symbols and myths of old
in search of his father's dead image

I'll always remember that year
when the child became the man

Sipho Sepamla   *Donga 8* March 1978

FORGOTTEN PEOPLE

Broken
rusty
and hanging gates
fallen leaves on unswept yards
where mangy dogs stretch out their empty beings
and where fowls peck fruitlessly at unwashed dishes
I saw him the old man on an old bench seated
leaning his old back against the crumbling mud walls
thoughts far off man's reach and sight
and like the setting sun
he gave way to the dying embers of life
and slowly he slouched in to bed
with a dry and an empty stomach
to await another empty day or death

Nkathazo kaMnyayiza   *Staffrider* March 1978

FACE

Your wrinkled face
Is a map of your case —
Your struggle for a place
Denied you under the sun
At the grin of a gun.

The system's cobwebs
Pulled in your eyes
Played in your mind
To the last beat of your heart.

You're the last of the moderates
Who've been waiting for a messiah —
A message so accurate
In measures of today's bitterness.

Mandla Ndlazi   *Staffrider* March 1978

LIKE A WHEEL

This thing is like a wheel
It turns
Today it's me
Tomorrow it's you

Today I'm hungry
Tomorrow it's you

Today I'm hungry
Tomorrow it's you
Today I'm homeless
Tomorrow it's you

Today I'm in prison
Tomorrow it's you

This thing is like a wheel

Oupa Thando Mthimkulu   *Staffrider* March 1978

FOR FATIMA MEER
SO MUCH LOVE

    they have taken you away
    and left you untouched
    they have locked you up
    and set you free
    they have silenced your voice
    and proclaimed your message

i raked rock with my fingers
battered my head to bone
for a long time lay senseless
heart shocked to stone

then the words of the Quran
stirred within me
i breathed again
knowing you were safe

    'Had we caused this Quran to descend
    upon a mountain, verily (O Muhammad)
    you would have seen it humbled,
    torn apart by the fear of Allah.'

you too accepted the weight of the Quran
of undefiled, unconquerable truth

of many-faceted, all-encompassing, overwhelming
                                                    love
for the whole of mankind

You too assumed, undaunted, that awesome trust
fulfilled steadfastly that formidable task
of being the eyes of a nation
the heart, the blood, the pulse of your fellow man

those who are trying to subdue you
would achieve success a million times greater
if they concentrated all their effort
on moving mere mountains

Shabbir Banoobhai   *Staffrider* March 1978

BLACK TRIAL

*i have crossed rivers and trudged the barren plains
from the hangman's noose i have stumbled tripped
and fallen hard on my back hauled myself up and
tried once again to face the world i've never been
knocked out but my soul is still scarred from the
pains sustained and my fingers still bleed from the
cuts received while trying to get a good grip on my
evasive roots my roots and mine alone*

   i heard them sing
   i heard them sing
   oh yes i did

   on my homeward way
   africa bound
   towards sunrise

it was hard
the road was steep
it was heavy
but i heard the beat
and i heard them sing
i heard it blown
the golden horn
i heard the echo
stirring my soul
i heard them cry
tears wetting dry earth
from eyes that have seen
the bitterness of life
i heard those voices
yes i heard them sing
i felt the pain
when my eyes beheld
how man can turn
his fellow men
into beasts of burden
i saw them struggle
i saw them kicked
and saw them die
i heard voices mourn
i heard them sing
when we buried them
i saw them pray
and by god they did
and the tears kept on raining
as they kept on screaming
to man the inflictor to show them mercy
i hit my chest
and a cry escaped my lips
god let it come to an end
i heard them sing

as we filled their graves
with red dusty soil
i heard them sing
as we turned our backs
and walked away

in my lonely room
in the dead of night
the world in repose
i lay still without sleep
and heard those voices
from beyond the grave
i heard them cry
my eyes were wet
i heard them sing
my soul in anguish
i heard them sing
yes i did

Ingoapele Madingoane

SO WELL TOMORROW

SO long we've been
     friendly and patient
          looking to the day when
     the trumpet of the Lord
          shall sound
          'ABOUT TURN'
               and
     the first be the last
          the bottom, the top
               the lowly, the worldly.

WE, the silent majority,
    freedom disappears like a mirage
    as we come.
  Our song is now hummed
    for it's been sung too long.
    We fail to cry
      for tears we've lost,
        we are guests to death
        strangers to life.

TO where? we don't know
    for the honey bird is lost in the mist,
  the lanterns shine not, for Herod
    rules in fear, afraid of the child,
      we hope for hope while
      bathing in showers of sorrow,
        we run
          we cry
            we hope
      'SO WELL TOMORROW'

Bonisile Joshua Motaung   *Staffrider* May/June 1978

A SONG OF HOPE

Black brother
Your lips are parched
and your mouth gapes an anger
wider than a scavenged minehole

Black sister
Your skin bleeds a pus
from a long weary battle
for existence and we lick

your wounds with tears
as long as tongues

Black mother
Your nipples of nutrition
have clogged and droop
down towards kwashiorkor

Black people
Our hearts beat to a lonely
acappella
But one day it will throb
to the rhythm of a drum
And all of Africa will dance

Christopher van Wyk   *Staffrider* May/June 1978

WHEN I DIE
A poem Sobukwe might have written

When I die
may my funeral (like my life) be political
and serve the struggle
may my people
use my coffin as a platform
to raise the banner

When I die
may my body be used
to awaken the indifferent and complacent tribe
my eyes, to trace dreams and hopes
shattered by injustice
my ears be used as drums
to recall the cries

of the dispossessed and downtrodden
When I die
may fiery speeches and freedom songs
replace passive hymns
may the Green and Gold and Black
fly at every mountain

May my loved ones take up the torch
and destroy the lies
written into our history
so that a new Brotherhood may emerge
to embrace our land

When I die
may some poet
write of the agony
and deep pain
that followed my days
and the inhumanity
of my captivity.

Muhammad Omar Ruddin   *Staffrider*
                                     May/June 1978

THE NEW ANTHEM

In our thousands we sang
requiem to the dying system
as they have done to falling dynasties
all through the continent.

We were amazed for it was like a soldier
going down fighting
faced with a colossal dilemma:

to fall in the battlefield
or to die a cripple in parliament.
Nevertheless we marched in glory
Higher still we raised our banners
Spelling salvation in black and white.

The kids were flag carriers
For mascots we never loved those hippos
but only the sensitive Soweto dogs at night
history had been done justice
we had our certificates as momentos
of a companion we never really approved.

T Makhetha   *Staffrider* March 1978

A YOUNG MAN'S THOUGHTS BEFORE JUNE THE 16TH

Tomorrow I travel on a road
That winds to the top of the hill
I take with me only the sweat
Memories of my youth
My heart aches for my mother
For Friday nights with friends
Around a table with the broad belch of beer
I ask only for a sad song
Sung by a woman with downturned eyes
And hummed by an old man with
A broken brow
O sing my sad song sing for me
For the sunset is drenched with red.

Fhazel Johennesse   *Staffrider* July/August 1978

THERE IS . . .
After Victor Casaus

Undeniably there is.

There is a truth
with rings wider than a poet's eye

There is a battling nature
Now threatened by pollution
and sprawling cities

There is, continually
nature's freedom
despite the moon landings
despite the heart transplants

There is, with all the odds against
a will to watch a child grow
Even if it is in a littered street
Or in a shack where rain pours
as water through a sieve

There is a laughter
brimful with the turbulence of man

There is a hope
fanned by endless zeal
decisive against the spectre
    of Sharpeville
hardened by the tears of Soweto

There is a thunder path
that stretches into jungle heights
where wolves whine and howl

where camouflage is nature's flak guns
where the dream of Pierre Mulele
   has revived

There is cause to stand
and utter words hurtful
to those who skulk
in the wilderness of lies
and bias

For there to be
For there to be facts 'other than'
is our human asset.

Mafika Pascal Gwala   *Staffrider* July/August 1978

LET ME BE AN APPLE

Hanging like a ball of flame,
the beautiful red apple glows
   between the cool shade of the
      curly green leaves.
Nursed like a baby and duly wet,
   the apple grows from beauty to
      export maturity.
Freely she hangs until ripeness sheds her from her
                        mother's womb.
Neatly wrapped and packed,
   freely she leaves the sunny
      shores of Africa for Europe
         without the fears and frustrations
            of an exit permit.
In banquets and at royal tables she becomes the
apple of everybody's eye.

So rather let me be an apple than a slave on an apple
farm.

Leonard Koza   *Staffrider* November/December 1978

PRISON SEQUENCE

1

At the first offer of judas-pay
his loyalty leaked
like yolk from an egg
leaving a scummy white
and our awareness alerted
by the cockroaching
of his eyes
as they met ours
his whisperings became
available to our ears
as another name was
added to the list
his masters compiled
he eluded our grasp
as he cowered in
the protective glare
of prison guards
waiting out his time
for an early release
while we remain
behind iron bars

2

The voice of

my brothers sustained
me in the dark
of my days
as we shared
confinement in the
solitariness of cells
the songs sung
were freedom songs
from which were
forged mail-vests
covering us from
their base assault
our songs reached
other brothers confined
in other parts
of the keep
freedom songs
became
a raging storm
and our voices
waves rushing forth
to drown those
who dared confine
men whose freedom
cannot be denied

3

I delighted
in the fear
cringing in their eyes
as they placed me behind
that iron door in a cell
they conceived will turn into my grave
My silence

silenced the shrill
accusations of their voices
demanding my voice remain mute
to the demands of the rights
rightful for an oppressed man to make

The firming
of my heart
was nurtured by their
fears as their hands trembled
ringing iron shackles around my wrists
to drain the power in my arms

Is freedom
only theirs to
have, i softly asked?
is it not for every man
to share and spread the need
of brotherhood's common creed in our land?

My mocking
laughter was louder
than their footsteps as
they fled from my cell
to bury the truth in their
hearts which their faces could not hide

4

The day i was taken from my office was as
    inauspicious as any other day except being the end
    of the month a little hotter than usual

The morning newspapers read that three more people
    had been detained — two women and a man.

Perhaps women's lib has asserted itself in the struggle for liberation

News of the arrest didn't startle me. It has been happening with regular monotony. Our Oppressor-doctors trying to cure our political fever with doses of detention; failures consigned to the disposal ward

Francis, our office typist, fright-filled face, said that two men wanted to speak to me at the reception desk. Her face told me that it was my turn. My fever must've reached a critical stage

I would've known them even if they hadn't identified themselves. Their odour wrinkled my nostrils. The oppressed can distinguish his oppressor even if he sends his hounds and the hounds have the same colour as the oppressed

Their voices droned as i was informed that i had to come along. I was to be detained under Code 100 of the Eternal Safety Measure to safeguard the fatherland from communists and agitating thoughts

My period of detention started from then and was to end six months later. I was to be held because the oppressor-doctors had decided that my symptoms were alarming and i would infect others if i remained outside

Health lecture completed, i was escorted by the hounds. An almost new car was parked at the kerb. I sat in the back. They didn't bother to lock the doors. A writer seems to have status among the hounds

Booked, listed and particulars taken, i was deposited
in a cell twice the size of my township toilet. The
smell of prison cells has become familiar and i
concentrated on six months in solitary
confinement with an occasional visit from an
oppressor-doctor

James Matthews   *Staffrider*
                              November/December 1978

MORALITY ACTS

We don't need people bloated by power
    hypocritical concern for the wretched
    honour being bought for a price
    business as usual.
We don't need peanut revolutionaries
    fat cats discussing the 'situation'
    smelling of twenty cent cigars
    indignation in voices
    abstention in hearts.
We don't need people with penis fever
    eager to cast the first stone
    hiding behind their guilt
    smearing our women with words
    their seed an improvisation.
We don't need Jekyll and Hydes
    transformed by cheap wines
    haunted by dreamless sleep
    agonising to view
    their escape an excuse for their inadequacy.
We don't need people ashamed of their beauty

enriching cosmetic firms
where features are measured
like articles in a store.
We don't need loveless sex
meaningless relationships
rushing to spread your legs
'baby it's the in thing.'
We don't need ripoffs
where life is cheaper
than the clothes you wear.
We don't need pseudo intellectuals
blinded by arrogance
fooling no-one in their ignorance
We need . . .

Keith Adams   *Staffrider* November/December 1978

VOICES FROM THE THROAT OF A DEAD MAN
For W in Johannesburg

1

Let me blow the horn
Let me whisper in the air
Let me sing a song:
Where you are now
You may hear it and recall
The past days of our youth,
You and I at the desk.

Remember those Sundays when I went to church,
You remained at home;
I can almost see you sitting on that stoep,
Sometimes waiting for a girl
Who did not come;

You complained about it to me;
I just eyed you and smiled,
And by your sullen smile
I knew you did not like it.

Do you still remember my dream,
That dream about your late mother?
You insulted me for being so silly
When I told you
That I saw her:
I saw her eating grass like a cow,
She walked on her knees,
She looked at you and cried —
You, so haggard,
Lean like a reed
On the banks of a dry river.

She wanted you to sing a song,
But you could not produce a note:
You sat there,
Looked at her
Wanting to talk,
But could not utter a word.

2

In a vision one day
You saw in tattered clothes
Your grandmother ablaze;
She jumped into the lake
But the fire would not die.

The grass started to burn,
Trees fell,
Mountains moved,
Rivers ebbed,

There was a thunderstorm:
She shivered with cold
And stood just there
Speaking to her ancestors.

I saw them
Streaming out of the donga
With broken ribs and jaws;

Others ran for their dear lives
And stood on the hills
Witnessing the policeman
Misusing the butt of his gun;

A girl ran around
Her dress pulled up
To stop the oozing gash on her forehead,
Her white panties soiled and torn,
Tears and blood blinding her eyes.

Heads swung like pendulums
Between the gigantic fists
And batons firmly gripped
To ensure a gaping, bleeding gash.

Like a chick
Trampled on by bulls on the stampede
They kicked him;
Yes, they kicked him,
Pulled him up from a pool of blood
His jaw broken,
Bible still in hand!

3
How do people explain their experiences in hell?

I remember this in trauma:
There is fire burning all day,
Fire burning all night,
You hear people gnash their teeth
While on your back you sleep
Facing the concrete ceiling above,
Nobody to talk to
And nothing to read,

The only music that of keys
That jingle even at midnight,
While women of the land
Are herded out one by one
To be used
Like the mat you are resting on.

Oh! my kingdom
Come back, my kingdom;
The kingdom that exists
And yet does not seem to exist:
Those days in my mother's belly,
Knowing neither reality nor oblivion
I love those days.

Yes, I have heard people bellow
Instead of cry,
I have heard people bark
Instead of talk,
Ask me when we meet:
I will tell you why.

Nthambeleni Phalanndwa   *Staffrider*
                                November/December 1978

CUSTODIAN OF OUR SPIRIT

oh Baobab
you stand firm
in the soil
in which you always stood
you stand firm
in the soil
in which you will always stand

your wrinkled bark testifies
to a memory
rich in times and events
long forgotten by man

you are not the rolling tide
you are not the changing cloud
you are neither the weeping willow
nor the departing ibis
you are not fallible man

you have never been colonised
you have always belonged
to the soil in which you stand
though your branches
may be chopped and pruned
you remain yourself
for your roots are secure
in the soil
which gave you birth

though your trunk is wide
and exposed to much
you can shield many
though the air about you may change

you will live forever

'Oh Africa, seek your Spirit in me'

Farouk Stemmet   *Staffrider* June 1980

WHOOPING THE FACETS OF KNOWLEDGE

Who are you, solitary dumb voice
so interminably hoarse like the
grass wafting on pink-cheeked graves?
Who are you, my dear comrade?

Who are you, barefooted 'mtwana
denied the nipples of Africa's breast,
cradled in the sunshine
of an alien intellectualism?

Who are you, my ebony-eyed inamorata
shading your sweet-breath into the
scented airs of spurious civilisations?
Beautiful lass, give me primal sanities.

Who are you, divinest brother of all,
warbling echoes of the spirits,
blending yourself with the clouds
that perplex the want of my soul?

Who are you, sponging snail-politician
asking for what you own and
embargoing your brothers' songs
sung in the pain of wounded throats?

Who are you, mysterious brother

eating and drinking brotherhood with me,
a mouthspear that excretes information?
Are you so cunning a chameleon?

Who are you, universal-famous humanity
so like me, so like him, yet so snobbishly
so inventively cosmetic, so blue
in the colour of your veins, O humanity!

Jaki waSeroke *Staffrider*
November/December 1978

HOW WAS I BORN?
For Mma's last born, Mapule

Was I born
a dearest object
of binding affection?
Or for a story and song
in an ill-harmonized and unmelodious land?
Or as a brother of Man
in the human family?
Or from my mother's womb
to a mute agony of despair
until I am entombed?
Maybe I was born
to live, and just be
me, myself.

Jaki waSeroke *Staffrider*
November/December 1978

THE IGNORAMUS

I live in the world of fantasy
My world consists of the little that I see around me
I accept everything without question
I am satisfied with everything for I know nothing
                                              better
I am ignorant.

I am happy I am living
I don't worry about anything for I know nothing
My major needs are food and sleep
I accept everything without reason
I take what I get for I know not what I ought to get.

I feel fortunate
Swimming in the abysmal sea of ignorance
I can read and write
Yet I am ignorant
I worry not about inflation and politics
My prime concern is where to get my next meal.

However ignorant I may be
I know *Mandela is on Robben Island*
But I know not why
I know there is *power in Soweto*
For all I know it has something to do with schools.

Oh! My people, help me before it is too late
Emancipate me from the chains of ignorance
Feed me with the knowledge of truth
If I know truth, truth will liberate me

And *Azania* shall be freed indeed!

Tshilidzi Shonisani Ramovha   *Staffrider*
                                    November/December 1978

EXHORTING MINORITY

Here's where we'll sustain repute
'neath the star-peppered african heaven
in chatsworth
lenasia
rylands
in times of fortune adverse
thrust into our faces
with impetus
abnormally precipitous
in times of gales flourishing
we'll cease to live each in our turn

we'll contend
over want of equity
with words spoken
africa's ears wax-haunted
that will still to sound
make impervious
our first love
genuineness
to her we'll let be seen
from our koran
bagavad gita illustrious
unshrinking
gloriously flaying brutality
here's where with offspring black
white

with minds of prejudice divested
ours will frisk
laboriously plod
like africa's most loyal sons of the soil
mindful
of saluting
sawubona now
goeie more
good morning then
'tis here neither coons nor boere
nor vets nor bruins
their recognition intuitive will apprehend
just africans
azanians
(by whatever other reputation renewed)
skylarks sky-born
singing daily
nkosi sikelela i-afrika

Africa will have been preserved
from damnation
in the white world
plunged
our kaftan
sari-clad damsels
deft
fluty
our loin-girded youth stirred up
from carelessness
she'll have been
to salute
salaam now

namasthe then

Shafa'ath Ahmed Khan   *Staffrider*
                                   November/December 1978

THE SILENT LISTENER

I hear voices
    Echoing throughout the dark forests of Africa
I hear voices
    Urging the plough-drawing oxen in the fields
I hear voices
    Chanting strange litanies and incantations at sunset
I still hear voices
    That were swallowed by the gurgling foreign seas
                              with *The Mendi*
I still hear voices
    That turned sighs in Rivonia
I still hear voices
    That sang from a dock in Pretoria
I still hear voices
    Screaming from dark dungeons on a cold island
I still hear voices
    That rose with black smoke in Soweto
I still hear voices
    Groaning blood-curdling death dirges beyond the
                              Northern Borders
I hear too many
                    voices . . . voices . . . voices . . .
In my foul and bitter life.

Chidi waPhaleng   *Staffrider*
                                   November/December 1978

THE EXILE

Father of my thoughts
sinew of my being
I relate to you as the moon to the sun

I've stood at the door
scanning the horizon for your return
unmindful of the load on my lone shoulders
I carry the scars of your wrenching
feeding hope with your homecoming

In those distant places
where my voice might not reach
know that I'm tanning a melody for you

They tell me
those lands have seasons too
but do the winters drag bodies through the snow
are summers meant for mourning
our past spring walked death a long way
leaving our spirits to droop long before the coming
                                                    autumn

I remember once
you spoke of a man's will-power
for me all that remains
some highfaluting balderdash
my life offers no alternatives
as I stand on shifting sands

but strength to your elbow
mother's child

Sipho Sepamla   *New Classic* 1978

CANDLE
For Caplan

Read brother read
    The wax is melting fast
    The shadows become obdurate
    and mock pantomimes of you
    laughing through crude cement
    in silent stage whispers.

Read brother read
    though the wax lies heaped
    in the saucer
    and the silhouettes of gloom
    grow longer.

Read brother read.
    Only the wick shines red now.
    But it is not yet dark.
    Remember brother,
    it is not yet dark.

Christopher van Wyk   *New Classic* 1978

WE KNOW LOVE

Oh people you shall not drown in your tears
But tears shall bathe your wounds.

Oh people, you shall not die from hunger
But hunger shall feed your souls.

Oh people, you are not weak in your suffering
But strong and brave with knowing.

Oh people, if you have known struggle
Only then are you capable of loving.

Oh people, be aware of the love you have

Let not your tears submerge it
Let not your hunger eat it
Let not your suffering destroy it —

Oh people, bitterness does not replace a grain of love:
Let us be awake in our love.

Noorie Cassim   *Staffrider* March 1979

DEATH WITHOUT COMPROMISE

He who has no heart knows no compromise,
He who knows change knows he cannot compromise
                                        change,
For the truth of change is the truth of growth,
And today Azania stands on the threshold of justice
                        and liberty.

Hearty men in harmony with justice
Experience the joyous pains of change,
But the heartless experience the sting of that pain.

Sweet are the fruits of pain,
And sour the fruits of pain:
For now Azania moves and the apples of life
Are at hand: Eat Brother! Eat Sister!
Be happy in suffering, for opium is sent packing,
And change is on the doormat of my father's house.

But for a heartless man life is vanity,
And vanity knows no compromise:
An enemy of mankind.
In vanity they move and monopolise,
And you and me are their objects.
But for reality we stand,
'For life is earnest' —
And for that we die, and must die.

How cruel death seems to be,
And how painless it is,
In it change is not compromised,
And great is the man who knows this fact,
And experiences this fact.

But woe to men of vanity
In the alleys of arrogance and ignorance they move,
In luxury they dance! dance! dance!
They don't know this fact: *a great man has died.*

Like the sun, Azania rose on that day, for a
Flower of progress died, and scattered
Its celestial seeds:
On fertile soil did they fall,
And the sun of Azania became hot
As it rose,
And it rained as the sun set.

Thamsanqa Zondo   *Staffrider* March 1979

DON'T DELAY

I am off to exile
Off to the land

that carnates
All afrika's flowers:

When i land there
Will i think of home,
When i reach there
Will i think of riches
Which i left behind?

I may:
And then I won't delay.

Matsemela Manaka   *Staffrider* March 1979

AFRIKA
My peace with life

Afrika
You are the horizon
To which I turn
To see the sun rise
To wean the poet
Who praises you daily
For baring your breasts
To these my seasoned lips
Do not desert me
For I love you
I want to cherish you
Take me into your heart
For you are the path
Whereupon treads my pride
Do not beguile me
For you are the sky
That measures my manhood

And spares me stars
To kindle my soul
Let me drink of you
For you are the river
That flows with vigour
Carrying the taunting tale
Our forefathers died to tell . . .
Afrika
You are my peace with life . . .

Eugene Skeef   *Staffrider* March 1979

AS A CHILD

I saw as a child
  A large and beautiful space
  With children and playing facilities
And I never knew why
  I was prohibited from the park.

I saw as a child
  A large double-storeyed building
  With children and compulsory education
And I never knew why
  I was prohibited from the school.

I saw as a child
  A large building with a cross
  With a minister and congregation
And I never knew why
  I was prohibited from the church.

I saw as a child
  A large advertisement-placarded building

With refreshments and meals
And I never knew why
I was prohibited from the restaurant.

Shadrack Phaleng   *Staffrider* March 1979

MY SANCTUARY
In memory of my comrades still buried alive

Where does time go?
Can't she be put back?
Like a spirit she's consumed
She vanishes with the speed
Of a closing eyelid
Where does time go?

In the small hours of the morning
I'll steal to the high window
To marvel at the beauty of the night
Bloubergstrand* my eyes discern in you
A beauty unblemished.

Like a monkey I'll sit on the railing
Feeling my inner eye ailing
Enjoying a beauty unsurpassed
Away from the misery of the grey walls
My eyes will cascade above the roof tops
Like a dry leaf on ripples of grey water.

There she lies
Her lights all golden
Like eyes of a billion giants
Holding council before an onslaught
What colours! What a panorama!

A spectrum, no, a signet of the gods.

Silence, and Atlantic waves
My soul swims in the cool waves of the night —
Below the murderous current of the grey walls
Why! I am floating backward and forward!
The current is gaining momentum!
An entanglement with an octopus.

Farewell! Bloubergstrand
Your snow-capped mountains are engraved
In my memory
You're the eye-witness
Of all my misery and woe
We share a sacred secret.

*Opposite Robben Island

Molahlehi waMmutle   *Staffrider* July/August 1979

DEMENTED

Do not let me see light
For I fear my sight
Do not let me see the light
For it shows me
What I lack
I fear the unknown
I desire the unknown
And yet I tremble
To think of freedom —
My desire
Do not give me light
For I do not know

How to hold light
But for once I will be bold
And blacken my sight

No more the blizzards
that blow across the face,
None of the heat
Raining from the sky
No giggle
Of laughter from the
Lips of taunting girls
Shuttered within walls
Waiting for the trudge of the boot
Bringing the truncheon
And insipid food
As a palliative
And the bludgeon at times . . .
And I shutter my consciousness
To keep out the knowledge
That my life is drawing to a close
Under the watchful eye
Of my tormentors,
I only know vaguely
The conspiracy with fate
That I will die
Sooner or later
Yet hoping faintly
That it will not come
I keep my soul shuttered
And through its windows
I see dull rain
Draining from her eyes
And I tell myself
I shall die
Before boys grow into men

For just then,
I feel the finger
Placed against my neck,
Draining away my life
And so I have lifted
My finger,
In anticipation of the moment,
And scratched with the nail,
Inside my heart
My final message,
To inscribe for the record
The agent of fate:
For like a sick dog
I have stolen myself away
To die in a secret place.

To be discovered,
When worms start to eat my body
For I like a mad dog
Have snapped and barked
At the wind
All my life,
For I like a chained dog,
Have been led from
My kennel
And left to die
To kill the menace inside me
For conduct contrary to nature.
Let my body be destroyed
And the evil inside me
Shall also die
And yet I shall wander about the face of
The earth
Like a ghost,
Haunting all the palaces

And shake their peace
Till we hear voices
Of women in the palaces
Shrieking and screeching in terror of my spirit,
Demented, shattered and destroyed,
The signal of my triumph.
I have then lifted my
Heart in my hand
And waved with it
Dripping with blood
Weeping for the land
And that you may learn.

Mafika P. Mbuli   *Staffrider* July/August 1979

AN EXILE'S LETTER HOME

I remember where I am
sitting
on cold cobblestone,
this is not home.

I cannot forget
where I am not,
for I remember
the place you built
for me
on the banks
of Swartkopsrivier,
whose breeze blows
stolen words to me.

Dear Sir,
have they forgotten me?

Have they built for me
no monuments
at Slagtersnek
or Hoenderkop
or Kaffirkraal?

Dear Sir,
I cannot forget
why I am here.

Achmat Dangor   *Staffrider* July/August 1979

THE JOURNEY OF A SLAVE

Toiling for a tot
I am hopelessly entwined
In the creeping vineyards.

But I have often dreamed
Of riding Ben Schoeman 3rd class
To the mother city
Whose fathers abandoned their curly-haired kids
To squat outside the periphery
Of the master's conscience.

But in the meantime
I can always ride Blue Train Express
To journeys that will always bring me back
To squeeze with chapped feet these succulent drops
To make the distinctive *Paarl Perlé*
So that I can drink the bitter sediment.

And when there's a little money sometimes
I can always drink *Ship*

And be lulled by the gentle waves
Be tossed by the violent storms
Only to be returned to the rocks of reality
To spend my days sweating
My nights in another toil.

But with the years
If there is no salvation
Like the lord Jesus Kristus promises
Every Sunday in the whitewashed church
And there's no journeying from this wasteland
And the wine is turned to water
In my seasoned gullet
I can always mix Rocket-Fuel
Astronaut to hell
And rest in peace.

Farouk Asvat   *Staffrider* July/August 1979

THE GARDEN BOY

He lives amid the floricultural attractions
Of the white suburbs.
He's unknown to his people and the state,
Known to his employer and to his duty.
He never schooled, but he can english.
He knows Verwoerd and has seen King George
And never forgets to say,
'How good they were'.

He is the only black rose among
The white daisies and lilies
The lawns he tends are greener
Than the grass he smokes.

'Keep off the grass,' he shouts
Whenever his brother comes for garbage.
He lives to see the happiness of others
Which is of his making:
The florist wears his dignity
And pockets his emoluments.

His possessiveness knows no law,
Colour or creed
They are all his,
My baas, my missis
My baas se vrou, my vrou se baas.
He sings the music of the birds,
Listens to the humming bees
And dances spade in hand as the flowers
Sway from side to side.

He prefers to be called
Jim, Dick, John or Petros
Rather than boy.
And whenever the missis shouts 'Boy! . . . '
He never responds,
But says, 'SHIT! . . . '
Without being heard.

Bonisile Joshua Motaung *Staffrider* July/August 1979

THE ABC JIG

   Anger comes in silence

Some of our brothers graduate
on Robben Island
in the Arts of Struggle;

Others graduate
on the plains of the African Savannah;
Others still,
in the malaria-infested bushes
of the Boerewors Curtain.

   Yet anger grows in silence

When they took us in
Steve Biko had resurrected
Onkgopotse, Mdluli, Mapetla;
I had seen them
give breath into the clay
of our liberated black manchild

   Black is alive & keeping

The S.B.'s swarmed over us
leaving their stings of State fear
in our Black-Star shoulders;
You'd swear
it was the Gestapo squads
on Jew hunts.

   The hunter shall be the hunted

They tortured our black souls
little knowing:
By detention
   they had sent us on a Black Holiday;
By assaulting us
   they were teaching us hate;
By insulting us
   they had told us never
to turn the other cheek.

We have no more tears to shed.

   Ours is the long stride

Mafika Gwala   *Staffrider* July/August 1979

BEHOLD MY SON
Fragment of an epic poem

behold my son
behold
and hear man's anxious call
awakening the new reality
behold the ancestors' wish
that a day shall dawn
in the annals of creation
to be known as afrika day
and before you have counted on your fingers
the onrush of the coming years
man's anger will emerge
the volcano will come to life
with africa day
as its background
behold my son
behold the last eruptions
of emergent afrika
with anger as sharp as Shaka's spear
sharpened on the pavements
of freedom road
where some of your brethren died
behold, let your stride
be set on a sure footing

behold my son

Time is a device
made by man
with a sound like your heartbeat
copied from nature's
chronological set-up
to register his downfall
and the time of your reign
behold my son
take note of the seconds
that were once my parents
your gods
take note that from them
i the minute was born to give way to you
as the hour of today
behold my son
for this hour
that is you
with the impulse
of your heartbeat
will come to be reckoned
as afrika day

behold my son
behold
'cause freedom is a distance
like a bridge too far
high above the tombs
of your ancestors
monuments
clustered on afrika's peak
like the pain that burned her neck
depriving her of
the right to navigation
rivers filled with tears
tears flowing like

mandela's sweat
as he crushed the stone
to tame afrika's
stubbornness

behold my son
behold the road
from nature's mould of creation
en route to the shelter
of existence
a place known to man
as home
take note my son
for you are the look of my love
lest you forget
that the road of life is called experience
and relax not my son
after freedom comes
'cause freedom
is not free without you
freedom is the land that fills you
even after death
go explore my son
the avenues of reason
before you enter
the last shelter
and i'll be your witness
when the spirits of mangaliso
refuse you entry.

Ingoapele Madingoane   *Staffrider*
                          November/December 1979

HOW LONG!

Through the rain
the night descends,

the occult darkness
balms the eyes,

the land in all its blackness
sings freedom songs
around the brazier.

How long!
before we sharpen
the blades of the hurricane.

How long!
before the dawning
of the black-green-golden sunrise.

Essop Patel   *Staffrider* November/December 1979

DOGS CONTINUE TO BARK

they flock in
faces like walls
with peeling paint
faces looking like
haunted graves
at phiphiḍi-waterfalls

at ṱhoho-ya-nḍou hotel
boys and girls complain
about 'the look in your eyes'

while pigs and people drink together
some bubbling politics
an agent next to them
sipping beer and lighting a cigar
for his drinking comrade

waiting for the hotel to close
old-timers snore in cars outside
dreaming about a school-girl in botsotso
who never worries about a bed
coin and fuel papa had

but down in papa's village
dogs continue to bark
while a baby continues to cry
mama sobbing and weeping inside
for a habit is like a stubborn germ

Nthambeleni Phalanndwa   *Staffrider* February 1980

FOR MY BROTHERS
(MANDLA AND BHEKI) IN EXILE

You have seen part of the world
Met some very nice people
Experienced the hardships of fresh air
Longed for the warm home-fires
Around which we sat on winter nights
Listening to pa tell us stories
Or reading passages from the Bible.
Those were the days, my brother Mandla,
Some days they were, my brother Bheki.
Do you remember those days?
When we were young and happy together

Playing cops and robbers, hide and seek,
Pinching bottoms whilst in hiding —
Young and happy together?
One day it would rain
And before the night was out
We'd be carrying brooms, sacks and buckets,
Urging the water out of our house.
You do remember those days?

Maybe I do not know where you are.
You left in the stealth of the night
Maybe hiked miles in fear but determined
To finally reach new worlds unknown.
Some days I happen to clean house
Exploring every nook and cranny.
I find here and there memories of our youth
Written on scraps of black and white photos.
I shake my head in pain of loss,
Say to myself, 'Gone are those days.'

The old woman is still around, brothers,
Heavy creases run down her mahogany face;
They are dry rivulets opened by heavy rains of pain.
At night, alone in the vaults of darkness,
She prays. In her prayer she talks about you.
Mama cries at night — by day she laughs,
Tending sisters' small children.
I know she longs to catch but one glimpse
Of her flesh and blood. Of her own womb.
Sometimes she talks about it,
Swallowing lumps, hiding tears behind eyes.
Mama is strong. Very tough. She was carved in teak.
In the evenings when we're together, she sometimes
Sings the songs we used to sing together.
Then she goes to sleep. I wonder if she'll sleep.

On Xmas Day mama makes custard and jelly,
Reminds us of how we all looked forward to Xmas
Because that was about the only day
We ever tasted custard and jelly.
Big bowls of jelly would be made
Then taken to the kindly butcher
(Remember, we didn't have a fridge).
Some time before our big meal
She'd send one of us to collect the bowls.
I remember we would handle those bowls gingerly
As though our whole life depended on them.

I do not know, maybe, what you're doing out there.
I know you're alive, yet longing for the home country.
You loved this country deeply,
So much that you could leave only to come back
When it has gained more sense.
Our neighbours (the ones you knew so well) are still
                                                    there.
We meet at the tap (it's still outside) and chat.
They ask about you. They care about you.
Those days you do remember.

In all our pain and agony we rejoice,
For the tensile steel strength of our souls
Transcends borders and boundaries.
However far apart our bodies may be
Our souls are locked together in a perpetual embrace.

Ben J Langa   *Staffrider* February 1980

INJUSTICE

Me, I cry easily if you're hurt

and I would've carried the crosses
of both the murderer
and the thief
if they'd've let me
and I'd've lived then.

I grasp helplessly at cigarettes
during riots
and burn my fingers hoping.

My nose has never sniffed teargas
but I weep all the same
and my heart hurts
aching from buckshot.

My dreams these days are policed
by a million eyes
that baton-charge my sleep
and frog-march me into a
shaken morning.

I can't get used to injustice.
I can't smile no matter what.

I'll never get used to nightmares
but often I dream of freedom.

Christopher van Wyk   *Staffrider* April 1980

TIME TO COME HOME

MAMA AFRIKA,
Mama, are you listening
to the sons of baNguni

weaving uqunge ancestral songs?
did you hear the veld grass labour
under the weight of dew drops
moonlit diamonds
scattered by shadows
moving in the womb of night?
Mama, did anyone tell your daughter
living in strange lands
of the bullet refrain
on the morning breath of goch street?
MAMA AFRIKA,
we hear choruses
we dig the refrain
chains clanking unjust justice justly
the vibe moves limb and mind
polyrhythmic war drum beat
MAMA AFRIKA,
do you hear the spears' conspiracy
with that cowhide drum speech?
MAMA,
Oh, MAMA!
tell Makeba and Masekela
Inkos'sikelele verse comes down
like summer rain Jol'inkomo,
'Tis time to come home.

Dikobe Martins   *Staffrider* June 1980

AFRIKA AT A PIECE
(On Heroes Day)

You can't think of a solution
Without your mind spelling revolution
Unless your mind is steamed with pollution

So much that you drop the notion

As our heroes die
As our heroes are born
Our history is being written
With the black moments given
Looking the storm in the eye
Our hope is not gone

Our blackman's history
is not written in classrooms
on wide smooth boards
Our history shall be written
at the factory gates
at the Unemployment offices
in the scorched queues of dying mouths

Our history shall be our joys
    our sorrows
    our moroseness
scrawled in dirty third class toilets
Our history will be graffiti
decorating our ghetto walls
where flowers find not peace enough to grow

Our history shall be written
on laps in the bush
Or whizz out of a smoking steel mouth

Our history is being written

Our history is being written
As the Bergies refuse to bend
    to white civilization
below Table Mountain

Our history is the freedom seed
being sown across the Karoos
With our Kaapenaar brothers
refusing to mix the milky way
But blocking blows
Right into 'die duiwel se skop'

Our present is the lavatory blues
we so love to sing
    in our matchbox houses

Our present is the Blue Light
flashing operations
high up at Groote Schuur
Our present is those heart operations
with guinea-pig donors from ghetto deaths
and from deaths called 'accidental'

Our present is naked ribbed stomachs
    and TB coughs
at Limehill, Dimbaza, Winterveldt
It is panga attacks and rape
at Tin Town, Malacca Road, Crossroads
It is ritual murder at Richmond Farm,
Rooigrond, Klipspruit

Our history glosses
the rail tracks
at Effingham and Langlaagte
Our history is black women marching
on Pretoria Building
    lifting fists
shouting:
    'Amandla!'

Our history is being written
with indelible blood stains
with sweeping black souls
in the streets at John Vorster
    where Timol dived thru the window
  at Auden House
    where Mdluli made a somersault stunt
  at Sanlam Building
    where Biko knocked himself against walls
  at the Kei Road copshop
    where Mapetla thought hanging was fun
  at Caledon Square
    where the Imam Haroon slipped on a bar of soap

We sing our present
We sing the dark-lit rooms
where the 'Free Mandela' chant is mounting truth
We sing the New Truth
The New Truth is!
Those 1976 bullets were not sacramental bread meant
for the faithful . . .
We've heard the Bullet Refrain vibrating walls at
                            Silverton

On the sidewalks of Goch Street
We shall sit down and sing
We shall sing songs Tiro would have loved to hear
Songs Ma Ngoyi would have sung
Songs Mthuli kaShezi would have composed
Songs
Songs that lead us on
And when it's Time To Rise
The Isle of Makana will be flooded
by the swelling tide of Kwancha

Batho ba Sechaba,
   hora e fitlhile!
The Hour has come!

Mafika Gwala   *Staffrider* September/October 1980

THE RUSTLE IN THAT TALL DRY GRASS

the rustle in that tall dry grass
the revolver
the cry of the bird
in the tall naked tree
struggling
and the groan from the people
to liberate . . .
the struggle, the rustle,
the sweating as years crowd into dust
the strangling
the killing
and death somersaulting like a vulture
on the people, the victims . . .
clouds and smoke gather in their sky revenge
the streets smeared with blood too young
unlike the streets of jerusalem golden
you walk not in haste in streets of gold city
soiled with corpses
you wish larvae were a commodity
to devour this murdering sight.

Lindiwe Mvemve   *Staffrider*
                      September/October 1980

GHETTO-BOY

1

i
am in the ghetto
tonight;
i
am the ghetto
this night.
the ghetto is me
me alone.
i
am the ghetto
me alone
in the ghetto.

2

when i sit
in meditation
in the night
to hear how the ghetto
snores,
i
hear the bark
the bullet
the cry
the scream
the movement in darkness
the devils in darkness
the looting of the tin-shop
the killing of mlungu ibrahim.
yes,
that
is me
that is you

the ghetto
the ghetto is you
we are the ghetto
we alone

                    3
in quietness,
i hear
the choir singing
you hear the bells ringing
the
drums beaten with fists sound
woman singing high
men leaping high like flames
girls
harmonizing the song.
then far away i
heard angels singing
with
their wings praising Him:
all of this
is us
the ghetto is us
we alone
tonight
in this ghetto.

                    4
when i lie
on my cold mat,
i lie in the
ghetto;
i dream of the
ghetto,
the squirrels

the lightning of storm
the moving shadows
the mourning songs:
when i wake up,
i find that
i
am the ghetto
the ghetto is you
the ghetto is us
us alone.

David Moja-Mphuso   *Wietie No. 1*, 1980

TRIP TO BOTSWANA

I had a taste
of freedom
the first cautious sip
causing
an unexperienced delight of
senses
my soul outpaced the girded
wings
transporting me from forced
confinement
my soul welcomed my
arrival
it stilled my trembling
flesh
as a woman and man embraced
though their colours were in contrast
no hostile hand ripped them
apart
love blossoming on their

faces
my eyes became an eager
spectator
to the manifestations of
freedom
where within my captivity i was
denied
filled with the fruit of
freedom
my return holds no
fear
of the horror of my slaughterhouse

James Matthews   *Staffrider*
                              December 1980/January 1981

EYES

I remember your eyes
when they spoke of me,
of my race, of my god,
of the way I danced.

They were not your eyes
but the eyes of years gone by,
shaped by sights of images
too big to see,
and left alone . . .
in the dark.

Those eyes, archaic,
of years gone by,
had to be plucked,
and in the unwanting sockets,

I put
mine in yours,
yours in mine.

I remember my eyes now,
when they spoke of you
of your race, of your god,
of the way you danced.

Kriben Pillay   *Staffrider*
                          December 1980/January 1981

PIETY

There was a time when
I did not drink wine,
for wine was the blood
of my brother

there was a time
I had forsaken flesh,
for flesh was the substance
of my soul,

now as I watch
the farmer plough and seed,
and reap with his hands
the young anaemic corn

I shall give up breathing,
for abstinence

is the sum of my virtue.

Achmat Dangor   *Staffrider*
                        December 1980/January 1981

THE SOLITAIRE

Captive cabined caged
He tenses against the encroaching walls
Built by the might of a state

His memory travels traversed territory
His tongue meditates
The implosion of thought
A contained atomic explosion
Rises spreads and excavates:
An eloquent stillness
Of blank whiteness on the pages of men.

His wife and children
Also under house arrest;
And through a window of despair
They watch the spring blossoms falling

Another hedged-in family
For yet another five years
In a peaceful state
Secured by soldiers in the street

Farouk Asvat   *USBC Newsletter* 1981

Chapter 2:
Songs in The Wind

TO THE FALLEN ...
A tribute to 'Drive Combo' duo at their tragic end

Like moaning calves
we hankered for horn milk
flowing from Henry's horn
very soothing and c-ear-essing

watery-eyed and mouth-agaped
we stood rooted
at
Upington . . Guguletu . . . Bhayi . . .
Kwa Mashu . . . Madadeni . . . Ratanda . . .
Jabulani . . . Rankuwa . . . Sibasa . . .
and Gaborone

As sharp as a snapping twig
lithe Luthuli's strings
twanged our souls apart

Thousand pairs of breasts
joyfully throbbed up . . . down and sideways
beards bobbed madly back and forth
teenies and oldies
bump-jacaranda-sikiza-ing
. . . all being 'Driven'

Henryless . . . Barneyless . . .
we will
still be driven

Vusi Mchunu

PUNCH-U-ATION

                    Why
                     ?
does africa resemble a continent of question marks?
                south america
               south of america
                 south africa
         are exclamation marks shouting!
       in agony inflicted by major nations
                   needling
                 for major power
                  the 3rd world
                  is overturning
                  emerging from
                   a comma,
            and will in a brief period;
   dot your dreary eyes and punch a full stop to all this
   anglo-owen-american double-carter-dealing internal —
        smith-settlement vostered-bantu pluralistic
                    bullshit.
                     period

Barolong Seboni   *Marang* 1978

FREEDOM

If the freedom I cry for
is beneath the big Marula tree
I'll use my hands to dig it free.

Makhulu waLedwaba   *Staffrider* April/May 1979

SONGS IN THE WIND

My Eye
   Ear
   Nose
And tongue control
Were on the horizon
Of Mount Kilimanjaro
I could now feel
Afrika
From above my sensual horizon
And my texture is in the
Sahara desert
The songs of
Namibian winds
Have the yellow mellow
Tone of Nubia
My car is an occan of sound
A translation box
To inform the continent
About this invading West wind
This trade wind
That made the slave songs
Of Congo and Benin
And to this very same day
We sweat through our eyes

We have seen the similarity
Of our sweat and tears
And the rain rhythms of
Equatorial Africa
That beat on our ear drums
To make us feel the latent
Power in Lake Victoria
And the Victoria Falls
Our victory is in our ears
Listen Listen
        Listen

Lefifi Tladi

TIME HAS RUN OUT

the bright eye of the night keeps whispering
when it paves and pages the clouds
it is knowledgeable about hideous nights
when it winks and keeps winking like that
it is like a breathing burning wood —
i feel looked at
walking and silent like this in the night
in this strange land which mutes screams.
the night
with its vague and bright eye-ball
which bears boot-prints and flags
eats away into the bone of the distance of my life
this i know,
and the night knows it too
so
the bright eye of the night keeps whispering and
                                        whispering
and the stars with their distance

keep whistling and whistling
throbbing on my memory about the distances we
                                                    made
yes —
We did make distances
whose milestones are, as we all know
broken droplets of blood which are now splashed
and are scattered on the streets
on fences
and on walls of houses we live in
and on ceilings
on floors and on desks
even on floors of land-rovers.
i said i feel looked at
walking this silent night like this
alone —
cars, with their treacherous big eyes
stare —
and speed past me, leaving their red glow with me
leaving me with the night
whose thick darkness touches my eye-balls
and keeps dancing into my face
with every footstep i make;
i walk the night of this land
i hear crickets chirp
and see prostitutes at street corners
feel shirt and underpants stick to my flesh
and i count the red lights along village road
smell the green of the tall grass
i'm all over this little town
and,
the stars keep whistling and whistling.
listen —
these fucking stars
whistled like this once long ago

when one man
walked like all of us do
and then he was naked
and then he was chained on the leg
and then he was on the floor covered with a blanket
in a landrover
destined to make 1 000 km in that state
to another cell
where he woke up one morning
naked
chained
alone
with brain damage, his blanket wet
his eyes strange as they said;
and i dare say
his damaged memory told him now, that he was going
         to die

in a cell
chained on the leg
wet and naked
alone
the 45th to have made it
into the hands of mad men who believe in God
yet these men did not know
that this man knew
he would make it for his funeral
that the people would claim his battered remains
that he would not be counted among the countless
who were stolen by these men
from their homes,
streets
fields
huts
and disappeared as if they were never born
except that they now float like a rotting corpse

                              would on water
on the memory of the people;
steve knew this
he had to, he was a bright boy
there was a funeral in kingwilliamstown
there have been many many funerals in my country
funerals
of bright babies
whose fresh and young blood was spilled in the
                                                    streets
by fire-power of God's children
there are commemorations all over the world
of my countrymen
some of whom fought and lost
some fell defenceless
we in my country fought and fell and keep fighting
ask blood river
and soweto will answer
that:
    school children took to the street one day. there
    will never be another soweto. nor, south africa.
    there are many kinds of deaths, and soweto knows
    them all, south africa too, and southern africa. you
    cannot kill children like cattle and then hope that
    guns are a monopoly. we were born like everybody
    else, and like everybody else, we know when it is
    too late or, to put it another way, when there is
    nothing any longer to lose. we made love in strange
    places: ghettoes. that is, we gave birth in these
    holes. we learnt from the pain and sorrow of
    having lost our children to so many and such cruel
    deaths as malnutrition or murder or sadness even
    dying while throwing spears or stones and being
    shot dead. we can now say, while we claim our
    land and die in the process: our history is a culture

   of resistance.
ask southern africa
mozambique
angola
zimbabwe
which we read while some men believe in god
and we know trouble
and say so, by scattering bloody milestones in places
where nobody would ever intend to die

since the types of deaths which are died in these
                                              places
ask us the price of liberation
and we ask ourselves nothing nice now
and south africa answers:
   europe took it from us. we fought and lost. the
   wheel kept spinning, slowly at first, whipping, as it
   spun us into position: landless. into mines.
   factories. tribes. race. ignorance. poverty. cogs of a
   machine, whose wheel spins and spins, ejects:
   insane, sick, ignorant, poor men and women,
   whose children were now caught, in a fast spinning
   wheel which whipped off more and more landless,
   uneducated, poor people. bloody. fast, insane. the
   wheel keeps spinning and spinning. it spins. had
   spun, and the union of south africa was born,
   whipping thousands and millions of landless,
   underpaid, ill-educated men and women, who
   build cities day and night and rest in ghettoes, if
   they ever do, poor, playing hide and seek with all
   types of deaths.
yes —
we did make distances
from blood river
to sharpeville to soweto

we know now
that oppression has been unmasked and will act true
                              to our expectations
we ask, why oppress us
to exploit us
why exploit us
and now we learn, and that is because we are born so
                              that we should live,
that the chain must be broken
whatever the fuck this chain was made for:
    days go by like everyday. we bury the dead who
    died cruel and strange deaths. yet, like we said,
    memory is like water which shores up rotten
    corpses.
yet,
that isn't enough
memories don't break chains
nor does dying like dogs or cattle
or throwing stones and bricks at mad armed men
nor do lies at the U.N., or anywhere else.
my people, tell me:
what does, what breaks the chains?

the bright eye of the night keeps whispering and
                              whispering
when it paves and pages the clouds
it is knowledgeable about hideous nights
when it winks and winks like that and the stars keep
                              whistling
it will see us one day
when children, mad at us, will spit and kick us in
                              public
they had their trouble; they ask us about the love we
                 made so that they could be born
for what?

soweto?
please, can someone, my countrymen, say a word of
                                        wisdom.

we need the truth not fiction
when we ask why;
we need to hear words
which, if the lips which make them, do tremble
they do so only because they know
they understand the perilous billows of our country
                        which we've learnt how to ride
not because they fear us our stare
or they are angry because we do not believe their
                                        report.

alas —
time has run out:
  too much blood has been spilled. please my
  countrymen, can someone say a word of wisdom.
  it is too late. blood, no matter how little of it,
  when it spills, spills on the brain — on the memory
  of a nation — it is as if the sea floods the earth. the
  lights go out. mad hounds howl in the dark; ah,
  now we've become familiar with horror. the heart
  of our country, when it makes its pulse, ticking
  time, wounds us. my countrymen, can someone,
  who understands that it is now too late, who
  knows that exploitation and oppression are brains
  which, being insane, only know how to make
  violence; can someone, teach us how to mount the
  wound, the fight.
time has run out —
period.

Mongane Serote   *Staffrider*
                        November/December 1979

THEY NO LONGER SPEAK TO US IN SONG
(in memoriam steve biko)

Excerpt from an unpublished work, 'Our flight in winter'.

i want to raise my voice in song
and sing a song
that won't be prey to the whims of the wind
but
a song that will remain carved and chiselled
on the lapidary spirit
that makes us what we are in this wilderness
for we all know that now is the time
now is the hour of the beasts
the green-eyed ghouls that gathered to gloat
the going away of the generous soul
of the beautiful brethren

i have heard many songs in my life
songs
that perished as soon as they knocked
from one deaf ear to the other
i have heard people sing to the glory
of a god who has one gigantic ear
that has never known how to hear
i have heard people sing about the children
who were mown down
like we mow down lawns and hedges
of the *baas* and his *missus* in the springtime
of our defeat
children who dropped down as though falling
from a great height
like all those multicoloured leaves that fall
down

at the ripe autumn that holds no promise
to the summer of our victory
we people who have never stopped preparing
for our flight in winter
in this hour of the beast
when the green-eyed ghouls gather to gloat
the going away of the generous soul
of the courageous sisteren

the children we sing about were shot down
in the midst of winter
and the leaden bullets that cut them down
were moulded and came from the cold hearts
of our cowardice

i have heard people sing about the children
who were mown down
i have heard songs that are sung in whispers
about those young maidens of africa still clad in school
uniforms who were forced at gunpoint to house the seed
of those men whose forebears are past-masters at taking
african virginity by force
those young girls our sisters our children our comrades
who died their bellies bloated with the filth
of the predators
and those who survived to tell the story
and give horrific accounts of this hideous tale
some birthing the lust of the savage in remote corners
of remote villages

some suffering untold agonies in spewing out
the continuation of the creed of men-beasts
i have heard songs that are sung in whispers
about those young captive men of africa
those young men our brothers our children our comrades

whose eyes
saw the sodomites ripping open canals of evacuation
and blood flowing trailing down the attenuated manhood
of the destroyers
yes —
they dug graves in avalon and doornkop to bury their
                                                compatriots
slain
in the most one-sided war mankind has ever witnessed
i have heard people sing about the children
who were mown down
and now we compose songs about those
who were transported thousands of miles
cold and naked and dead
in cold and naked and dead chains and leg-irons
which the captors exhibit in court with savage glee
yes, it is time now for them to gird their loins
those green-eyed ghouls who gathered to gloat
the going away of steve
i have heard my kinsfolk's voice stolen
by the thieving breeze
to reverberate against stolid hills
that have neither ear for music nor feeling for mourners
and were certainly born barren
and without the power
and without this redoubtable blessing
of giving birth and nurturing a new life
that will soon be food to the marauding wolves
for it must be said now so blessed are those in these hours
whose wombs never felt the kick of life
in these hours when everything
alive and small and black and beautiful
can be plucked like the yellow flowers they pluck
                                                every day
to decorate the offices that are in fact death cells

of the inquisitors of barberton
and leeuwkop and john vorster square

i have heard many songs in my life
men
divested of the last crutch and all qualities
that make people members of the human race
men robbed of their manhood: singing
their leathery faces raised to the broiling sun
men singing
to the accompaniment of the curse and the chain
and the gun and the whiplash
under the midday sun
singing
these men these outcasts singing in the mute cadence
of the damned
their voices trailing and spiralling upwards like smoke
and becoming one with the cloudless sky
these men singing
about how they are going to lay down their heavy loads
by and by

i have heard our women sing a lullaby
rocking
the nameless and pinkish and yelling bundle
in their arms
a bundle
that will in the course of time be transformed
into the greediest urchin
and lounge in darkened doorways with terrible and
                                                    lustful
eyes
and a rumbling belly whose only friend is emptiness
and a shrivelled body that knows the entrance
of a sharp blade

and the bone-rattling kick so well aimed
from
the heavy boot of the white policeman who will
                                        always remain
innocent and well-meaning until the end of time
yes —
i have heard the voices of our women singing on grave sites
without headstones
as they witness the final passage of a young one
who has been helped
into this earth that is only silent in its groaning
by our crime of silence

i have seen the faces of my people
my people
showing the curiously-shaped scars branded as though
with a hot iron
on their faces
is it any wonder then that our faces
are never described positively
in that queer lexicon of our captors?
these well-wishing masters who have literally stamped
on the dark brow such gaping wounds
that can never heal
the same men who say they cannot understand
what it is in fact that we want
what it is in fact that weighs heavily
like a millstone
round the neck of our hearts and our minds

i have watched us: you and me: like a man watching
a movie re-run of his twin brother's drowning
i have watched us singing
songs to the attainment of our freedom
our fist raised like one black monument

to whatever glories might have remained hidden
in the cryptic meaning of our past
all of us: the singers and the raisers of the fist
wondering
at the final meaning of these gestures and these
                                                chanted words
all of us
we children who emerged from the same fiery womb
thinking
thinking whether we understand the price we have to pay
to make concrete these sung words
all this singing is happening now at this hour
before the dawn of black liberation
when the sun is still in deep slumber
and the moon is awake and staring with one bright
                                                eye

now i want to sing a song
i want to raise my voice in song
and sing a song
that won't be prey to the whims of the wind
a song
that will still make me want to ask you
in this hour when our most beloved brothers
are lying naked on alabaster slabs
isn't it time now
to stop the green-eyed ghouls from gathering
and gloating over the going away
of brother steve?
isn't it time now
to gather and gloat over the death
of an obscenity?

i ask you africa
i ask you all my brothers and sisters
in the diaspora

my brothers and sisters
   in all these lands
my brothers and sisters of the dark race
give me an answer
a sign
for i also want to be free

Mandlenkosi Langa   *Staffrider*
                            November/December 1979

THE FACE

The face
Behind my face
Twists in agony at the thought of our people
Twisted by various forms of constriction
The mirror
Behind the mirror
Reflects me in my deeper crisis
Of being, unbeing, and becoming
Tasting the bitter pill
Of unhappy happiness
I tell myself stories
Of my ancestral heroes who
Fought undaunted until
I feel bitter
Till itchy fingers and feet sprint
In the arena of change
On the bleeding edge
Of experience
From these narrow confines
The voices I hear
Are whips on my back
Urging me to survive

To maintain my sanity

The face
Behind the face
The mirror
Behind the mirror
The voice
And the echo
Which is the voice repeating
The cry of my people's struggle . . .

Pitika Ntuli   *Index* January 1980

THE REVOLUTION OF THE AGED

my voice is the measure of my life
it cannot travel far now,
small mounds of earth already bead my open grave,
so come close
    lest you miss the dream.

grey hair has placed on my brow
the verdict of wisdom
and the skin-folds of age
bear tales wooled in the truth of proverbs:
if you cannot master the wind,
flow with it
letting know all the time that you are resisting.

that is how i have lived
quietly
swallowing both the fresh and foul
from the mouth of my masters;
yet i watched and listened.

i have listened too
to the condemnations of the young
who burned with scorn
    loaded with revolutionary maxims
        hot for quick results.

they did not know
that their anger
was born in the meekness
with which i whipped myself:
it is a blind progeny
that acts without indebtedness to the past.

listen now,
the dream:
i was playing music on my flute
when a man came and asked to see my flute
and i gave it to him,
but he took my flute and walked away.
i followed this man, asking for my flute;
he would not give it back to me.
how i planted vegetables in his garden!
    cooked his food!
how i cleaned his house!
how i washed his clothes
    and polished his shoes!
but he would not give me back my flute,
yet in my humiliation
i felt the growth of strength in me
for i had a goal
as firm as life is endless,
while he lived in the darkness of his wrong

now he has grown hollow from the grin of his cruelty
he hisses death through my flute

which has grown heavy, too heavy
for his withered hands,
and now i should smite him:
in my hand is the weapon of youth.

do not eat an unripe apple
its bitterness is a tingling knife.
suffer yourself to wait
and the ripeness will come
and the apple will fall down at your feet.

now is the time
    pluck the apple
and feed the future with its ripeness

Njabulo Simakahle Ndebele   *Staffrider*
                              December 1980/January 1981

MAYIBUYE iAFRICA*

like the memories
of fatherless black children
become fathers of desire
in fox-holes before
they are old enough to build
rattle by the riverbank
the dancing road
uncoils in the ear
pierced by the finger
of the slender smile
of tight roots . . . these
retrieved eyes across the tight

* Come back Africa

belly of a pregnant drum
these are the words
of an ancient dancer of steel
— the children of a person
share the head of a locust —
and who cannot say
life is an unfolding proverb
woven around
the desire of the memory
of the belly dance

I remember
the taste of desire
crushed like the dream
of ghetto orphans rendered
speechless by the smell
of obscene emasculation
but this morning
the sun wakes up

laughing with the sharp-edge
birth of retrieved root
nimble as dream
translated memory rides
past and future alike

Keorapetse Kgositsile   *Poets to the People* 1974

CHILD OF THE CRISIS
For Zeke and Dennis

Child of the crisis
Sons of sirens knuckles and boots
Tongues pronounce judgements yes

And so do guns and grenades
Armed peace is an act of love
We now know. We now know
— *Somewhere a mother will rejoice* —

These voices gather
Like rainclouds over the land
We must reclaim. Under any sky
They gather as they whisper in your eye
Or where the smile could have been
Somewhere a mother must rejoice

Wanderer with embers on your tongue
These voices gather to tame
Or fuel the furnace in your eye
On the long road that will nourish soul
And purpose with a simple
THIS LAND IS MINE
Because we now know
— *To know our sorrow*
Is to know our joy —

Keorapetse Kgositsile

THE POLITICAL PRISONER

I desired to talk
And talk with words as numerous as sands,
The other side of the wire,
The other side of the fortress of stone.

I found a widow travelling
Passing the prisoners with firewood.
It is this woman who forbade me to sleep

Who filled me with dreams.

The dream is always the same.
It turns on an anchor
Until it finds a place to rest:
It builds its cobwebs from the hours.

One day someone arrives and opens the gate.
The sun explodes its fire
Spreading its flames over the earth,
Touching the spring of mankind.

Behind us there are mountains
Where the widow is abandoned.
She remains there unable to give birth
Priding herself only in the shadows of yesterdays.

Mazisi Kunene   *Poets to the People* 1974

FIRST DAY AFTER THE WAR

We heard the songs of a wedding party.
We saw a soft light
Coiling round the young blades of grass
At first we hesitated, then we saw her footprints,
Her face emerged, then her eyes of freedom!
She woke us up with a smile saying,
'What day is this that comes suddenly?'·
We said, 'It is the first day after the war'.
Then without waiting we ran to the open space
Ululating to the mountains and the pathways
Calling people from all the circles of the earth.
We shook up the old man demanding a festival
We asked for all the first fruits of the season.

We held hands with a stranger
We shouted across the waterfalls
People came from all lands
It was the first day of peace.
We saw our Ancestors travelling tall on the horizon.

Mazisi Kunene   *Poets to the People* 1974

EMBRACING EXILE

Yes
We drift
Country to country: drift?
I move!

Yes I move on
Upon, depending on
Ideal tides
But even in the fashioning current

As it furnishes
I gather moisture
To carry me ashore

Sometimes too much
And then I weaken
From the weight
Also
Of blood and water-home, home screaming blood

Sometimes too little
As when it takes slow years
To rock
Again

Together in long warm embrasures of the sunlit,
                                    running sands

THERE
you can see
The piercing of wounds better
Than
You can pierce

A fish
High on its sunlit crest
Of awesome beauty.

Lindiwe Mabuza   *Poets to the People* 1974

SACRIFICE

We need money
to buy our birth
   so to say.

We need money
to buy our death.

We have no faith tall enough
to pluck the stars
   and buy our country
   with diamond.

But we have blood to lose
to retain all;
tenacious, they shall stick to us

in the wind.

Klaus Maphepha   *Poets to the People* 1974

THIS PATH

Child of the soil
Child of own destiny
cross this path
cross the sword
ride the lion's back and hold the mane
bound on with shoulders high
sky in heavens light the path
echoes from this thorny bush guide the way
Luthuli, Kotane, Mandela, Sisulu trod this path
Pull hard, hack the prickly shrubs
burden beads on your brow
pilgrim yoke on your back
will balm the people's tortured heart
and bid the sod to seed freedom.

Rebecca Matlou   *Poets to the People* 1974

AT THE DAWN I SAW AFRICA

*(When, in July 1879, the British defeated the
Zulus and captured King Cetshwayo,
Mkhabayi, a centenarian and the doyen of
Zulu royalty, publicly slit her own throat on
hearing news of the defeat)*

At the dawn I saw Africa,
And pride moved in its body

As I moved;
And the light which we breathed
Was strong.
Our King was our people,
And the king, Ngonyama,*
Moved without fear;
And the light in the sun
Shone on the birds, the trees,
And the voices of children.

Yesterday my people were fierce,
And smiled that all things moving,
In all the lands,
Beyond all seas,
Held no fear for us.

Today the king is dead.

Where is that dawn I woke to,
When the sun was round,
And breathed life from the earth?
We do not move.
Where are the voices of the birds and trees,
And the light shining on our children?
My child's voice is strong
But I do not hear.

Yesterday when we were proud,
And knew that we lived
In all the lands
And beyond all seas,
The earth lived in us.

*Lion, a royal title

Today the king is dead.

I, of the Nation,
Have no king.
Today I see
No light in the sun,
And today,
Before you, the Nation,
I am no longer living.
Before you the Nation
I say that I am dead,
And will live again only
When our Nation is free,
And the sun sings in the eyes of my child.

And as I rise,
My king shall rise,
And Africa will come back.

Today I have died.

John Matshikiza   *Poets to the People* 1974

REMEMBER ME

Remember me
When the azure sky
Sighs with grief
And the ash-pale lips
Tell of my existence
Remember me
When the green fields of home
Cover my deep wounds
That urge me on

Into the fire of life
Where the whining bullets
Draw me closer to the dawn of freedom.

Victor Motapanyane   *Poets to the People* 1974

I AM THE EXILE

(Works by Dennis Brutus are banned in South Africa.
This poem can be found in Poets to the People:
South African Freedom Poems, *Edited by Barry*
Feinberg, Heinemann, London, 1980.)

Dennis Brutus   *Poets to the People* 1974

Chapter 3:
Azanian Love Song

OUR POINTS OF VIEW

I goofed.
You can't do anything right.
She said nothing about that.

I am argumentative.
You are belligerent.
She enjoys a lively discussion.

I am a creature of many moods.
You are temperamental.
Mama, she is real cool.

I have a healthy sense of self-esteem.
Who do you think you are, anyway.
She is not conceited.

I am unavoidably detained.
You have no consideration for other people.
She is inexcusably late.

I am 'me'.
You are 'you'.
She is Azania.

Jaki waSeroke   *Staffrider* July/August 1978

THE SILENCE OF THE ROCKS

Oh my earth,
I have come to terms
with you.
I no longer sow
the seeds of my youth
in your womb

It is not
that my youth is gone
but your womb
is no longer a place
for youthful dreams
to grow

And all that falls
from the sky
onto your barrenness
are tears,
and whispers
of fear and pain

Once,
In the rain-filled mornings
of our love
we heard the seeds burst
and stir the roots of our lives

Now the hard and
poisonous bushes that grow
take nothing from
the light of day
except the deadly life
that it gives,

clutches to its bosom
the photosynthesis
of doom

The wind laments
that I no longer
sing with the
lyrical voice of the poet
that my tongue
has become as hard
and sharp
as the silence
of the rocks

Let the wind, then too,
go into the ghettoes
of my kind,
and listen to the silence
as hard and sharp
as the silence of the rocks

Achmat Dangor   *Wietie No 2* 1980

IN THE SHADOW OF SIGNAL HILL

in the howling wind
by the murky waters
of the sea
children of colour
gather shells
and hold them to their ears
and listen to the lamentations of slaves
in the dungeon of death

in the howling wind
by the murky waters
of the sea
sons of langa
gather at the ruins of district six
and sharpen the spears of the night
and the heroes from the island urge
go towards the fiery dawn . . .

Essop Patel   *Wietie No 1* 1980

AZANIAN LOVE SONG

Like a tall oak
    I lift my arms to catch the wind
    with bruised fingers,
    and somewhere in the ghetto
    a Child is born,
    a mother's anxiety and pain
    hide in a forest of hope.

Like a straight pine
    I point my fingers at God
    counting a million stars
    of my dreams
    and somewhere in the ghetto
    a Child is weeping
    a woman writes her legacy
    on leaves of despair.

Like a weeping willow
    I drop my soul into a pool of fire
    somewhere in a dark sanctuary
    I hear the sound of a Freedom Song:

The Child has risen
and walks defiantly
towards the lion's lair
undaunted, unafraid . . .

Muhammad Omar Ruddin   *Staffrider*
                        December 1980/January 1981

Chapter 4:
The Return of
The Amasi Bird

DO NOT ASK ME

Do not ask me, mother, if they're gone
I fear to tell you
they left in the middle of the night
turned their backs on the warmth of the hearth
and for the last time
heard the home rooster crowing

Do not ask me, mother, where they went
Tracks on watery dew-bells
as puny feet brushed the morning grass
have evaporated in the heat of the sun's kindness
and the hunting bloody-snouted hounds
have lost the trail

But to you I will whisper:
Look where the willows weep
The willows of the Mohokare River
have seen the forbidden sight
tiny feet in a mad choreographer's dance
from shore to shore
wading on the sandy bed
And the waters washed and leveled up the sands
Nor will the willows point their drooping limbs
to say where they've gone

Do not ask me, mother, why they left
Need I tell you
They took the amasi bird out of the forbidden pot
and bade it fill their clay-bowls to the very brim
they'd been so hungry
so long

Then an army with giant boots
came towering over them
Brand new guns
made to silence little children who cry
glinting in the African sun
The gun-toters threw the amasi bird
back into the pot
and wrote on it with the government's ink
        For white children only
and henceforth it was guarded night and day
by one hundred bayoneted soldiers

And the children raised their fists
and shouted:
Amasi! Amasi! We demand the amasi bird!
Amandla! Amandla! Ngawethu!

Now they've been gathered up
in the wings of the Giant Bird
to the place of circumcision
far, far away

And the village waits
for the day of their return
to conquer

Daniel P Kunene

Index

ABRAHAMS, Peter
  The Call of the Sea, 84
  The Negro Youth, 85
  Freedom, 94
  Heritage, 100
  Little Grease-Men, 102
  Freedom's Child, 110
  Self, 113
  To White Workers, 114
  Spring in a Coloured Woman,
    115
  Lonely Road, 272
ADAMS, Keith
  Morality Acts, 323
A.C.K.
  The Spirit Song of Mehloka-
    zulu, 38
'Alpha Beta'
  Bars, 50
Anon.
  Amagunyana's Soliloquy, 35
  Emakhaya, 46
  A Zulu Thought, 77
  On Some White 'Friends', 116
  Salang Ka Khotsa, 126
  Shantytown, 145
ASVAT, Farouk
  The Journey of a Slave, 346
  The Solitaire, 368

BANOOBHAI, Shabbir
  God, Please, 231
  The Border, 250

For Fatima Meer: So Much
  Love, 309
BRAND, Dollar
  Africa, Music and Show Busi-
    ness, 190
BRUIN, John
  Light, green-yellow, 279
  I Might be a Better Lover, 279
BRUTUS, Dennis
  I am the Exile, 397

CASSIM, Noorie
  We Know Love, 336
CHOONARA, I
  Letter to Mamma, 205
CITASHE, I.W.W.
  See Wauchope
CLARKE, Peter
  In Air, 274

DANGOR, Achmat
  An Exile's Letter Home, 345
  Piety, 367
  The Silence of the Rocks, 399
DHLOMO, Desmond
  How Soon They Pass, 161
  Rise Up, 162
DHLOMO, H.I.E.
  Sweet Mango Tree, 119
  Drum of Africa, 129
  Not For Me, 138
  The Harlot, 139
  'That Their Praise Might Be

Reported', 146
Drought, 152
Lindiwe Laughs, 159
O Mystic Love, 161
DHLOMO, R.R.R.
My Country, 57
The Wailings of Rolfes,
R.R. Dhlomo, 64
DIKOBE, Modikwe
A Worker's Lament, 181
These Black Hands, 297
Counter 14, 298
Time, 299
Asseblief Baas, 299
Dispossessed, 300
DOUTS, Christine
My Township, 245
DUBE, Mrs A.C.
Africa: My Native Land, 41
DUBE, John
Welcome to our Supreme
Chief, 39
DUES, Mike
My Fishing Village Is, 245

E.M.
See MPHAHLELE, E.
E.M.G.
Ohlange, 40

FABER, S.C.
The Scolly, 92
FANELE, E.
Spring, 92

GRENDON, Robert
Tshaka's Death, 19
'Ilanga', 26
A Glimpse of Umkomaas, 27
To You Abantu, 30
A Tribute to Miss Harriet
Colenso, 41

GWALA, Mafika Pascal
Just to Say . . . , 221
There is . . . , 317
The ABC Jig, 348
Afrika at a Piece, 358

H.D.T.
To Satan, 58
HEAD, Bessie
Things I Don't Like, 176

JALI, E.C.
Despair, 68
The Poet's Defiance, 71
J.M.
The Firm Hand: An Un-
finished Story, 66
JOHENNESSE, Fhazel
Extra, 258
The Bullfight, 261
A Young Man's Thoughts
Before June the 16th, 316
JOLOBE, J.J.R.
To the Fallen, 142
J.R.S.
Onward, Ever Onward!, 104

KGOSITSILE, William
Innuendo, 189
For Melba, 275
My People No Longer Sing,
283
Mayibuye iAfrika, 388
Child of the Crisis, 389
KHAN, Shafa'ath Ahmed
Exhorting Minority, 332
KHUNDOU, Theodore
Our Future, 88
KOLISANG, G.M.
A Game of Guessing, 165
KOZA, Leonard
The Street Lamp, 257

Let Me Be An Apple, 318
KUNENE, Daniel P.
   Do Not Ask Me, 403
KUNENE, Mazisi
   To Be Proud, 276
   The Echoes, 277
   Farewell, 278
   As Long As I Live, 278
   The Political Prisoner, 390
   First Day After the War, 391
KUNENE, Obed
   Apartheid Falling, 254
KUNJBEHARI, Kissoon
   Housewives, 228
   Vulgar Neighbours, 229
   Children Playing, 229
K.V.M.
   The Burly Sop, 159
KWANKWA, Mavis
   'May Be', 127

LANGA, Ben
   For My Brothers (Mandla and
      Bheki) in Exile, 354
LANGA, Mandlenkosi,
   They No Longer Speak To Us
      In Song, 379
L.D.R.
   The Struggle, 83
   The Defeat, 87
waLEDWABA, Makhulu
   Freedom, 371
LEKHELA, S.M.
   A Bantu Lament, 72
LETSEBE, J.W.L.
   Africa is Calling, 109
L.H.P.
   Remember, 79
L.R.
   'Civilised' Labour Policy, 70

MABONA, Mongameti

Dead Freedom Fighter, 280
MABUZA, Lindiwe
   Embracing Exile, 392
MABYANE, P.M.
   A Dying Man, 207
MACKAY, Ilva
   It's Not There!, 221
MADINGOANE, Ingoapele
   Black Trial, 310
   Behold My Son, 350
MAKHETHA, T.
   The New Anthem, 315
'MAKINDAN'
   Basuto Mother's Prayer, 76
MALULEKA, S.P.
   My Mother's Dream, 93
MALOY, Shep
   Farewell My Lady, 78
   Dawn on Africa, 99
MANAKA, Matsemela
   'Let us create and talk about
      life', 289
   Don't Delay, 338
MAPHEPHA, Klaus
   Sacrifice, 393
MAREE, P.J.
   Upon the Dealings of Man,
      103
MARTINS, Dikobe
   Time to Come Home, 357
MASOKOANE, Ujebe Glenn
   A Cry from the Cells, 293
MATHER, Farooqi
   My Country, 211
MATIBELA, A.F.
   Ohlange is our Shield, 55
MATLOU, Rebecca
   This Path, 394
MATSHIKIZA, John
   At the Dawn I Saw Africa
MATTHEWS, James
   Prison Sequence, 319

Trip to Botswana, 365
MAZIBUKO, Fanyana
    The Voiceless Ones, 295
MBULI, Mafika P.
    Demented, 342
MBUTI, Mafika
    Out, 205
MCHUNU, Vusi
    To the Fallen, 369
MEER, Unus
    Gazal II, 210
MESSAN, Joshua
    The Beggar and the Lady, 164
MFEKA, Zini,
    Hark! My Lonely Heart, 128
M.G.
    Black and White, 80
waMMUTLE, Molahlehi
    My Sanctuary, 341
kaMNYAYIZA, Nkathazo
    The Durban Indian Market
        Fire, 227
    Do They Deserve It?, 242
    A Day in our Life, 266
    Forgotten People, 307
MODISANE, Bloke
    Lonely, 273
MOGOBA, Stanley
    Cement, 220
MOJA-MPHUSO, David
    Ghetto-Boy, 363
MOLEFE, Z.B.
    Jerusha's Dance, 215
    To Paint a Black Woman, 247
MOOKI, Obed
    Dedication to the New Offices
        of the 'Bantu World', 96
    Mother Maxeke, B.Sc, 107
    The African National
        Congress, 141
MOSIA, Lebona
    Sister Sing the Blues, 256

MOTANA, Nape 'a
    My Organs, 253
    Another Black Boy, 291
MOTAUNG, Bonisile Joshua
    So Well Tomorrow, 312
    The Garden Boy, 347
MOTJUWADI, Stanley
    Taken for a Ride, 198
    White Lies, 199
MUTLOATSE, Mothobi,
    Sir, 223
    Wa'reng?, 224
    On Marriage, 225
    Mamellang, 225
MOTOPANYANE, Victor
    Remember Me, 396
MOTSISI, Casey
    The Efficacy of Prayer
MPHAHLELE, E.
    The God of Formal Ways, 156
    Exile in Nigeria, 167
MPHAHLELE, M.
    In Commemoration of the
        Pass System Martyrs, 47
MTHIMKULU, Oupa Thando
    Like A Wheel, 308
MTHOMBENI, Alexander
    A Mum Calls For Her Children,
        244
    The End of the Dragon, 244
    The Highway Road, 245
MTSHALI, Oswald Mbuyiseni
    Reapers in a Mieliefield, 202
    The Washerwoman's Prayer,
        203
    I Will Tell It to My Witch-
        doctor, 204
    Handcuffs, 222
    Carletonville, 235
    The Cross-Bearer, 238
    The Miner, 242
MVEMVE, Lindiwe

The Rustle in the Tall Dry
    Grass, 362
MZAMANE, Mbulelo
    South of the Border, 246

NDEBELE, Njabulo
    I Hid My Love in a Sewage,
        213
    More Impressive on the Mind,
        217
    The Revolution of the Aged,
        386
NDLAZI, Mandla
    Face, 308
N.G.M.
    An African Star —
        R.T. Caluza, 52
NGUZA, A
    The Village River, 290
    Black Art, 291
NHAU, Clifford
    The Widow, 215
NHLAPO, Walter
    The Revolution Song, 85
    Up! My Race, Up!, 86
    Black and White Before God,
        90
    They Are Gone — Gone For-
        ever More, 90
    Late Queen Lomawa, 95
    A Prayer for Africa, 98
    The Mendi, 101
    Mrs Charlotte M. Maxeke,
        B.Sc., 106
    Amanzimtoti Institute, Fare-
        well, 107
    First Romantic Night, 108
    War Dancer, 117
    Africa, 151
    Come, Freedom, Come!, 157
    How Long, O God, 157
    Tomorrow, 158

NKONDO, Zinjiva Winston
    Always My People, 263
    Africa, 264
NKOSI, Lewis
    To Herbert Dhlomo, 163
NOBLE, Claude
    Significant Change, 252
NORTJE, Arthur
    Nothing Unusual, 182
    Thumbing a Lift, 183
    Discovery, 187
    In Exile, 275
    Poem: South African, 281
    My Country is Not, 282
    Promise, 284
NTHODI, Motshile
    Ghost, 249
NTULI, Pitika
    The Face, 385

PATEL, Essop
    Baby Thembisa, 248
    Limehill, 292
    How Long!, 353
    In the Shadow of Signal Hill,
        400
PETJE, Rahab
    Africa's Song of Freedom, 118
PHALANNDWA, Nthambeleni
    Voices from the Throat of a
        Dead Man, 324
    Dogs Continue to Bark, 353
waPHALENG, Chidi
    The Silent Listener, 334
PHALENG, Shadrack
    As a Child, 340
PHETO, Finn
    It is Night, 184
PIETERSE, Cosmo
    Song (For Being), 286
    Two Scenes: Boland and Cape
        Town, 287

District Six (Cape Town), 287
Song (We Sing), 288
PILLAY, Kriben
Eyes, 366
PLAATJE, Sol. T.
Song, 45
Mzilikazi's Song, 45
Song of the Baca, 46
In Praise of Langa, 49
Sweet Mhudi and I, 49
PLAATJE, Violet
'What is in a Name?': In
Memory of Sol. T. Plaatje,
73
P.Q.R.
A Game of Chess, 51
Post Mortem, 53
Three Folk Poems, 53
The Death of a Zulu, 55

RACHILO, Sol.
The Anonymous Houseboy,
261
RACHITANGA, Tenda Robert
The Shadows Behind Me, 219
RADEBE, Gaur
An African to his Country,
136
RAMOVHA, Tshilidzi Shonisani
The Ignoramus, 331
RIVE, Richard
Where the Rainbow Ends, 155
'ROLLIE REGGIE'
See R.R.R. DHLOMO
RUDDIN, Muhammad Omar
When I Die, 314
Azanian Love Song, 401

SAMUEL, John
Now We Shall Stand, 252
SEBONI, Barolong
Punch-U-ation, 370

SEME, P. KaI.
The Regeneration of Africa,
35
SEPAMLA, Sipho
Feeling Small, 230
The Start of a Removal, 232
Nibbling, 233
Darkness, 250
Beyond this Moment, 265
I Remember Sharpeville, 269
Manchild, 306
The Exile, 335
waSEROKE, Jaki
Whooping the Facets of
Knowledge, 329
How Was I Born?, 330
Our Points of View, 398
SEROTE, Mongane
Alexandra, 216
Lost or Found World, 218
My Brothers in the Street, 239
Listen to Me, 240
To Don M — Banned, 241
Time Has Run Out, 372
SIDIQUE, Safee
To This Day, 212
SIKAKANE, Joyce
An Agony, 200
SILWANA, Stanley
Compensation, 80
Ode to Dr W.B. Rubusana, Ph.D,
81
I Sing of Africa, 82
SKEEF, Eugene
Afrika, 339
SMALL, Adam
And the Flesh was Made
Word, 188
Body, 196
But O . . . , 208
SMUTS, Colin
Doornfontein, 259

SOGA, A.K.
    Ntsikana's Vision, 17
    Death and Life, 18
    Santa Cruz: The Holy Cross,
        18
    Daughters of Africa, 47
SOMHLAHLO, Basil
    Naked They Came, 196
STEMMET, Farouk
    Custodian of our Spirit, 328
SWARTS, A.B.
    Be of Good Cheer, 75

THABEDE, W.J.
    Winter and our Little Poor, 88
THEMBA, Can
    O Ghana, 164
    Ballad to the Coffee Cart, 166
    Dear God, 180
TLADI, Lefifi
    Notes from an African
        Calabash, 249
    Songs in the Wind, 371
TWALA, James
    A Sad Case, 226

VAN WYK, Christopher
    Agrarian Reform, 251
    A Riot Policeman, 296
    A Song of Hope, 313
    Candle, 336
    Injustice, 356
'VESPERTILIO'
    See Grendon
VILAKAZI, B.W.
    In the Gold Mines, 131
VILAKAZI, Paul
    Portrait of an Intshumentshu,
        232

WAUCHOPE, I.W.
    Your Cattle are Gone 15
    To Us A Son Is Born, 16

ZONDO, Thamsanqa
    Death Without Compromise,
        337
'ZULU'
    Teachers' Meeting, 59
    Our Dying Speech, 61
    The Three Aborigines, 62